# THE LOUIS L'AMOUR COMPANION

I'm just a storyteller, a guy with a seat by the campfire. And I want to share with people what I have found, and what I have seen, and the wonderful old voices of men and women talking of those bygone times.

Louis L'Amour in "Louis L'Amour: Man of the West" by Harold Keith
*The Roundup*, January 1976. Reprinted by permission of
the Western Writers of America

# The
# LOUIS L'AMOUR
## Companion

by Robert Weinberg

**Andrews and McMeel**
A Universal Press Syndicate Company
Kansas City

Designed by Edward D. King

Library of Congress Cataloging-in-Publication Data

Weinberg, Robert E.
    The Louis L'Amour companion / by Robert Weinberg.
       p.   cm.
    Includes bibliographical references and index.
     ISBN 0-8362-7996-4 (ppb) : $12.95
     1. L'Amour, Louis, 1908-   .   2. Novelists, American—20th
century—Biography.    3. Western stories—History and criticism.
4. West (U.S.) in literature.    I. L'Amour, Louis, 1908-   .
II. Title.
PS3523.A446Z95    1992
813'.52—dc20
[B]                                                                92-5595
                                                                        CIP

Frontispiece illustration copyright © John Hamilton.
For an extension of the copyright page, see page 305.

# Contents

## Part 4: Audio and Video

## Appendices

To the memory of my father, David Weinberg,
who always liked a good Western

# Introduction

I READ MY first Louis L'Amour paperback in the fall of 1962, when I was sixteen years old. In those days, living with my family in Hillside, N.J., I was an omnivorous reader who devoured books by the shelf, sometimes reading three or four in a day. My tastes ran mostly to science fiction and mystery. I had little time for Westerns, having sampled and rejected old standards including Zane Grey and Max Brand. Louis L'Amour changed all that.

The book, bought at the Valley Fair Department Store in nearby Irvington, N.J., was *The Daybreakers,* the first Sackett novel. Why I purchased it I don't recall, though I am sure the blurb, mentioning "An Epic Novel of the Opening of the West," had something to do with it. I do remember racing through the book, finishing it in an hour. As was my habit at the time, I passed the book along to my father, whose appetite for good books matched mine. Like me, he was hooked. From that day forward, whenever either of us saw a Louis L'Amour novel, we bought it immediately.

In L'Amour's books, I found a mythic quality that seemed to define the Old West. Most prominent in *Flint,* my choice for L'Amour's best novel, it appears throughout all of his stories, elevating many of them (including most of the Sackett novels, *Bendigo Shafter,* and *The Lonesome Gods*) out of the realms of genre fiction. That L'Amour has not received much critical attention reflects more on the elitism of the literary establishment than the importance of his work. The two hundred and thirty million copies of L'Amour's books sold are a strong statement of his enduring literary legacy.

This book is the culmination of more than twenty-five years of collecting Louis L'Amour material. It is my attempt, now that L'Amour is no longer with us, to provide a little something extra for his fans throughout the world. There are numerous interviews with L'Amour on a wide range of topics from the pulps to his last few novels, rare unreprinted articles and letters written by him, and even his first published short story, never before in book form. Accompanying these rarities are new articles by well-known Western, mystery, and fantasy authors on various aspects of

L'Amour's writings, and detailed annotated checklists of all of his work. Without question, it is a book that even the most hardcore L'Amour fan or collector can pick up and find exciting material on his favorite author unavailable anywhere else.

Though I have nothing but the utmost respect and admiration for the L'Amour family, this volume is not connected in any way with them or the L'Amour estate. It was written and published without their cooperation, suggestions, approval, or authorization. Any biases or opinions expressed in the book are mine or those of the various contributors.

Any book like this is the result of the work of many people. I am extremely grateful for all those who helped make this the best work possible.

First and foremost, I have to acknowledge my wife, who not only helped in a thousand ways, but who also put up with my long hours spent on this volume without complaint. This book would never have appeared without her assistance. A word of thanks, also, to my son, Matthew, who was very patient sharing his father with a computer.

I am indebted to my agent, Lori Perkins, who helped shape the basic idea of this volume and who sold it for me.

Donna Martin, my editor at Andrews and McMeel, deserves special thanks for her suggestions and support.

My close friend Stefan Dziemianowicz has to be thanked for his invaluable assistance in all phases of this volume. Without his many tireless hours researching rare and obscure L'Amour material, this volume would have been much less complete.

The same holds true of Joel Frieman, chairman of Argosy Communications, Inc., whose input and expertise proved invaluable many times during the course of assembling this book.

I owe a great deal to all the contributors to this book: Jon Tuska, Harlan Ellison, Lawrence Davidson and Richard Lupoff, Bob Sampson, Stefan Dziemianowicz, Bernard Drew, Scott Cupp, Ed Gorman, R. Jeff Banks, Judith Tarr, Victor Dricks, Hal Hall, and Jim Hitt. Special thanks to John R. Hamilton for use of his tremendous photos.

My personal thanks also to Jack Schiff, Ryerson Johnson, and Frank McCarthy for answering questions about their work. My thanks to Kent Carroll for agreeing to be interviewed. Many thanks to Shirley Steeger for permission to reprint an excerpt from the interview with her husband, Henry Steeger, one of the true giants of twentieth century American publishing.

I am especially thankful to the following people, all of whom had a hand in this volume: My brother-in-law, Doug O'Boyle, whose research proved invaluable; George Hocutt, John Gunnison, Mike Pellow, Albert Tonik, Richard Wald, Arthur Hackathorn, David T. Alexander, Walker Martin, Leonard Robbins, Bill Blackbeard of the San Francisco Museum of Comic Art, Frank Robinson, and Steve Miller for their help with my research on L'Amour's pulp work; Gary Lovisi and Grant Thiessen for their information on rare L'Amour paperback editions; Ray Walsh for his encouragement and loan of a very special item; Paul Dale Anderson, Bernard Drew, Robert T. Gale, and Nancy Hamilton of the Western Writers of America for making available to me a number of rare articles and books that provided a great deal of necessary information about L'Amour's career; Joe R. Lansdale and Beth Gwinn, who put me in touch with the right people; Debra Weaver, who loaned me some important letters; Thomas Bauduret for his information of the French editions of L'Amour's work; W.O.G. Lofts for his help with L'Amour's British editions, and Mike Ashley for putting me in contact with the right person; Paul Schulz for the photos; Joe Desris for the phone number; and John Jakes, who almost made it.

For their help and permission to reprint from their publications I am indebted to Gary Ink of *Publishers Weekly;* Nancy Hamilton, president of the Western Writers of America, publisher of *The Roundup;* Michael Greaves of Fawcett Books; Caroline Mahla of McFarland & Co., Inc.; and to Denise Singleton of Gale Research, publishers of *Contemporary Authors.*

In any undertaking this size, it is always possible accidently to forget someone's help. To anyone I might have overlooked, I extend my sincerest apologies.

Robert Weinberg
Oak Forest, Illinois

# Part 1:
# His Life and Times

If I had a thousand years, I could not tell the
stories, nor put into words half of what I feel.

Louis L'Amour in "Louis L'Amour: Man of the West"
by Harold Keith, *The Roundup*, January 1976
Reprinted by permission of the Western Writers of America

# Introduction

LOUIS L'AMOUR led a life more incredible than most of the characters in his novels. A high-school dropout, he sailed around the world before his eighteenth birthday, worked at a dozen odd jobs from mining to logging, and hobnobbed with many old-timers who remembered the glory days of the Old West. Largely self-educated, he taught himself how to write. He sold his first short story when he was twenty-seven, but did not start placing fiction regularly until 1940, when he was in his thirties. His first paperback, *Hondo*, appeared when he was forty-five years old. His books sold in the millions of copies, and by the time he died at age eighty, L'Amour was by far the best-selling Western novelist of all time.

In this first section of the *Companion,* we look at Louis L'Amour the man and his history. A chronology of the important dates in L'Amour's life is followed by an appreciation of his work as the most popular Western author of all time.

After that we have reprinted two of the earliest and most important biographical pieces written about him, by Walker Tomkins and Harold Keith. These two articles helped promote and establish many of the legends about L'Amour that grew larger and larger over the years.

Contrasting those pieces, "Louis L'Amour—the Man Behind the Myth" is a long biographical sketch of L'Amour that cuts through much of the hype surrounding his career, separating fact from fancy. It is the most accurate biographical sketch of the author ever published.

L'Amour's many letters to *Rob Wagner's Script* are the focus of another piece, which presents details of L'Amour's wartime experiences, unavailable anywhere else. This long series of letters written during the 1940s is the only record of L'Amour's thoughts on World War II and his time overseas. They provide a rare glimpse of this great writer during the most difficult period of his life.

Articles about L'Amour by Jean Mead, Jon Tuska, and Harlan Ellison continue the section. Each deals with a personal meeting between L'Amour and the author. Concluding the section are two short pieces on the special honors bestowed on L'Amour during his lifetime.

# Chronology of Louis L'Amour's Life

**1908**  Louis Dearborn LaMoore is born on March 22, in Jamestown, N.Dak., the son of Louis Charles LaMoore and Emily Lavisa Dearborn LaMoore. He is the youngest of seven children.

**1923**  In December, his father sells his business and moves the family to the Southwest. Louis leaves high school and strikes out on his own. He loses contact with the family, and after a series of odd jobs in the Southwest ships out as a sailor on a ship for the Caribbean. After shipwreck and rescue, he ships out for Liverpool, England. He spends most of the next fifteen years as a merchant seaman or working at odd jobs all across the world.

**1926**  "The Chap Worth While," his first published poem, is printed in the *Jamestown Sun*. Throughout the next decade he manages to sell a number of poems and short articles to small-press magazines with limited circulation.

**1935**  After several hundred rejection slips, he sells his first short story, "Anything for a Pal," to *True Gang Life* magazine. It is published in the October 1935 issue.

**1938**  L'Amour settles down with his family in Choctaw, Okla., determined to become a professional writer. He places a boxing story, "Gloves for a Tiger," with Standard Magazines, and it is published in the January 1938 issue of *Thrilling Adventures*.

**1939**  His first book, *Smoke from This Altar,* is published by Lusk Publishers, Oklahoma City. According to the copyright information in *Yondering,* the collection of poems was "privately published by the author."

**1942**  Drafted, he spends two years in the United States before being sent to England. He serves with the transportation corps in France and Germany, rising to the rank of first lieutenant.

**1946**  Released from the army with an honorable discharge on January 6 at Long Island. He calls Leo Margulies, editor of Standard Publications, who suggests that he write Western stories for the Standard pulp chain. L'Amour adopts the pen name "Jim Mayo," which appears on approximately one-third of his work.

**1950**  He writes four Hopalong Cassidy novels as work-for-hire for Doubleday Books. His first Western novel in book form, *Westward the Tide,* is published by World's Work in England.

**1952**  His short story "The Gift of Cochise" is published in *Colliers* magazine. Screen rights to the story are bought for four thousand dollars by John Wayne, to be made into a film by his newly formed production company.

**1953**  The novel version of "The Gift of Cochise," now titled *Hondo,* is published and released the same day as the film. Fawcett prints 320,000 copies of the book and signs L'Amour to a contract for future Westerns.

**1955**  L'Amour signs a contract with Bantam Books for two books (later revised to three books) a year.

**1956**  He marries Katherine Elizabeth Adams on February 19.

**1958**  His first original novel for Bantam Books, *Radigan,* appears.

**1960**  Bantam publishes *The Daybreakers,* first novel in the Sackett family saga.

**1961**  His son, Beau Dearborn L'Amour, is born.

**1964**  His daughter, Angelique Gabrielle L'Amour, is born.

**1969**  He wins the Golden Spur Award from the Western Writers of America for his novel *Down the Long Hills.*

**1972**  L'Amour receives the Theodore Roosevelt Rough Rider Award from the state of North Dakota.

**1975**   He becomes Bantam's best-selling paperback author, passing John Steinbeck's total of 41,300,000 books published.

**1977**   His novels *Hondo* and *Flint* are voted among the best twenty-five Western novels ever written by the Western Writers of America.

**1978**   L'Amour is awarded the Great Seal of the Ute Tribe.

**1979**   "The Sacketts," a two-part TV miniseries, is aired. It is the first adaption of L'Amour's work for television. It is later voted the most authentic Western of the decade by the Cowboy Hall of Fame.

**1980**   L'Amour tours the United States in the "Overland Express" for three weeks, celebrating his one hundred million books in print.

**1981**   He is presented the Western Writers of America Golden Saddleman Award for his contributions to the Western genre.

**1982**   Congress votes him a National Gold Medal (presented to him by Ronald Reagan in 1983).

**1984**   L'Amour is awarded the government's highest civilian honor, the Medal of Freedom.

**1988**   Louis Dearborn L'Amour dies on June 10, at the age of eighty.

# Louis L'Amour—All-American Author

ENGLAND has Robin Hood and King Arthur. The French have Joan of Arc, while the Swiss speak of William Tell. The Japanese look to their samurai. Throughout the world, every country has its historical figures whose character and exploits help define the identity of that nation. In the United States, those archetypes are the heroes and heroines of the Old West. And the greatest chronicler of their exploits was Louis L'Amour.

America has had many heroes. They range from real historical personages such as George Washington, Abraham Lincoln, and Martin Luther King, Jr., to the imagined greatness of folklore legends Pecos Bill and Captain Stormalong. Oftentimes, the line between real and imaginary blurs, as in the cases of Johnny Appleseed, Davy Crockett, and Buffalo Bill, real people who became legends. Or, in the cases of Zorro and Paul Bunyan, characters who first appeared in print became so well known that they were assumed to be based on folk legends. One and all, they share certain defining characteristics that make them uniquely American.

These same unique traits can be found in the heroes who populate the novels and short stories of Louis L'Amour. It is what makes L'Amour's novels so popular and makes him the most popular Western author of all time. His stories, while historical and technically accurate, are rooted in the basic myths of the American frontier. They strike a responsive note in anyone who still believes in the American dream and the ideals that guided this nation.

Over the years, critics have never ceased to wonder at L'Amour's incredible popularity. When he first started, L'Amour was ignored by reviewers, who labeled his work as typical "genre" writing. It was only after his sales climbed into the tens of millions that many of these same critics were forced to admit that perhaps a writer who sold that many books deserved some attention. But, try as they would, the critics never could understand why Louis L'Amour's Westerns sold in record numbers.

The literary establishment complained about the lack of complexity in L'Amour's characters. The protaganist and antagonist acted from basic, simple motives without any deeper, darker psychological motivations given to explain their actions. By and large, while there was always romance in the books, there was little sex. And the heroes were whole-some and true, not bent and twisted with little quirks and traits that made them "more believable."

L'Amour's plots were similarly attacked as being too straightforward. They lacked the sordid believability of modern life. Too often, the novels centered around a battle between a strong moral hero and an equally strong, but inherently immoral, villain. L'Amour's heroes were never filled with doubts. They knew what was right and they followed their consciences, no matter what the consequences.

The lack of ambiguities in L'Amour's Westerns baffled the critics. They searched in vain for some common element that linked all of his novels and made them best-sellers. Finally, almost in frustration, they latched onto the fact that L'Amour's novels were historically accurate, that the books were technically correct in every aspect of the Old West. Because of that accuracy, they proclaimed, L'Amour's books sold better than any other Western writer before him.

Other Western authors who had been writing authentic stories of the West for years shrugged their shoulders and kept on working. L'Amour, as was his fashion, ignored the critics. And his readers kept on buying his books in record numbers.

The critics were right that L'Amour worked hard to maintain the historical truth in his novels. His descriptions of the time and place and people are meticulous and worked out to the last detail. But, as mentioned above, many other Western writers are equally careful. Louis L'Amour's secret was no secret at all. He wrote the type of Westerns that people wanted to read.

The reviewers are correct in their assessments of L'Amour's books and stories. L'Amour's characters and plots are not believable by today's standards. However, people reading Westerns are not looking for main-stream novels disguised as frontier fiction. They want stories of the mythic West, the legendary West as defined by tall tales, John Wayne movies, and television series. They want the West that Louis L'Amour defines in clear-cut, straightforward narratives that bristle with action, color, and most of all, heroism.

L'Amour's heroes are all larger than life. They are strong, silent men who know the difference between right and wrong and are willing to fight for the right. Uncompromising in their belief in justice, they always do the right thing, whether they have to or not.

In chapter five of *The Daybreakers,* Tyrel and Orrin Sackett, Cap

Rountree, and Tom Sunday come across a small wagon train destroyed by Indians. Hidden in the wagons, they find over a thousand dollars in gold, along with a few letters. Tom Sunday wants to keep the money. But Orrin Sackett has other plans.

> "Maybe somebody needs that money," Orrin suggested. "We'd better read those letters and see if we can find the owner."
>
> Tom Sunday looked at him, smiling, but something in his smile made a body think he didn't feel like smiling. "You aren't serious? The owner's dead."
>
> "Ma would need that money mighty bad if it had been sent to her by Tyrel and me," Orrin said, "and it could be somebody needs this money right bad."

In that brief exchange, the basic difference between the heroes and villains of every Louis L'Amour novel is defined. Tom Sunday thinks only of himself. Orrin Sackett thinks of what is right.

Louis L'Amour took American ideals and gave them life in his characters. His men are strong individualists, who believe in freedom, equality, and independence. They are free-spirited pioneers who want to go their own way, manage their own business without interference, make their own plans. However, one and all they know the value of cooperation and the importance of working together with others for the common good of all. Above all, they are fair, just, honorable men, even when they are dealing with rascals, Indians, or outlaws. They embody the spirit of the frontier.

That does not mean they aren't tough as nails. L'Amour constantly subjects his heroes to beatings, stompings, brutal fistfights, multiple shootings, stabbings, and even an occasional fall off a cliff. And yet they survive, refuse to give up, and always return to pay back their tormentors in kind.

Take for example Jim Flint. In L'Amour's finest novel, *Flint*, voted one of the twenty-five best Westerns ever written, James T. Kettleman, alias Jim Flint, has returned to the Old West to die. Believing he has cancer, Flint wants only to mind his own business and die alone. But Port Baldwin and his men won't leave Flint alone.

In chapter six, Flint comes into town to buy supplies. Before he can leave, Baldwin and his cronies brutally beat Flint to a bloody pulp. However, they don't kill him. Which is a big mistake, they discover, as Flint soon regains his gun.

He swayed, half-falling, then pushed himself erect and staggered through the swinging doors of a saloon. The Baldwin riders, some of them at least, were there.

Their laughter died, their half-lifted drinks stopped in midair, and Flint fired. He opened up in a blinding roar of gunfire, fanning his gun, for the range was close and there were a number of them.

One man grabbed for a gun and was caught by a bullet that knocked him sprawling. Panic-stricken, another man leaped through a window, carrying the glass, frame, and all with him. Another bullet smashed a bottle from a man's hand, and another—it was a face he remembered—struck a man in the spine as he dove for the back door.

Flint staggered to the bar, catching a glimpse of a bloody and broken face in the mirror. He picked up a bottle, took a short drink, and started for the door.

Flint is perhaps L'Amour's most dangerous hero, a man who believes he is dying and has nothing to lose. But his refusal to give up, to admit defeat, is typical of all of L'Amour's heroes.

In *Conagher,* Conn Conagher is a middle-aged cowboy who has never been very successful. He has little money and nothing to show for his years riding the range. But when he is paid, Conagher "rides for the brand," no matter what the odds or the circumstances.

After fighting his way through a blizzard, without food for days, Conagher stumbles across a group of rustlers who have been stealing cattle from his boss. Though barely able to stand, he confronts the three members of the gang. Holding them at bay with his six-gun, he makes his feelings known to the leader of the outlaws:

"Now, Smoke," he said, "I'm going to ride out of here. You boys are then going to get up and leave the country, and if you stop this side of Tascosa or Trinidad, you're crazier than I think you are. You've had your try at me and you failed, but as of noon tomorrow I'm hunting you, and I'm going to shoot on sight, without any warning whatsoever. I am going to ride your sign until you've killed me or I've put lead in all of you."

Parnell stared at him. "You're loco! You're plumb, completely loco!"

"Maybe . . . but you've given me grief, and I'll take no more from any man. All I'm going to give you is a running start."

Only a few minutes later, Conagher collapses from lack of food and rest. Lying there, unconscious, he is at the mercy of the outlaws. One of the band asks the leader if he plans to kill the cowboy.

"Kill *him*?" Smoke Parnell turned around sharply. "Kid, you don't know what you're sayin'. I may be an outlaw, but I never yet murdered anybody in cold blood, least of all an hombre. And there, as my friend Casuse will agree, is an hombre that *is* an hombre."

Even the outlaws in L'Amour's stories, no matter how vile and wicked, have their own code, their own brand of ethics, their own sense of honor. They are men of the West first, and villains after.

To his detractors, L'Amour too closely followed a formula, rarely tried anything new and different. They seem annoyed that he did what he did best. L'Amour wrote for his fans and supporters, not for his critics. His books sold in the millions because he aimed them not at the reviewers but at the readers.

Though L'Amour wrote nearly a hundred novels and several hundred short stories, most of his fans bemoaned the fact that he didn't write even more. The immense Sackett saga of nearly fifty novels was not even half finished. The adventures of Parmalee Sackett were never told. Nor was the long-promised novel of the American Revolution featuring the Sacketts, Talons, and Chantrys. And what of the sequel to the adventures of Bendigo Shafter, with its many loose ends and mysterious happenings?

Louis L'Amour was the greatest Western writer of all time because in over a hundred books about the American frontier he consistently delivered the goods. He wrote stories that people enjoyed reading, and enjoyed rereading again and again. He told stories that could be enjoyed by both truck drivers and presidents, teenagers and senior citizens, whites and blacks, men and women. And he did it with characters who remained true to their ideals, refused to compromise their beliefs, and fought for what was right no matter what the odds.

Louis L'Amour filled his books with heroes who lived the American dream. He is the most popular Western writer of our time because his books define the ideals that make America great. And as long as people believe in those goals, those dreams, Louis L'Amour will continue to reign as the greatest all-American author.

# Meet Louis L'Amour

*by Walker A. Tompkins*

*("Meet Louis L'Amour" was originally published in* The Roundup, *the official organ of the Western Writers of America, in December 1954. Tompkins, at the time, was one of the major names in the Western field, while few people had ever heard of Louis L'Amour. This article was the first major biographical sketch of L'Amour ever published and helped establish many of the myths about him and his career that were to become part of the L'Amour mystique in years to come.)*

LOUIS L'AMOUR—alias Jim Mayo—is the only Western story writer I know who has the physique and the background to play the hero of one of his own novels. Six foot one, two hundred pounds, around forty but looks thirty, he resembles John Wayne, for whom he wrote *Hondo.* I'm sure he's the only WWA member whose personal life is faithfully reported by Hedda, Louella, and other Hollywood columnists.

The guy's story is fantastic. All a biographer can do by way of profile is to catalog a few high spots. Louis L'Amour (the name is his own) was born in Jamestown, N.D., but before his sixteenth birthday he had explored the West Indies and Europe, panned gold along the Agua Fria, rode a raft through a canyon in a flash flood, worked in a circus, shocked hay in New Mexico, picked fruit in the Southwest, and become a professional prize-fighter.

"I'm very poor at mathematics," Louis admits. "The only thing I can count is money. With my background I should have a beard, deep bass voice, and a scar on my cheekbone. I look like hell with a beard and my only visible scar is through an eyebrow. Fell on my head twice as a child. Had it been three times I might have been a senator."

He's been a tugboat deckhand, a longshoreman, an AB on a round-the-world freighter. Between voyages he mined all over Arizona, Nevada, Utah, and Colorado—boxing on the side. After a look at South America, he tried his hand at lumberjacking and flume-building. A year later he was in China and India, finally wound up sailing a dhow in the Red Sea, and later was a tourist guide in Egypt. Finally, back in the States, he took up writing. Two-line jokes, fillers. A book of poetry—which was a financial success. He reviewed books, and lectured at thirty-seven universities, although his formal schooling ceased at age fifteen.

His original "career," prizefighting, is behind him now. He fought fifty-nine bouts professionally, winning thirty-four by KOs, and lost only five. World War II found him an officer in the Tank Destroyer and Transportation Corps; he was in every major action from D-Day on except the Battle of the Bulge.

Satiated with living adventure, Louie started writing about it in earnest after the war. He has sold around four hundred stories, five books, and four movies to date. He's unmarried—although he may be a bridegroom before this comes out in *The Roundup*—and his first hobby is Western story writing. Others include mountain climbing, tracking game, photographing ghost towns, and amateur archaeology. As I say, these are only random high spots of a career that you wouldn't believe if you read it in a pulp magazine.

You'd never guess all this meeting Louis L'Amour for the first time. The guy who once walked sixty-nine miles across a desert in midsummer without a canteen is as at home on the range as he is decked out in white tie and tails at a Hollywood party with a big-name actress on his arm. I'll leave that facet of Louis L'Amour to the gossip columnists; suffice it to say he knows everybody who's anybody out in the film capital.

As to his writing, Louis has this to say: "I believe in absolute authenticity in Westerns as well as any book. I believe the Western novel is only beginning, that its stature is growing, and that it can be and occasionally has been literature. No writer can ever know enough. Everything he knows will someday be of use, and if he's any good at all he'll always wish he knew more.

"The West as a source of material has been barely tapped. The picture is too stylized and this is the fault of both writers and editors. Western cowhands and gunmen weren't of a type. Many were educated men of excellent background. The men who went west came from everywhere."

The Louis L'Amour you'll have a chance to swap yarns with at the 1955 convention in Santa Rosa is the most quiet-voiced, self-effacing, thoroughly likable fellow you could hope to meet. I'm proud to call him my friend and to have brought him into the Western Writers of America.

# Louis L'Amour: Man of the West

*by Harold Keith*

*(This series of three short articles by Harold Keith was published in* The Roundup, *the official organ of the Western Writers of America, in 1975 and 1976. As in the case of the Walker Tompkins piece, these articles helped embellish the Louis L'Amour legend. Most biographical studies of L'Amour that followed relied on the Keith and Tompkins articles for information, never questioning the authenticity of the data. Unfortunately, many of these facts were based on L'Amour's recollections of the past, which did not always jibe with accounts published previously or much later in his autobiography.)*

People ask me how I can do so much, and
I wonder why I have done so little.

Louis L'Amour

ALTHOUGH Louis L'Amour, the subject of this sketch, was born in North Dakota and never attended school beyond the tenth grade, the University of Oklahoma has had a profound influence upon his writing career.

"I found there an appreciation and understanding of the West that was rare in academic circles," L'Amour says today. As a boy of fifteen, he had first come to Oklahoma City to visit his brother, Parker LaMoore, private secretary to Governor M.E. Trapp. He later lived at nearby Choctaw, Okla., on acreage with his parents.

Among his acquaintances on the Norman faculty in those times were Dr. Walter Campbell and Foster Harris of OU's professional writing school, which L'Amour says is "far the best and I've seen lots of them"; Dr. E.E.

14

Dale and Dr. Carl Coke Rister, noted historians of the Indian and the Southwest; Dr. Joseph Brandt, director of the university press, who later became president of the university; Dr. Savoie Lottinville, who later would succeed Brandt at the press; Ben Botkin; Elgin Groseclse; Dr. Paul E. Sears; and Dr. Kenneth Kaufman.

All of them wrote books, mostly about the West or the Southwest. "A great, great bunch of people," L'Amour still rates them.

The one who had the greatest influence on him, he says, was Kaufman, lean-faced, keen-eyed chairman of Oklahoma's Department of Modern Languages who was a Christian Scientist, wore spectacles with plain gold rims, spoke five languages fluently, and whose wisp of a mustache punctuated the look of mischievous inquiry that livened his somewhat ascetic features.

Not only did Kaufman write a column, "The Way I See It," which graced the editorial page of the state's largest newspaper, *The Daily Oklahoman* of Oklahoma City; he also edited that newspaper's book review page. L'Amour secured an advance copy of the novel *Anthony Adverse,* wrote a review predicting its success, and sent it to Kaufman. Kaufman published the review, sent L'Amour more books, and invited him to Norman for a visit. That led to the meetings with the others.

L'Amour started as a poet. His *Smoke from This Altar* (1939, published by Lusk Publishing Company of Oklahoma City) is a small gray volume of thirty-six poems, many of them well-structured sonnets. They deal with his roamings over much of the world and are dedicated to "Singapore Charlie . . . who couldn't read."

Kaufman also wrote poetry. When he signed for young L'Amour a copy of his own volume of verse, *Level Land,* he wrote: "To Louis L'Amour, who will be heard from some day." However, L'Amour believes that the professor thought that he would be heard from as a poet rather than a novelist.

L'Amour educated himself. Although he never went to college (he has since lectured at thirty or more colleges or universities), he has always considered the University of Oklahoma his school and Oklahoma his second home. "It was there I dug in and really started to write," he says. "I'd been trying to write while wandering around the world. But one doesn't get far at writing when loose-footed. It was my early acquaintance with Professor Kaufman that led me to settle down."

He had started life at Jamestown, N.D., in a small house in the middle of town. There his father, Louis Charles LaMoore, a veterinary surgeon, owned a farm machinery store, occasionally served as a deputy sheriff, and became a city councilman and an unsuccessful candidate for mayor. His mother, Emily Dearborn, came from pioneer stock.

"Our real name is L'Amour or Lamour," he says, "and has been spelled in various ways by generations of the family. Few names are now spelled as they once were, a check of genealogical records will prove. My first names are Louis Dearborn. I keep the middle name but do not use it. It makes the name too long."

L'Amour describes Jamestown as a "town of about seven thousand, a very attractive and pleasant place." The most pleasant place in it for him seems to have been the "very good" town library "to which I had constant access," he recalls. He went through its shelves as if their contents were food delicacies and he was starving. His first reading had been done at home where there were several hundred books, "a mixture of fiction and fact with much history and poetry."

Bad times shortened his schooling, which stopped permanently in the middle of his sophomore year at Jamestown High School. All of his father's business customers were farmers who went broke and couldn't pay their debts. L'Amour adds: "So we moved away, and I was already discovering that I could advance faster by educating myself. When I am asked by other kids about dropping out, I tell them they should drop out only if they have read from fifty to one hundred nonfiction books per year for three years, for fun. I never graduated from high school or anything else."

But he read hungrily and voraciously, storing everything away in the files of his neat and orderly mind. Before he was twelve, he had read forty Dumas novels, several by Victor Hugo, *Westward Ho!* by Kingsley, *Scottish Chiefs* by Porter, and all he could find of Stevenson and Defoe. At twelve, he read his first book of nonfiction, *The Genius of Solitude*. In the next three years he digested books on natural history, botany, mineralogy, geology, military science, and many volumes of history including part of Gibbon. He read a treatise on submarines, and another on aircraft, starting with the first kites and balloons. "I often fell asleep reading," he remembers. "My mother would take the book from my hands and put it on the table."

He began living a man's life at age fifteen, passing for twenty-two. He made most of his own living from age twelve when he hustled his first job as a messenger boy for Western Union. Before he was fourteen, he began to box, working with professionals.

As he grew, he began to travel. From age fifteen to eighteen, he worked in Texas, New Mexico, Nevada, California, and Oregon. He made a five-and-a-half–month trip around the world. He worked in the mines in the western states, and on construction gangs. He bummed around the oil fields. Off and on, he'd go to sea. While waiting for his turn to ship out on the waterfronts of San Pedro and San Francisco, he bucked rivets and rough-painted in a shipyard, swamped on trucks, and "slept in empty boxcars, lumber piles, or wherever. But I was still reading all the time."

What brought on the wanderlust? "I was born with it. In the fourth and fifth grades I used to trace out routes on the maps of my geography that someday I hoped to travel. The reading I did provided understanding of what I was to see. When traveling, I absorbed more by osmosis than by questions. I liked to sit somewhere and watch people go about their affairs, listening to them talk. Things seemed to happen right for me. I had what I call the adventure-type mind. I was geared for change, at going off on the tangent. Often the way seemed to open up before me, and where another might have hesitated, I went ahead. Not because I had more nerve, but simply because I had the feeling I could cope. And when times were bad I always found solace in the thought that it would work for me in a story someday."

He kept coming back to Oklahoma City, where, using an "old beat-up Underwood," he resumed writing. He got a lot of rejects but always kept eight to ten stories in the mail. His first check was for $6.50. It was paid by a magazine called *True Gang Life*. L'Amour says: "My story was a short-short about a gang killing. A hit man killed a witness against a gangster, and the witness he killed proved to be his own brother whom he had been sending to school for years."

Soon he sold a boxing story. As a boxer in small towns and mining camps, L'Amour fought under several names—"largely to earn a buck." He never seriously intended to make it a profession. "I never lost a fight when I was eating regularly," he says. In fifty-nine fights, he lost five, knocked out thirty-four. He coached a Golden Gloves boxing team at Choctaw, Okla., at one time.

What did he learn from his fighters? "That it was easier to take a beating yourself than to see a kid you've trained take one." In World War II, L'Amour went into the army from Oklahoma as a buck private and emerged as a first lieutenant with a tank destroyer unit. He also served in the merchant marine.

When the war ended in 1946, he moved to California, his roving largely finished, and began to write.

"Hit your reader on the chin. So he knows he's in a story. The reader doesn't want to know what's *going* to happen. He wants to know what's happening *now.*"

That was Louis L'Amour talking June 7, 1967, to the University of Oklahoma's annual professional writing conference at Norman. Meachem Auditorium was nearly packed with embryo writers wanting to hear the curly-haired spinner of Western yarns. Liking what he said, I made notes on the small white cards I carry in my shirt pocket.

L'Amour seemed to operate on the theory that not much of life is truly exciting, that it's mostly slog and drudge. "People want to read something that will lift them out of themselves," he maintains.

So he begins with action, or events immediately preceding action. "Action connected with the story," he insists. "Make something happen. Ideas are all around. Think. Develop. Get the reader interested. Then the plot will carry you along.

"You've got to get the reader in the first two minutes."

That's advice you'd expect from a boxing man who had horizontaled thirty-four opponents.

L'Amour's precepts brush every facet of the writing art. "Suspense that the reader feels clear down to his guts is the most important word in the writer's book," he told our writing group. "There has to be a goal, a thing desired. The hero's goal must be important. . . . A striking adjustment to a difficult situation is the character's lot. . . . Small things characterize better than great ones. . . . Just before the climax, a terrific setback. . . . Every sentence must have a feeling as well as a fact, like 'Chip rode with caution.' . . . Every word of the dialogue must move the story. . . . We must put sight, sound, and smell in every thing we do."

An arresting facet of L'Amour's technique is that his heroes bypass the principle that to be interesting the protagonist must undergo some gradual character change, either growth or deterioration, and must possess weaknesses as well as strengths or he won't seem real. L'Amour builds many of his stories around a self-sufficient hero who excites curiosity and admiration in a unique way. Hondo, Shalako, Trace Jordon of *The Burning Hills*—they're all desert-roving supergunmen who undergo little if any character change themselves but work such a profound change upon the main female character that she often becomes the most interesting person in the book.

For example in *Hondo,* Angie's introspection, her looking within herself, especially in the first third of the story, is the best part of that book.

L'Amour never plots a story. "I always write off the top of my head, although the story locale and character have often been in mind, or partly so, for some time," he says. "I do jot notes which is a sort of thinking on paper, giving me a chance to examine the thought."

His first draft is his finished draft. "I go over it to correct typos. No editor has ever given me advice or suggestions. They just ask when they will get the next book."

He rarely researches a particular book except to verify some isolated fact. "I do research as a continuing project which never stops," he says. "I believe one should absorb research material until it becomes a part of one. I saturate myself in background, seeking not only to understand the times, but the people, the thinking, the work methods, the tools, and so forth. I look for all this in research and never stop looking."

L'Amour still reads enormously. "I read twenty-five books a year," he estimates, "carrying them in my pocket while I wait for the dentist to arrive, or while waiting for my wife at the supermarket. One has to know what other writers are doing. Libraries are the caves of Aladdin. My own large library solves my needs. I have poetry in mine over five thousand years old. I have twenty books on costume alone."

Who first urged L'Amour to write Westerns? Leo Margulies, then editor-in-chief of *Thrilling Adventures* and forty-seven other magazines. Margulies had bought L'Amour's second short story. After his discharge from service following World War II, L'Amour went to New York. He phoned Margulies who invited him to a party. "At the party there was a discussion between us as to what I intended to do," L'Amour remembers. "I replied I was not sure. He suggested I write some Westerns for him."

L'Amour did, all of them short stories. He also wrote one for *Colliers* magazine, a quality slick. Fawcett [Books] suggested that he expand the story into a Western novel. Thus *Hondo,* which actor John Wayne, who played Hondo in the movie, said was the "best Western novel I ever read," was born. And L'Amour's career was launched. His first novel sale to a slick was *The Burning Hills,* which the *Saturday Evening Post* purchased in 1955.

On February 19, 1956, L'Amour married Kathy Adams, an actress who attended Westlake School for Girls and UCLA. "She's the perfect wife," he says. "In nineteen years I haven't found one thing I'd change or want other than it is. She is beautiful (acknowledged so by everyone), intelligent, reads a lot, and is always busy with needlework and quilting. Now she is supervising the construction of a wing where I will work. She has a sharp business mind. She has many interests, principally her home, her children, and me. I am not exaggerating about this, although she would say that I was."

The L'Amours have two children, Beau, a son, now fourteen, and Angelique Gabrielle, a daughter, eleven. "Both read constantly," he says.

Since 1946 he has lived almost continuously in Los Angeles. He likes it because it is his wife's home, because all her friends, and many of his, are there, and because he likes the climate. There's another reason, too.

"Los Angeles accepts creative people," he says. "The writer here is not a strange creature; he is not special for there are many of him. The movies have brought an enormous array of talent to the area, not only actors, actresses, composers, directors, and cameramen but artists, set decorators, fashion designers, and special effects people.

"The activity in the sciences is far greater than realized. There are seventy thousand scientists living in the area of greater Los Angeles, Orange County, etc. That of course takes in Cal Tech, Scripps, the several Hughes firms, Kaiser, Lockheed, and others. I doubt if anywhere in the world there has been such a gathering of talent of every kind. The atmosphere is one of creativity."

L'Amour knows people in all these fields. His best personal friends are the vice president in charge of production at Columbia Studios, Michael Jackson, who has an excellent radio talk program in southern California; a contractor who builds malls, stadiums, etc.; a successful stage and screen actress; an attorney who handles Ann-Margret's business affairs; the owner of a primitive art shop; a television producer; a highly successful actor-director; and a scattering of others.

The L'Amours have a wide acquaintance in the film colony but go to few parties. They entertain at home occasionally. They have many friends from Asia who come to visit or who exchange dinner invitations, several from Japan (all of Chinese birth), and from Thailand, Iran, and India, among other countries.

L'Amour is aware that many find fault in what they designate as "Hollywood," which he says is simply a name for a climate, rather than a place. But there are thousands of working professional writers in the area, he points out.

"By and large, I think writers are the best company in the world," he says, "but if they talk together too much they begin either writing the same stories, or writing for each other. A writer should write for people, not critics or other writers."

Although some of his output is hardcover, he prefers paperbacks.

Hard covers get a better critical reception, he concedes, but he doesn't share the reviewers' belief that paperbacks are second class. "The only measurement of a book lies in the writing, not the covers," is the way he sums his opinion.

Agents? He doesn't use them. "I like direct contact with my publisher," he says. "I don't share movie rights with anybody. I like to keep them for myself. For many writers an agent can be an asset. Certainly they know the markets, the going prices, how to make the deals. An agent might have been good for me but I am happy in my ignorance."

L'Amour writes best in the morning, but "I can work anywhere, any time, under almost any circumstances, and do." He uses an electric typewriter, ten years old.

"I work all the time," he continues. "I love it and can't stay away from it. I am a man intoxicated with my country and its people. If I had a thousand years, I could not tell the stories, nor put into words half of what I feel.

"People ask me how I can do so much, and I wonder why I have done so little."

---

*The Roundup* asked Louis L'Amour for a photograph of him at his desk, working.

He didn't have one, and anyway, "it wouldn't be typical," he wrote back.

"At the moment," he explained, "I am building on an addition in which to work, but for the present am just making do on a borrowed table. Soon I'll have a very fine place to work and can have all my books around me. Over the years I have gathered a lot of books, many manuscripts, some old mining town and cow-town newspapers, and a good many locally published memoirs on which I draw for pictures of the times. . . . Soon I'll have them housed properly."

L'Amour spends a part of every year hiking in the mountains. For the desert he sticks to vehicles with four-wheel drive. "I still love to hike," he reports, "but don't find the time so much as in the old days."

No writer I know has had as complete and varied a saturation in Western life as Louis L'Amour.

His novels of the Western frontier, as well as of the cowboy West, are as authentic as a Charley Russell oil, filled with emotion and vitality.

L'Amour says, "The West was wilder than any man can write it, but my facts, my terrain, my guns, my Indians are real. I've ridden and hunted the country. When I write about a spring, the spring is there and the water is good to drink."

His whole background is pioneer and Western. "My great-grandfather, Lt. Ambrose Freeman, was killed and scalped by the Sioux while with the Sibley Expedition far out on the Dakota plains," he reveals. "There are several accounts of it (in five different books), the best written by George F. Brackett, who was with him at the time, and escaped.

"I grew up on that story and those of my grandfather, Lt. Abraham Dearborn, who was with the 3rd Minnesota and saw a lot of Indian fighting. Sioux Indians who fought against him used to visit him afterward at the house. I often heard them talking. I was very young at the time but the picture is vivid."

He also heard stories at his home by an uncle who punched cattle in Montana and Wyoming. Another uncle roamed all over the West. From the late 1870s on, he and L'Amour's aunt wandered from British Columbia to Sonora, Mexico. They drove a mail route in the Star Valley of Wyoming and managed a big cattle ranch there.

This uncle knew Tom Horn, Butch Cassidy, and most of his gang. They often swapped horses with them at the ranch corral in the dead of night. L'Amour listened to all these stories and also to other old-timers talking to him, "or more often, to cronies and friends," as well as studying old newspapers, diaries, and journals. A hard worker with a retentive memory, he wanted to learn all he could about the West. He says, "I can tell stories off the cuff about the West for days on end."

L'Amour's personal Western experience was characterized by much variety. When he was fifteen, he helped a wolf hunter skin dead cattle on the range of west Texas. He baled hay in the Pecos Valley of New Mexico. While working around Fort Sumner, Ruidoso, Socorro, Las Vegas, Santa Rosa, and Las Cruces, he knew two women and five men who had known Billy the Kid and all the major participants in the Lincoln County War.

"I never punched cows but a lot of my pals did," he says. "When I was around Kingman, Ariz., several of my friends were cowpunchers from the

Big Sandy. I went to dances with them, less for the dancing than the fighting."

You have to believe that L'Amour liked a fight and therefore can write about one. He had curly hair, dressed as well as possible, bore no facial marks, and often was taken for somebody soft.

"I was in a lot of brawls," he says, "one big one in Shanghai when the crews of two destroyers, a cruiser, and a couple of freighters took on almost half the British navy. And the next night we were all having drinks together. One brawl I missed: in Liverpool, four big Norwegians picked a fight with us in a fish-and-chip shop. But the Dutch second cook on our ship whipped all four of them before I could get the girl off my lap."

At sixteen, he was caretaker of a mine in Arizona, living in the desert of the Bradshaw Mountain area, feeding the dogs and chickens and making sure that nobody walked off with the tools. "I'd have to write a book to give you all of it," he says, "but I worked on mining claims south of Death Valley in the Owl Head Mountains, in the Monte Cristos of Nevada, near Jarbridge in Nevada and in Vallecito Canyon in Colorado." He also worked in lumber camps and sawmills. "It sounds adventurous and romantic but it was simply a way to keep going then," he says.

During the period of his travels, many old-timers still lived. "I met Jim Roberts, whom Zane Grey wrote about in two books. He was the last man living in the Tonto Basin War and marshal of Jerome and Clarkdale, Ariz." L'Amour talked to such well-known Oklahoma frontier marshals as Bill Tilghman (the man who captured Bill Doolin) and Chris Madsen, was introduced to Frank Canton, and knew Billy Colcord a little.

Tilghman, a state officer at the time, was a friend of Parker, Louis's brother. Hearing that they were interested in the subject of shooting from the hip, Tilghman took them down into the North Canadian River bottoms and showed them how to draw and shoot. ("I was actually a bystander, although he liked kids and knew how to talk to them," says L'Amour).

Tilghman shot as simply as he pointed a finger, looking right at the target, both eyes open. "He also made the important comment that a gun in the holster was more dangerous than one drawn," recalls L'Amour. "Especially the holster of a man who knows how to shoot, and who others know can shoot."

L'Amour says his main reason for writing about the West is the West itself. "My story people live with the country, not against it," he says. "They fit themselves into the land and become a part of it. They are rocks among the rocks, dust in the dust. They are the sound of streams and the shadows of trees. They are the smell of gunsmoke, and fresh hay, and sweat, and the taste of blood. They are hands, stiff from working, burned by ropes, gnarled by the years and by arthritis.

"They are poetry, because their land is poetry, and their lives are a harsh reality that was poetry and epic all in one. They gave sweat and blood to the country to make it grow. I write about them because I live them with a deep, undying love, for I have heard and read their words, felt what they felt, and I've walked out there in the grass, and up in the mountains alone, and down through the trees.

"I write about it because I think it needs to be said, and because in these later years, despite what some may feel, I know that the same blood is here today, the same guts, the same nerve. I write because now that things are so good I want people to understand what it was like when times were bad, and that no matter what hardship they encounter, there was a greater hardship before. This country was born of failure repeated a thousand times over until it became success, because the people who failed did not think they had failed, and would not believe it.

"I know that at this point my stories are inadequate, but they improve a little now and then. Some day maybe people will understand a little better what happened here because of what I have said.

"But don't put me down as a novelist, and don't say I'm an author. I'm just a storyteller, a guy with a seat by the campfire. And I want to share with people what I have found, and what I have seen, and the wonderful old voices of men and women talking of those bygone times.

"I listened, and I just wish to God that I could have caught the sounds a little better."

# Louis L'Amour—
# The Man Behind the Myth

> I think the grandest thing ever said was that
> crack about "Know the truth and the truth
> shall make you free."
>
> Louis L'Amour in a letter to
> *Rob Wagner's Script* magazine

"A LOT OF THINGS were happening in 1908 when I was born—place, Jamestown, N.D.; date, March 22nd. Earthquakes in Calabria and Sicily killed 76,483 people, there was a financial panic in the United States, a revolution in Portugal, an independent monarchy established in Bulgaria, and Chicago won a World Series."

Thus began the incredible life story of Louis L'Amour, as told in his own words, and first published in the pages of *Thrilling Adventures* magazine for October 1940. For little over a year, the monthly pulp magazine had been running a column titled, "They Write as They Live." Each installment focused on the life story of one of the regular contributors to the publication. L'Amour, who had been selling stories to *Thrilling Adventures* since January 1938, was well known to the readers of the pulp for his series of stories about "Ponga Jim Mayo." The column, several thousand words long, was filled with details of L'Amour's early adventures, only rarely mentioned in later interviews.

In fact, this early memoir was one of the few places where L'Amour actually mentioned his actual date of birth. As his popularity as an author grew, so did his reluctance to mention his age. In a letter in 1973 to one of his many correspondents, L'Amour stated "... as to my age, nobody

**25**

knows, not even my wife, and she doesn't care." Later, in that same letter, he stated, "Age is of no importance and death is only the anteroom to another life."

The son of Louis Charles LaMoore and Emily Lavisa Dearborn LaMoore, Louis was the youngest of seven children. His actual name was Louis Dearborn LaMoore. He shortened his last name to L'Amour when he started writing professionally. His sister, the oldest child of the family, Edna LaMoore Waldo, grew up to be a well-known nonfiction historical writer.

According to L'Amour, he could trace his family history in North America back to 1638. In the *Thrilling Adventures* column he declared:

"Most of my family before me had divided their time between fighting the wars of the world and writing, and all of them moved west. A lot of them were original settlers, and naturally, some of them got around to fighting the American Revolution. (It was a soldier in the company commanded by an ancestor of mine who fired the first shot at Bunker Hill.)

"As for the moving, that seems to have been a family trait. Probably some of my ancestors had a lot to do with the sea. One, I hear, was with Sir Francis Drake, but if he got any Spanish gold he knew what to do with it, because there's none left!"

In addition to his more famous relatives, one of L'Amour's great-grandfathers had the distinction of being killed and scalped by the Sioux Indians. The author often mentioned this fact in his many interviews with the media, as if offering actual proof of his unique ties with the Old West. Robert T. Gale, in his book for the Twayne United States Authors series, *Louis L'Amour*, identified the Indian fighter as Ambrose Truman Freeman, who died in a battle with the Sioux in North Dakota on July 24, 1863.

Louis's father was a state veterinarian, working mostly with horses and cattle. According to L'Amour, his father was active in civic affairs, serving as a deputy sheriff, policeman, and alderman in Jamestown.

"Somewhere along there," L'Amour continued in his pulp autobiography, "I stumbled across the stories of Stevenson and that led me to those of Jack London, Herman Melville, and Rudyard Kipling. Most of the time, I was going to school, and during the first six or seven years, getting good grades.

"After that I lost interest. I'd put on a lot of height and weight, to say nothing of a lot of ideas. There were too many places I hadn't seen, and too many books I wanted to read—and, or so it seemed, too little time for them."

Dissatisfied with school, L'Amour continued attending classes until he was fifteen. During that time, he spent much of his time reading on his own. A large family library at home provided him with hundreds of titles. The well-stocked city library offered an even greater selection.

While working as a Western Union messenger boy, L'Amour discovered the pulp fiction magazines. Like many youngsters, Louis was fascinated by the science fiction stories he found in such titles as *Argosy* and *Science and Invention*. The strong thread of fantastic elements that ran through much of L'Amour's fiction probably had its roots in the heroic adventures of John Carter of Mars as related by Edgar Rice Burroughs.

Along with reading, another interest dominated Louis's thoughts—boxing. Again, according to his account in *Thrilling Adventures*:

"Right now, I can't remember a time when I wasn't boxing. My father and two brothers took a swing at it, and so I just about grew up with gloves on my hands. By the time I was thirteen, and already starting to grow up fast, I was working in the gym with professional fighters.

"No kid stuff, for I was sparring with some boys who had a lot of stuff on the ball. Billy Petrolle, afterwards one of the best lightweights and welterweights the country ever saw, was just starting then, and we worked out nearly every day together."

In 1923, L'Amour's whole life changed. The relentless tide of progress put his father out of a job. As farmers turned more and more to machinery, there was less and less work for a farm veterinarian. In December of that year, a few months past Louis's fifteenth birthday, Dr. LaMoore sold his business and moved with his family to the southwest. That was when Louis first struck out on his own.

"When I was fifteen," he wrote, "I'd missed connections with my family and when they next heard from me, I was in Liverpool, England. I'd hitchhiked to Phoenix, hoping to catch them there, but when they didn't show up, I joined the Hagenbeck-Wallace Circus, stayed with them to El Paso, then rode freights and blinds to Galveston. There, I helped unload a banana boat, eating eighteen bananas in the process (the first food in two days) and then went on to New Orleans. There I had a fight on the docks and wound up by shipping out and going to sea."

L'Amour shipped out on a four-mast bark sailing the Caribbean. According to his description, the ship was barely able to make it from port to port. Still, over the next few months, he worked as a seaman on the boat as it visited Haiti, Santo Domingo, Ponce, San Juan, Kingston, Tampico, St. Kitts, and Martinique.

Then, unexpectedly, the boat ran into a hurricane. The boat piled up on a reef, with L'Amour and two other crew members the only survivors. They remained on the reef for three days until they were rescued by a sponge fisherman.

Returning to Galveston without a cent, L'Amour shipped off for Liverpool, England, on the SS *Steadfast.* Afterward, he worked as a carnival barker, picked fruit in California and Arizona, worked in a mine, and held a wide assortment of other jobs. All of that time, he continued to box, sometimes as an amateur, others as a professional.

In between trips back to the United States (where he reestablished contact with his family), L'Amour sailed to Japan, China, Borneo, Java, Sumatra, New Guinea, Ceylon, Burma, Egypt, Morocco, and a number of other spots in the near and far east. He kept busy, as related in his pulp column:

"[I] sailed a dhow from Aden to Port Twefik through the Red Sea. . . . In China, I boxed a couple of times, ran a machine gun for Chiang Kai-shek, and left stoking coal on a British Blue Funnel boat bound for Balikpapan, Borneo.

All this time, L'Amour was trying to write professionally. Like many young authors, his first efforts were poems. According to Robert T. Gale, Louis's first sale, a poem entitled "The Chap Worth While," was to the *Jamestown Sun* in 1926. Over the next ten years, he would regularly submit poetry, short articles, and stories to a multitude of magazines. A few sold. Most did not.

By the mid-1930s, L'Amour had come to the realization he wanted to be a full-time professional writer. And, while roaming the globe gave him plenty of background, it taught him little about the craft of composing a story or poem.

"Adventure is just a romantic name for trouble," L'Amour stated in 1940. "It sounds swell when you write about it but it's hell when you meet it face to face on a dark night in a lonely place. But you take it, and after a while you like it. . . ."

In 1935, L'Amour sold his first short story. Titled "Anything for a Pal," it was bought by *True Gang Life,* probably at the rate of a half cent a word, paid on publication. The short-short was published in the October 1935 issue of the magazine and is reprinted for the first time anywhere in the second section of this book.

*True Gang Life* was anything but true. The stories were all fictitious, and the pulp not considered a major market. Still, it was a step in the right direction.

Deciding that the only way he would become a full-time writer was to put an end to his traveling, L'Amour settled down on his family's farm in Choctaw, Okla., in the late 1930s. It was there that he finally devoted the necessary time to learn his chosen profession.

L'Amour taught himself to write by reading what he wanted to sell. He took a number of stories that appealed to him as a reader and analyzed why they worked. As the pulp magazines were the largest and easiest market for a beginning author to crack, he made sure he included a good supply of pulp efforts among his choices.

It didn't take L'Amour long to discover what made a story click in the pulp marketplace. Adventure tales needed to start immediately, with action occurring in the first paragraph. The hero had to be on the scene from the beginning, and everything in the story had to revolve around him and his problems. And endings had to wrap up all the loose ends and conclude the story with a snap. It was a basic, commonsense approach to writing, but one that worked.

In January 1938, "Gloves for a Tiger" appeared in *Thrilling Adventures* magazine, published by Standard Magazines. According to L'Amour, the story was bought by Leo Margulies, one of the best-known editors for the pulps. Actually, Margulies was in charge of the entire Standard line, and while he kept close tabs on all the magazines, "Tiger" was most likely purchased by senior editor, Jack Schiff.

Selling a story to Standard was a major step upward for L'Amour. Unlike his first sale, he was paid on acceptance, and probably at a penny a word. More important, Schiff and Margulies evidently liked what they read. Soon, Louis L'Amour was selling regularly to *Thrilling Adventures*.

Later that year, L'Amour managed to convince a small Oklahoma City firm to publish a slender collection of his poetry. The book, *Smoke from This Altar*, appeared early in 1939. It contained thirty-six poems, and most copies of the book were signed by the author. L'Amour scholars have speculated for many years whether or not the author actually helped finance the project. Giving some credence to that theory was the fact that Lusk Publishing Company shared the same address, 217 N. Harvey, Oklahoma City, as *Lands of Romance* magazine. L'Amour was a regular contributor to that magazine in 1937 and 1938. Also, on the copyright page to the hardcover version of his book *Yondering,* a poem from the book was credited as having appeared in a book that was "privately published by the author."

While not a major work, *Smoke from This Altar* was a hardcover book and was reviewed in the local newspapers. Coupled with his pulp successes, the volume confirmed that Louis L'Amour was a professional writer.

"Gloves for a Tiger" was a boxing yarn, reflecting L'Amour's firsthand knowledge of the ring. He followed it up with a novelette, "East of Gorontalo," an adventure story set in the Far East featuring a tough, two-fisted skipper named Ponga Jim Mayo. Published in the January 1940 issue of *Thrilling Adventures,* the yarn was quite popular and led to a whole series of Ponga Jim stories. The hero's nickname came from the Ponga River in Africa, and the authentic background to the stories came from L'Amour's own knowledge of the Far East.

L'Amour wrote nine adventures featuring his seafaring hero. All of them appeared in *Thrilling Adventures.* Seven of those stories were collected many years later in the paperback *West from Singapore.* Not included were two longer novelettes, "Voyage to Tobalai" (July 1942) and "Wings Over Brazil" (November 1943).

Shortly after selling the first Ponga Jim story, L'Amour broke into another market. *New Western Magazine,* one of the Popular Publications pulps, printed "The Town No Gun Could Tame" in its March 1940 issue. Originally titled "The Marshal of Basin City," the novelette earned L'Amour thirty-five dollars, paid at the rate of half a cent per word. This story was the first Western yarn Louis ever sold. However, once he began contributing regularly to Standard Publications, Louis submitted infrequently for other pulp chains. He appeared with only one other story in the Popular chain during this period.

With one character already established in *Thrilling Adventures,* L'Amour naturally tried another. Turk Madden was similar to Ponga Jim in all aspects but one. Where Mayo was the skipper of a ship, Madden was the owner of an airplane. Otherwise, the two heroes differed little in their adventures, actions, or personalities.

The first Turk Madden story, "Pirates of the Sky," appeared in the

February 1941 issue of the pulp. It was followed by "Coast Patrol" in the November 1943 issue. Unfortunately, that was the last issue published of *Thrilling Adventures*. The magazine was discontinued by Standard, effectively ending the career of Ponga Jim.

However, Turk Madden survived. His adventures continued in *Sky Fighters*, another Standard pulp, through 1949. In all, there were nine Turk Madden stories published. Of those, four stories were reprinted in the collection *Night over the Solomons*.

L'Amour had other things on his mind than the state of Standard Publications. As early as 1940, he wrote to *Rob Wagner's Script* magazine about his likelihood of being drafted: "It looks like I'm to be in uniform for a year. Having tried writing at sea I know how tough it will be trying to write in camp, for it never worked very well in the fo'c'sle. Naturally, I'm not very happy about it."

L'Amour was correct, though he was not inducted until 1942. In the meantime, he hired a New York agent, Jacques Chambrun, to handle his magazine sales during the war. Chambrun remained L'Amour's agent until mid-1946.

For his first two years in the service, L'Amour stayed in the United States, teaching winter-survival techniques in Michigan for part of the time. In 1944, he was shipped overseas. As noted in an interview with Lawrence Davidson (reprinted in this volume) L'Amour did *not* participate in the D-Day landing. He did serve as a lieutenant in the transportation brigade in France, hauling fuel for the advancing armored divisions. Louis received four Bronze Stars during his years in the service and was honorably discharged on January 6, 1946.

Back in the New York area, L'Amour called Leo Margulies, editor of Standard Magazines. Pulp writers were a gregarious bunch and gathered together weekly for informal parties and bull sessions. Margulies invited L'Amour to attend one that same evening.

At the party, Margulies broached the idea of L'Amour writing Westerns for Standard. Adventure magazines were on the decline, but Western pulps were selling extremely well. Though L'Amour had only sold two Western stories in his entire career, he readily agreed.

However, Margulies had strict ideas about names of Western writers. He didn't mind if L'Amour used his real name for some of the stories he sold to Standard. However, he felt that readers preferred reading Western and frontier tales composed by an author with a more "he-man" type name. Casting about for a pen name, L'Amour settled on Jim Mayo, the name of the hero he had created for Margulies six years earlier.

L'Amour set out to write with a passion. In less than a year, he sold nearly forty stories to the pulps. Not all of the material went to Standard. Louis submitted work to all of the major pulp publishers. Nor were all of the stories done under the name Jim Mayo. His use of that name became highly exaggerated in interviews done years later.

Of the twenty-six stories written by L'Amour that appeared in the pulps during 1946–1947, only seven were listed as by Jim Mayo. Of the forty-five stories he sold in 1948–1949, sixteen were by Mayo. A majority of L'Amour's stories were published under his own name, including the popular Chick Bowdrie series written for Standard's *Popular Western* magazine.

Unlike most pulp writers, L'Amour did not stay in New York to write. Instead, he moved to Los Angeles, where he lived for the rest of his life. L'Amour led an active social life in Hollywood and he was prominently mentioned in the gossip columns of the time. At one time, he was engaged to actress Julie Newmar.

In 1950, L'Amour sold his first novel, *Westward the Tide,* a Western adventure very much in the pulp tradition, to World's Work, a genre-oriented English publisher that issued the book in hardcover in Britain. Though he had sold over a hundred short stories and novelettes to the pulps, L'Amour could not find a U.S. publisher for the story.

Late that same year, L'Amour signed with Doubleday to produce a series of Western novels featuring Clarence Mulford's famous Western character, Hopalong Cassidy. The stories were done as work-for-hire and thus were published under the name Tex Burns, which was owned by Doubleday. Four novels were published in hardcover, of which the first two were printed first in abbreviated form in pulp magazines.

Years later, L'Amour angrily denied authorship of the novels to every-one who asked him about them. He refused to sign copies of the books and denied using Tex Burns as one of his pen names.

In a radio interview with Lawrence Davidson, L'Amour finally spelled out the problem. The novels, as he wrote them, were true to the original character as portrayed by Mulford in the Cassidy novels. Evidently, Doubleday wanted stories that reflected the sanitized character as seen on TV and the movies. An unnamed editor rewrote the stories, changing L'Amour's character to fit the proper mold. Because of this rewriting, L'Amour felt the books were no longer his work. The Tex Burns name was not his pen name, but entirely the creation of Doubleday Books.

Despite L'Amour's strong personal distaste for the Hopalong Cassidy novels, Bantam Books recently began publishing the books under L'Amour's name. They are being reissued with all the usual fanfare associated with any L'Amour release. And the first novel in the series was a national best-seller.

By the early 1950s, the pulps were beginning to die. Paperbacks and television were driving the cheap fiction magazines out of business. Casting about for new markets, L'Amour managed to place a short story, "The Gift of Cochise," with *Colliers,* an upscale slick-paper magazine. The short was published in the July 5, 1952, issue. It proved to be the most important sale of his entire career.

Film rights for "The Gift of Cochise" were bought by Robert Fellows and John Wayne from L'Amour for four thousand dollars. It was Wayne's first venture into film production and he was unofficially assisted by his friend John Ford. The screenplay, despite later claims by L'Amour, was clearly identified as being based on the short story, and was written by James Edward Grant, Wayne's favorite screenwriter.

L'Amour wrote a novel version of the movie that was released the same day as the film. It was published by Fawcett–Gold Medal Books and featured a quote on the front cover by John Wayne, proclaiming the novel to be "the finest Western I've ever read." However, in a letter to Western film historian and critic Jon Tuska, Wayne admitted years later that his endorsement of the novel was supplied entirely at the publisher's request.

*Hondo* proved to be a best-seller for L'Amour, with Fawcett doing an initial printing of over three hundred thousand copies. It was hailed as a Western classic, and over the years has proven to be his most popular book. In the mid-1980s, Bantam Books estimated that more than three million copies of the book had been sold.

Meanwhile, L'Amour managed to sell several other novels in paperback. Ace Books, which had begun in 1952, bought four Western novels from L'Amour that appeared in late 1953 and 1954. It seemed quite likely that the books were sold before the success of *Hondo* because the first two novels, *Showdown at Yellow Butte* and *Utah Blaine,* both appeared under the pen name Jim Mayo. It wasn't until mid-1954 that Ace published

*Crossfire Trail* as by "Louis L'Amour, author of *Hondo."* A fourth Ace title, *Kilkenny,* was issued later that same year.

Though L'Amour continued to sell stories to the pulps for another two years, he had finally made the jump to the paperback field. On the strength of *Hondo,* L'Amour signed with Fawcett–Gold Medal and they published four novels from 1955 through 1957. During the same period, L'Amour sold hardcover rights to two novels to Jason Press, one to Appleton–Century Crofts, and another to Avalon Books. Reprint rights for all four books were bought by Bantam Books.

Along with his success in the book field, L'Amour continued to do well with movie sales. Two films were made from his work in 1955, and two more movies were issued in 1956. Over the course of his career, more than thirty of his works were produced for the movies or television.

It was in 1956 that L'Amour settled down to married life. He was introduced to his wife, Katherine Elizabeth Adams, by actress Julie Newmar. Twenty-two when she wed the author, Kathy Adams had been an actress with appearances on "Gunsmoke" and "Death Valley Days." After their marriage, she left acting and devoted herself full-time to her husband and his career. A son, Beau Dearborn, was born to the L'Amours in 1961, and a daughter, Angelique Gabrielle, in 1964.

In 1955, Louis left Fawcett and signed a contract with Bantam Books that marked a relationship that would endure for the rest of his life. Bantam was looking for a Western writer who could produce two or more books every year. L'Amour, who had produced at even a faster clip than that for the pulps, fit the bill. His first original novel for Bantam, *Radigan,* appeared in October 1958.

The next year saw two new books in print, as was the case in 1960. In 1961, only one novel was published under L'Amour's name, but there were four in 1962 and four in 1963. And so it continued, with two, three, or four books appearing every year as Bantam paperbacks. From time to time, L'Amour sold hardcover rights to a novel, but the paperback edition always appeared from Bantam.

As the number of L'Amour's titles increased, so did his reputation and following. In a shrewd move, Bantam marketing executives decided to keep all of L'Amour's books in print. While first printings on his early novels were not extremely large, continual reprintings resulted in tremendous numbers of copies after a few years. In 1975, L'Amour surpassed John Steinbeck as Bantam's best-selling author with over forty-one million copies of his books in print.

Much of L'Amour's success was attributable to his style of writing. His novels were fast moving, entertaining Westerns with larger-than-life heroes and menacing villains. Most of his books were comparatively short and could be read in one sitting. Psychological insights were few and the books were free of gratuitous sex and violence. There was action but not senseless killing or gore.

In reality, L'Amour's books were Western pulp novels done in paper-back form. Though his marketplace evolved from magazine to paper-back, L'Amour's writing remained the same. The type of stories that won him fans in the pulps continued to work in paperback. Very much in the pulp tradition, L'Amour went back to series characters for many of his novels. His best-known heroes were members of the Sackett family, and he wrote seventeen novels about their adventures. There were also novels about the Chantrys and the Talons. And three books featuring Lance Kilkenny.

Also contributing to L'Amour's success was his own personality. An outgoing, extremely charming man, he worked hard at promoting his work. An excellent speaker, he was always available for interviews for newspapers, magazines, radio, and television. His fascinating life story provided plenty of copy for articles that rarely dwelt on his stories but instead focused on the author himself.


As L'Amour's success grew, so did his plans. It was in the mid-1970s that he outlined his ambitious plans for a series of thirty-four novels fea-turing the Sackett, Talon, and Chantry families, covering forty years of American history. As the decade continued, the number of books rose to fifty and the span of history changed to cover the entire westward move-ment in America.

Equally ambitious was L'Amour's plan for a historical Western town, done of the scale of Williamsburg, to be built in Colorado. Plans for the village, to be named Shalako after one of L'Amour's popular Western characters, called for it to be a both a tourist attraction and a movie set. However, though the project was mentioned in a number of L'Amour interviews throughout the 1970s, it never progressed much beyond the planning stages.

In 1980, to celebrate one hundred million copies of L'Amour's work in print, Bantam sent L'Amour on a three-week publicity tour of the United States. But this was no ordinary author tour. Instead, the company rented a bus, much like that used by touring rock singers, refurbished it, com-

The only time I got to meet Louis L'Amour was at a reception for him and myself right at the time when my book [of Western artwork] was published in 1981. He and his wife came to a reception at a motel right next to Universal Studios in Los Angeles. I found that I'm not that much of a politician or social goer or whatever. But there have been few people in my life in all my experience who I've seen that were like him. There were only two, really, L'Amour and John Connelly, the ex-governor of Texas, who ran for president. They're the type of person who would stand in the middle of a room—he was a pretty big guy—and for some reason or another, people just seemed to circulate around them. He had a certain aura, a certain mystique about him.

Western artist Frank McCarthy, whose paintings were used as covers for a number of L'Amour novels, interviewed by Victor Dricks.

plete with Western murals on the sides, and dubbed it the Overland Express. On the twenty-one-day trip, L'Amour met thousands of fans and autographed books wherever he went. At seventy-two, he showed no signs of slowing down.

L'Amour became a legend in his own time. In 1981, he was awarded the Golden Saddleman Award by the Western Writers of America for his contributions to the Western genre. In 1982, he was voted a Congressional Gold Medal. It was presented to him by Ronald Reagan at the White House on September 24, 1983. L'Amour was only the second writer ever to receive the award, the first being Robert Frost.

Less than a year later, L'Amour returned to the White House to receive the United States Government Medal of Freedom, the highest award for an American civilian. He was again given the award by Ronald Reagan, an avowed fan of his writings, at ceremonies held on March 26, 1984.

All the time, he continued to write. Along with one or two new L'Amour novels per year, Bantam began issuing collections of his pulp stories in paperback as well. And Bantam secured rights to L'Amour's earliest novels done for Ace and Fawcett Books and added those titles to their line as well.

Most of these books still appeared as original paperbacks, but that was not always the case. In 1981, Bantam issued *Comstock Lode,* one of L'Amour's longest novels, as its first trade paperbound book. Two years later, Bantam published *The Lonesome Gods,* L'Amour's longest and most ambitious novel, in hardcover. The book leapt to the top of the best-seller list and was one of the best-selling novels of the year.

The same year saw L'Amour involved in a legal battle with Carroll & Graf Publishers. The New York paperback house discovered that a number of L'Amour's pulp stories were in public domain and decided to collect them in several paperback editions. L'Amour and Bantam sued to stop publication.

After much publicity, the case was settled out of court. Carroll & Graf's right to reprint the stories was upheld. L'Amour had been lax in protecting his work and had no one to blame but himself. However, Bantam rushed out paperback editions featuring the same stories as the C&G books, using the same titles, and with harsh statements by L'Amour about unauthorized editions. Both publishers' versions of the books made best-seller lists.

After years of writing short to midlength books, L'Amour was now concentrating on longer books, aimed at both the hardcover and paperback buyers. Though *Son of a Wanted Man* came out in 1984, it was a rewritten version of a pulp novel from more than thirty years earlier. Distinctly minor L'Amour, it still made the paperback best-seller list.

More impressive was *The Walking Drum,* a long historical adventure published in hardcover the same year. It was the first of a trilogy, a rather ambitious undertaking for a man seventy-six years old. Actually, the novel had been written over a decade before, but Bantam had refused to publish it at the time, feeling that L'Amour's market was only among Western fans. Needless to say, *The Walking Drum* made it to the top of the best-seller list in hardcover and later in paperback.

For the next three years, L'Amour produced one new book a year, each published in hardcover as a best-seller, and then later in paperback to the same reception. He had finally become so popular that his name on a book insured its sales. L'Amour was an American institution.

His fans numbered in the millions. Ronald Reagan read Louis L'Amour, as did Jimmy Carter. According to L'Amour, Dwight Eisenhower had been a fan as well. Willie Nelson, Tom Landry, and numerous other celebrities from all circles of American life purchased every new L'Amour book as published. He was the subject of numerous magazine articles, talk-show interviews, and even a profile on "60 Minutes."

Louis L'Amour died on June 10, 1988. Though he had never smoked a day in his life, the cause of death was lung cancer. To the last, L'Amour was working on a book, proofreading the typescript of his memoirs, *Education of a Wandering Man.*

Yet even death could not slow down the L'Amour legend. His memoirs made the best-seller lists in both hardcover and paperback. A minor collection of pulp Western stories, *The Outlaws of Mesquite,* followed in hardcover and was also a best-seller.

According to publicity releases from Bantam Books, the L'Amour estate has enough L'Amour material on hand to publish books well into the 1990s. The recent announcement of the Hopalong Cassidy series seems to indicate that all future Louis L'Amour books will be reprints from his pulp career. Ironically, L'Amour's first published work will become his last.

# Louis L'Amour and Bill Tilghman— An Interview

*(The following is part of a long interview with Louis L'Amour conducted by Lawrence Davidson, Richard Lupoff, and Richard Wolinsky for KIOU radio in San Francisco in 1986. In this section, L'Amour discusses his meeting with Western lawman Bill Tilghman.)*

**LAWRENCE DAVIDSON:** In the profile of you in the WWA journal, Harold Keith mentions that there were members of your family who knew Bill Tilghman, Tom Horn, Butch Cassidy, and Frank Canton.

**LOUIS L'AMOUR:** No. Part of that is wrong. None of us knew Tom Horn that I know of, unless—there is a possibility there. I couldn't say for sure but I had an uncle by marriage. He was the one who knew Butch Cassidy very well, who may have known Tom Horn. He could have known him, because he was superintendent of a ranch in Wyoming at the time and Butch Cassidy and his crowd used to ride across their territory, heading for the Hole in the Wall. They would sometimes switch horses out there in the field. If they were in a big hurry, they would leave their horses and take some of them out in the pasture.

**RICHARD LUPOFF:** What was this uncle's name?

**LL:** His name was Lashow. He was superintendent of a ranch out there. He was a man who traveled all over the West and was dead set against success. [Much laughter] He didn't want anything to tie him down. This ranch he was managing was owned by an Englishman. He came over here and he said, "You know, since you've been managing the ranch, I've made money out of it for the first time. If you will stay on, I'll give you a third of it." My uncle quit the next day.

**RL:** Sounds like a Louis L'Amour character.

**LL:** Yeah, he just said the money would tie him down. He wanted to wander you know, and property, he thought, was a weight on his shoulders.

**LD:** Did he ever make any mention of whether Butch Cassidy might have survived?

**LL:**  I know that he did.

**RL:**  Could you elaborate on that a little?

**LL:**  Well, in the first place, in the 1930s I was looking for a job. At this particular time, I've forgotten the exact year, I was traveling across the country in a car with another guy and we were hunting a job on a ranch where we knew the fella. We were also, I might say, riding the grub line as they used to say, where, if you hit the ranch at mealtimes, they would always invite you to stay. And we didn't have that much money. We couldn't afford to miss a meal. We showed up and we were talking to this rancher and Butch's name came up as a lot of others did, and it was mentioned that something was said about him being killed in South America. And the rancher said, "That's a lot of nonsense, he was here about three weeks ago and traded some horses with me."

**RL:**  Where was this?

**LL:**  That was in Wyoming. However, his [Cassidy's] home at the time was in Spokane, Wash. And he was running a printing office up there. He wrote his own story, but wrote it very badly.

**LD:**  Is that around?

**LL:**  It is around, yes, but it's . . .

**RL:**  Larry Pointer wrote *In Search of Butch Cassidy* and took excerpts from that.

**LD:**  It also says that you met Bill Tilghman.

**LL:**  Bill Tilghman taught me how to use a six-shooter. My brother was secretary to the governor of Oklahoma. Bill was a state officer. My brother also in his job was chairman of the Prison Board. Bill was transporting prisoners to the penitentiary at the time. Bill and my brother had become very good friends. He was a fine gentleman. I was just a kid. I came to visit my brother and my brother at the time was living in a hotel. He wasn't home yet, and we were going to go out to dinner as soon as he got home. I was waiting there in the room reading. I was reading *The Passing of the Oklahoma Outlaw,* written by Bill Tilghman. It was a paperback book, not the kind we have now, but it was published in paper, locally published. I was reading and there was a knock at the door. I opened the door and there was a nice-looking man in a white hat and white hair and white mustache and very beautiful blue eyes. He asked me if my brother was there and I told him he was not back yet and he said, "Well, I'm Bill Tilghman. We had an appointment." You could have knocked me over with a feather you know. [laughter] I'm a kid, I had just been reading about this guy, so I invited him in to wait and he sat there and told me a few stories. We talked a little bit, then we went out to dinner, the three of us—my brother and Bill and myself. He found that Parker was interested in shooting too so the following weekend he took us out in the north river bottoms and showed us how it was done and taught me how to use a six-shooter. I started from there.

**LD:**  Do you ever get tempted to write one of your novels dealing with an historical character like that?

**LL:**  I do once in a while have them in my stories. But I don't deal with them because their lives are known and set and I don't want to write biographies you see, so I use my own characters. But I knew Bill's wife later very well too. I didn't know her at the time. She was a writer.

# L'Amour at War:
# Selected Letters by Louis L'Amour
# to *Script* Magazine

*edited by Stefan Dziemianowicz*

BETWEEN 1938 and 1946, Louis L'Amour was a regular contributor to *Rob Wagner's Script,* a "Western" magazine somewhat different than the ones we associate him with today. *Script* (as it was popularly known) was conceived as a weekly for the citizens of Beverly Hills, most of whom were involved with the film industry. Thanks to the wit and humor of its eponymous editor, it quickly became recognized as something of a cross between *The New Yorker* and *Variety,* a thinking-man's paper for the entertainment trade.

The success of Wagner's magazine, which published between 1929 and 1949, is an example of how sometimes who you know is as important as what you know. A minor director during the silent-film era, Wagner cultivated his relationships with movie stars and celebrities and convinced many to write for *Script.* Thus, it was not unusual to find interspersed between the magazine's movie reviews, society page, and gossip column a humorous article by cowboy star Tom Mix on women's bathing suits, cinematographer James Wong Howe discussing the educational uses of film in his native China, criticism of movie musicals by operetta composer Sigmund Romberg, or Lillian Gish commenting on the difference between acting in silent films and "talkies."

Though elitist by Hollywood standards, *Script* reflected Wagner's own liberal thinking during an era of great social and political ferment in America. Muckraker Upton Sinclair wrote regularly for the magazine, and articles by Charlie Chaplin and screenwriter Dalton Trumbo tended to focus on the plight of the blacks or the example of communist Russia. At the same time, *Script* consciously burlesqued the pretensions of the community it served. Its wry editorial tone was attributable in part to Wagner's close friendship with humorist Will Rogers, and Wagner was not above running cover titles for such nonexistent articles as "Do Germs

Have Souls?" "How Wives Can Protect Husbands from Clara Bow," and "Ten New Commandments by Cecil B. DeMille."

*Script* also printed a healthy sampling of fiction: poems by Jessamyn West, a play by Ben Hecht, and short fiction by Pulitzer Prize–winner William Saroyan. Two yet unknown pulp writers, Louis L'Amour and Ray Bradbury, both contributed fiction to the magazine.

Along with selling *Script* a number of short stories, L'Amour was a regular contributor to the letter column—"Voice of the Village." These letters date from the very beginning of L'Amour's writing career and continue through his wartime experience.

In this chapter, we present L'Amour's letters written to *Script* dealing specifically with the Second World War. They begin with L'Amour's feeling on the conflict and continue on with his actual experiences overseas, when he served as an unofficial war correspondent for the publication. These letters offer a unique look at the author and his opinions during an extremely important period of his life. They are reprinted here for the first time.

Letters appearing in "Voice of the Village" were always given a title by the editor and that title is included with each piece, along with the date of publication.

## *From a Fighter*

March 9, 1940

Dear Rob:

I once read a history of the world in five volumes. A fair job, but too much concentration on war, the battles and bloodshed of history. Fortunately, somewhere I acquired the good sense to be more interested in the steps man took to crawl out of the original swamp.

There is a good deal more satisfaction in the struggle of man to find shelter, food, comfort, and beauty than in the account of his warfare. Funny sentiments, probably, from a man who has made fighting a hobby. But my sort of fighting is the sort, whether for fun or for keeps, that concerns only two men. At worst it is scarcely more than a healthy form of exercise.

However, writing that paragraph inspired a very civilized thought: may it not be wrong to fight at all? Can violence, even for fun, be right? There's an angle worthy of consideration. Games excepted, of course.

I become impatient with the defeatist attitude of people who say we've always had war and so always will. We had family feuds, tribal warfare, and duels, too. We don't now. Once it was believed that justice could not exist without torture.

What was it Baudelaire said? "Torture, as the art of discovering truth, is barbaric nonsense; it is the application of a material means to a spiritual end."

A lot of common sense in that.

Good stuff in *Script*. I liked your editorial very well and the Tree stories were good. Also Al Cohn. Of course, "Horrible Hollywood" is always good, and all of it. Why try to name names? Just read them. I liked the whole layout from cover to cover.

## *L'Amour et la Guerre*

September 28, 1940

Dear Rob:

It looks like I'm to be in uniform for a year. Having tried writing at sea I know how tough it will be trying to write in camp, for it never worked very well in the fo'c'stle. Naturally, I'm not very happy about it.

No one could be more against war than I, and no one could appreciate its futility more, yet in a case of national emergency, I'd be more than ready to serve as things stand. Yet, now, in peace time, and when its going to hit me where it hurts, I'm not exactly happy about it.

War is never necessary, and whenever a nation declares war its statesmen are admitting their own incompetence. Recently, I was reading Carl Sandburg's very fine biography of Lincoln's war years, and in Abraham Lincoln's first inaugural address I found this:

> "Suppose you got to war, you cannot fight always; and when, after much loss on both sides, and no gain on either, you cease fighting, the identical old questions as to terms of intercourse are again upon you."

Could there be any more complete confession of futility?

Since sending you the last story I've met several friends of yours. I had the luck to hear Helen Gahagan speak to the Council of Social Welfare when she was here last spring, and then to help show her a few of Oklahoma's sore spots. It was a rare treat, and she was so interesting that one didn't realize how lovely she was until she stopped talking. Certainly, her talk had them hanging on the ropes, and if she were to campaign for him I believe she could elect Steinbeck Governor of Oklahoma, despite all the violent things the local papers have said—and some others.

A friend of mine here, Alice Jeppe (a reasonably tall blonde), met you in Australia. She's a swell person.

## *Toujours L'Amour*

October 5, 1940

Dear Rob:

Having some months ago taken Ralph Block to task on the subject of "Mr. Smith," I am naturally pleased now to agree with him completely on his article in the issue for September 21. He has certainly said something worth saying, and something that should be said loud, and often.

I believe the most essential thing we need now is the one that will be hardest to get. I mean intellectual integrity. In these days two-thirds of our existence is based upon falsehood. In the past weeks I have heard men attack principles they know to be good because the opposition is for them. I have read editorials that were deliberate misrepresentations, and all to advance a party or plan, or to attack one they do not favor.

Every day men and women attack democratic ideals because they have not been the person, or their has not been the party, to advance the ideal in question. A bill that is good for the country is advanced by Democrats and viciously attacked by Republicans, and vice versa. And this is not because of difference of opinion, but only because of party politics.

The recent deal for naval bases is a case in point, but only one of many. Men whom I heard criticize Roosevelt for not moving fast enough, for not preparing soon enough, attacked him bitterly when he wrote an executive order and made the deal. They were the same men who a short time before were in favor of something of the kind.

We need now men who will take the advice of Polonius, and be true to themselves, and to their own ideals, and who will honestly stand by what they believe regardless of person or party.

Block did a grand job, and we could use some more of the same sort of thing.

## *Napoleon and Hitler*

November 8, 1941

Dear Rob:

Just to clarify a point: in the Voice of the Village recently Mr. Chadwick quotes Napoleon to the effect that he had no strategy for defeating snowdrifts. No doubt the Little Corporal was willing to give General

Winter credit for his defeat, but a reference to history will show that such was not the case.

Napoleon was defeated before winter set in. It was a late season, and he was advised not to delay in Moscow, but he did. The snows did not set in *until he was already in full retreat.* They put on the finishing touch that turned into catastrophe.

Actually, it was the scorched earth policy and guerrilla warfare that defeated Napoleon. The Russians refused to meet the Little Corsican in a major battle, knowing him a master tactician. However, they continually harassed his columns, and they left the earth barren of all supplies. They stripped and burned the cities, leaving him nothing.

Napoleon, like many another man, has needed an alibi. The winter has, for a long time, been his. As a matter of fact, Napoleon the great general was already a thing of the past, and there in Moscow he wavered and was uncertain. He possessed a fault then that he never had in his younger years, fatal indecision. Hitler has it, too. He decides easily when his armies are winning, but this war he lost at Dunkerque. Then, despite the fact he hadn't planned it, despite the fact his men were tired, he might have won.

The world, including Britain, had been deeply shocked by his overwhelming victory in France, by his success in Poland. If he had struck then at Britain, he might have won. But once the British rescued their army, and withstood the shock of air attack in that fatal September, the tide had turned. History will record that Hitler lost the war at Dunkerque.

## *The Greatest Soldier*

January 31, 1942

Dear Rob:

In his recent letter to Voice of the Village, Mr. Adrian Johnson says: "Louis L'Amour calls Napoleon a master tactician. Quite, after Ney and Murat supplied the ideas." His letter continues with an attack on conquerors in general.

I am no lover of conquest nor of conquerors, nor of any form of destruction. Yet dislike of a method does not imply lack of ability in the use of that method. One may decry cheating at cards, yet can admire the cheat's dexterity. Certainly, however, if I were naming the great men of the world I would list no soldier among them.

As to Ney and Murat supplying Napoleon's ideas, there is no evidence to warrant such a statement. Ney himself remarked that he was a musket to be fired when Napoleon willed, and Murat was noted for lack of intelligence, being a lover of elaborate uniforms—Goering-like. Ney blundered unforgivably at Quatre Bras when he had a chance to use any ideas he may have had. Whatever one may say of Napoleon, the Corsican was a soldier. One many not admire his art, but in his field he was a genius. Major Thomas R. Phillips, editor of *Roots of Strategy,* says of him: "He is, beyond any doubt, the greatest of European soldiers."

I am a lover of peace and believe that most wars can be avoided. Yet in a world where ambitious men and nations resort to force, soldiers have their place, as we are now discovering.

As to the ideas of Napoleon: war develops by evolution, as all things do. The methods of Napoleon were developed by him from previous material. Improved highways was one of the greatest factors in his success, but even more he realized in military fact the developments of De Saxe, De Broglie, De Guibert, Du Teil, and Bourcet.

Mr. Johnson says that Napoleon triple-crossed Josephine. That statement is open to doubt. The lady from Martinique was given to playing around and had no claim on anyone's loyalty, even if she might have had on friendship. It is probable that she was treated as well as she deserved.

I think a study of the Corsican's life would prove that loyalty was a virtue to a fault. His brothers, and the leaders who aided him at the beginning, failed him time and again, yet he always forgave them, rewarded them and started again. Ney deserted Napoleon before Elba, going over to the Bourbons. When Bonaparte's star was again in the ascendant, Ney returned, deserting the Bourbons. Murat was often a traitor and often a fool. Yet even at the end Napoleon remembered these men with pleasure.

Like Mr. Johnson I dislike conquerors, but there is such a thing as justice.

## *Soldier Comes Home*

March 18, 1944

Dear Florence:

It has been years since I've written anything for *Script*. The Army hasn't left me much time. Now, I think I shall have more, and will be sending something like the stories that Rob used to like.

For the first time in several years, I'm on the Coast—with the Transportation Corps at Ft. Mason. I am living at the St. Francis Hotel, and would enjoy meeting any of the Scripters.

It was like coming home to return to San Francisco, the city of Jack

London, George Sterling and Ambrose Bierce. Crossing the Bay from Oakland the air was bright with sunlight, and the green hills, the glittering towers, all of it looked familiar, and very clean and bright.

There have been so many changes, so many different lives jammed into one. I've worked at so many things, lived in so many countries—all the Japanese occupied zones, and about everywhere else but Alaska and Australia.

## A Call to Poets

July 15, 1944

To Florence, to *Script,* and to Ann, the Mason of Circulation . . .

Somewhere on the trail behind me, in a bewildering chain of lost addresses, my copies of *Script* no doubt follow. Yet, I am here, without Sunshine, without laughter, without *Script.*

Here one is working. One returns "home" and tumbles into bed and sleeps. One awakens, digs out the typewriter, and battles a bit desperately with an idea. Eventually, something happens.

But there were a few days of shifting around through a maze of APO's, until I reached here, days when I saw Chester, Exeter, Oxford, and Riegate, not to mention Stonehenge and a lot of the most lovely countryside in the world.

The reading has mostly been odds and ends, books picked up here and there, and not many of them, and not many that are any good.

One of the best things about this war is the Red Cross set-up. These girls are the salt of the earth, a bunch of swell kids, taking a fearful beating, and doing a swell job. Most of them would be much more at home dancing somewhere, yet here they are, often sleeping in cold tents, lying on boxes and sacks, getting a few minutes of sleep before the next bunch of helmeted soldiers come in to be fed, given coffee and doughnuts and speeded on their way.

For many a man the last woman they will ever see are these kids from the States, and with all due respect for English girls, and on previous trips I've known some fine ones, I still haven't seen one to compare to these.

But what these men need is a poet. They haven't any buildup. What they need is somebody who isn't writing for the few, but for the many, someone to give them some glory and make them feel proud. Men die easier when they die for a cause, and they haven't been sold so far. Most of them think of one thing only, getting it over and going back. They want to go home. But not any of them would go without winning it, all the way.

To hell with the pretty, intellectual stuff. This isn't the time for an intellectual bust. It is the time for something these boys can believe, something they can remember. Something with a swinging, powerful rhythm and a catchy sound. They need to glorify themselves.

These kids have guts and stamina, and they go out of here laughing, yet every man who has ever seen action knows how they really feel inside.

And they're doing a grand job, wherever they are. Napoleon's crossing of the Alps was a romp compared to the crossing of the Kokoda Trail in New Guinea, and the beaches of Tarawa, Anzio, and over here at Cherbourg were something any fighting men the world ever saw could be proud of. And they shouldn't be passed off without more notice than they've had. The job is anybody's, the field is wide open.

Best wishes, and lots of luck with *Script* . . . always glad to hear from any Scripters in England, or any Americans over here. But Lord knows they've almost taken over some sections of England. Anglo American relations should be good after this . . . or is the word, plentiful?

## *Letter from France*

October 21, 1944

From my seat by the window I can look across a fine sweep of forest and meadow toward the long rows of poplars that line the distant highway. They are tall, graceful trees, shaped like candle flame, but against the late afternoon sky they resemble the spears of a marching army.

It is quiet here, and one can relax. These past weeks have left us but little time for that, for they have been hard, driving weeks when we often went thirty-six to forty hours without sleep.

Coming from a combat outfit as I did, I am afraid I had some of the usual lack of respect the combat soldier feels for supply outfits, but all that has changed. There has never been better work done than has been done by those QM truck companies, nor against greater difficulties. More than once I've seen these men crawl from their beds on the ground, sodden with weariness, and climb into their trucks to roll away. Through rain, mud, and enemy strafing (at first), over shell-torn roads, and often through narrow streets scarcely wide enough for the big *camions*, these men have worked long and without complaint.

Now, for a few hours, I have a measure of tranquility. The Count has been considerate, and I can sit by his window, in a pleasant room lined with books, and try to reorder my thoughts for a little writing.

The war passed lightly over this area, leaving it scarcely touched. It is different from the earlier days of the invasion when every bomb-pitted highway was lined with the scorched and blasted carcasses of vehicles that had gone before. Somehow they always reminded me of a line of marching ants that had suddenly been seared by a blow torch in the hands of a passerby. Here and there a huge tank lay on its back, grotesquely impotent, like some gigantic beetle.

One speaks with the people and finds many viewpoints, yet it seems that a large percentage favor De Gaulle. The Count and a friend of his, a member of the stock exchange, and themselves not too favorable toward him, admit to sixty or seventy percent. The Professor, who seemed to have observed the occupation with some gift for analysis, believes the percentage higher. At least, no less. His comments on the occupation are interesting.

The first year, he has said, was very bad. The Germans took most of the crops and many people were near to starvation. Many lost thirty to forty pounds in weight. But the following year there was a change. Somehow, the crops the Germans took were not quite so large. They returned what they thought the people needed, but in every case, when the grain was threshed or the fruit picked, there was less than before. Eggs apparently grew fewer, indicating that even the hens showed less eagerness to lay for the Germans.

Food parcels began to filter into crowded cities. Many city dwellers had friends in the country, and a black market began to flourish. So the succeeding years were not so bad. Even so, the children are thinner, and there are indications that four years of eating improper food has had its effect. Tuberculosis has increased enormously among children.

The French have been more than hospitable, and the country itself is a pleasant, lovely place. The soldiers seem to prefer this country to England by a great deal, at least that is the response one gets to questions, and it has been my own reaction.

Censorship rules have been relaxed somewhat of late, and places not close to one's present location can be mentioned. For a time we were near Chartres, and I became curious about the two steeples on its cathedral. Curious, because they did not match.

The new tower is about thirty feet taller than the old, and very different in style. Each, in its way, a thing of beauty. The old tower has a simplicity that is marked and bears no resemblance to the Renaissance tower designed by Jehan de Beauce. The new tower is the tallest in stone in France, reaching to three hundred and seventy-seven feet. The last four were added in 1690 by Claud Augé. On the spot where the Cathedral stands the Druids once worshipped, and the Cathedral itself has withstood many fires, storms, and much trouble, and many additions have been made since it was first completed.

Such things are seen only in passing now. One has an hour, a few minutes, one stops, and then one is rolling along again, for when there is war, one can think little of the creative arts, either as creator or observer.

Paris is still one of the world's most beautiful cities, and the closer to Paris one gets the prettier the girls . . . so many fine roads (although they don't last under the terrific volume of traffic they get now) with long avenues between tall poplars or sycamores . . . apples in Normandy . . . the wine of Anjou . . . the winding streets of Chartres, built for defense . . . the frightfulness of empty, dead St. Lo, her heaps of rubble cold and still under an autumn moon . . . the graciousness of the French people . . . the stone farm buildings and walls, all built like forts, and somewhat in principle like some rural farms in China . . . the hedgerows . . . Mont St. Michel . . . the French people returning home, pushing carts, prams, riding bicycles. And so many pretty girls on bicycles . . . the bedraggled German prisoners . . . A big guard who shouts, "Hey, Joe! Send over a couple of those Supermen to sweep these rocks off the road!"

And two of the Supermen came; two men from a country that said the Democracies were soft, that they couldn't take it. And the big guard who called Joe, with his bronzed hands and keen gray eyes, would have looked just as well under a coonskin cap, and would have walked with assurance beside the men of Concord, Gettysburg or the Alamo.

## *Letter from France*

February 3, 1945

We started for home in a driving rain storm. All the rivers were up, and so I left my place at the tail of the convoy and ran ahead in the jeep. There were several crossings of the river to make, and some of the temporary bridges didn't promise well.

But when we came to the Seine the end of the bridge was a quarter of a mile away over rushing water. Poles marked vaguely the sides of the road. Between those poles ran the pavement. I tried to remember how shallow that passage had been, and it seemed the water was probably not deep enough to stop us. If the jeep would make it, I knew the big trucks would.

So we rolled in. We had disconnected the fan so it would not splash water, and we moved ahead in low. We knew there was a chance the pavement had been undermined and broken, that we might run off the pavement into deeper water.

Rain whipped and lashed at the jeep, and the water tugged at her wheels, but she kept moving. Once she sagged sickeningly, and I was afraid she was going under, but the hood lifted bravely, and she went through. Behind us the big tankers roared steadily through. It was the third stretch of water we had navigated in the past day, but the others had been on the way up to deliver the gas. Now we were headed home, or what passes for it now.

We made it, and there was plenty of turkey, cranberry sauce, mashed potatoes, and all the usual fixings. Guitou came over from her chateau, and we convinced her that it was an old American custom to eat until we had to be carried from the table.

Later, in Paris, to the Club 44 with Guitou, and some dancing and champagne, with more lovely women than I've seen this side of California or Texas. About every fourth man was an American, and the rest as scattered a hodge podge of nationalities as one could expect to find. Much interesting talk with Willy of Budapest about the Corso, Margit Island, and the Arizona Club, and the many fine horses of Hungary. And talking with a French lieutenant of the old life around Shanghai in the thirties.

And then an argument with Delia, from Dublin, about the Irish question.

After Normandy's ruined walls and cities of debris, Paris was like something out of a dream. It isn't, of course, the old Paris. The Paris of before the war. Yet it is Paris, and like no other place on earth. Perhaps the girls are wearing dresses made over for the third or fourth time, perhaps the hats were created from extremity, but Paris is still Paris.

The dinners aren't as lavish, the dishes are fewer, and the wines not always vintage, but the company is some of the best to be found in the world.

It doesn't have the bewildering cosmopolitan variety of Cairo or Shanghai, nor the Victorian memories of London. It lacks the faded glamour of Vienna or the gypsy-like air of Budapest, or the Anthony Hope mannerisms of Bucharest, but it has the youth of the world in its atmosphere, and the feeling that in Paris it is always spring.

In the tiny village of Champeaux there is a priest who never accepted the German occupation, and who was never careful about what he said to them. In the floor of the church was a swastika, left there many years ago, possibly about the year 900.

Seeing it, a German officer remarked: "Ah, I see the Germans have been here before! No doubt some German is buried here?"

The priest replied: "No doubt. We have buried many Germans in France, and we shall bury many more!"

My first meeting with him was at Andrezel, a nearby village, on Armistice Day. I'd been asked to speak there, to say a few words at the monument to the men who died in the first World War. The priest was there, and he liked what I said, so we became friends, and talked many times thereafter, and he showed me through his church, and pointed out the old house where Abelard and Heloise are reported to have met many times.

Later that day some flying forts passed over, and we went to the door to watch them pass. Guitou told me how they used to watch them when the Germans were still there. "We always like to see them, even when we knew they were coming to drop their bombs near us."

Movies were shown in France of the death of the generals and others who plotted against Hitler. One, a general who used Vaux le Vicomte for his headquarters for awhile, was hung through the chin and throat by a steel hook, much like they use in hanging sides of beef. He took, they said, a long time to die.

And so many are saying even now that it wasn't Germany, it was only Hitler, only the Nazis. There is nothing Hitler has done that Germany hasn't advocated for centuries. Read Fichte, Gneisnau, Bismarck, Scharn-horst, Clausewitz, Treitschke, Spengler, Nietzsche, or any one of fifty others over the hundreds of years Germany has been in the making. Read, if you wish, Tacitus. He described the German as he was then. Is there a difference?

Mail call treated me well this evening, and among others came one from Don Blanding, dated from Carmel, which seemed like a breath from home. Don was his usual cheerful self, and that was a help. Even seeing the post mark is a break over here.

Not that we dislike France. On the contrary, everyone seems to be enthusiastic about the country, and according to the rumors drifting down this way, they like Belgium also.

In the past few weeks we've had a chance to look around a little. At first, back before Isigny, La Haye du Puits, St. Lo, Domfront, Avranches and Mortain, there wasn't much time for looking around, and very little to look at but the shells of stone buildings and hedgerows.

In some ways, it was better back there. We had the added incentive of danger. Snipers fired on our convoys, and I had my own little experience of going into the woods after them, and one of our convoys was cut off when the Germans struck toward Avranches from Mortain, and again we had to take our gas tankers through a town in flames. It kept us all keyed up and on the ball. Now it is just long hours of hard, driving work, and sleepless hours.

Oddly enough, we who are close to it hear little of the war's progress. At home we heard much more. Here scarcely one man in twenty can tell you the day of the week or month. Despite that, and the fact that we all want to come home, I doubt if there is a man in the ETO who would settle for anything less than unconditional surrender.

In this company there are several California boys, and one of my best squad leaders, Cpl. Rockdale, is from Hollywood Boulevard. I expect we should all get together and talk about the weather. Here sunshine is only a memory, and a vague one at that. Every day and night it rains. There is mud clear up to here . . . that's right.

In Paris you can get a very good meal, black market, for 1,000 francs, which is twenty dollars of anybody's money, too much for a G.I. Even not a very G.I. lieutenant. Everyone is looking for cameras. And a few can be had. I'd buy one from home if I could get a good deal on something worthwhile.

Knowing something of combat and with several months of it behind me, I came to a Transportation Corps outfit with some skepticism, but have remained to learn respect and admiration. No one, not even the boys up front, know what these men go through. They don't have any glamour, they never get medals, but I've seen them come in dropping with fatigue, get a few hours sleep, and roll on again. I've seen them sleep in the cabs of their trucks when they could sleep at all, and time and again we have had to stop convoys and get the boys out to wake them up by running in the rain before starting on again. Yes, it's rough, but it's a job that has to be done.

Incidentally, everyone in France is looking forward to seeing "Gone with the Wind." I think everyone over here has read the book in translation, and so far everyone I've met has liked it. That, I think, and Chaplin's "The Great Dictator," are the films they look forward to most.

But there was another day, and I had a convoy to consider, and some long miles ahead of me, and all the work and trouble that comes with it. There is pleasure, but it comes only in moments between long hours of cold rain, and endless mud.

P.S. As for pin-up girls, don't let anybody kid you. The boys still like them best, and will always go for them. I do, myself, and the only trouble is that the only ones I see are occasionally in *Yank*.

## A Soldier's Ode to Cooking

April 14, 1945

Being Mess Officer, among other things too humorous to mention, I have to think about eating, and thinking about eating makes me think about home, and thinking about home makes me think about eating. All of which is no doubt very clear and takes me somewhere close to the borderline of Dick Sharpe's field. Personally, I think he is a public benefactor of the highest type, and should have a statue somewhere in Beverly Hills, probably not too far from the famous Peterless Pans.

Whether Napoleon ever actually said anything about an army marching on its stomach is open to question. The truth of the statement is not. And the art of eating as well as the art of cooking are too little regarded in this world. Along with music, painting, sculpture and writing, cooking should be ranked as one of the major arts.

In fact, there is some reason to believe that it is *the* major art. Would Shelley have written his poetry on a diet of spinach or would Chopin have composed his nocturnes on C rations? Probably if Napoleon's stomach hadn't bothered him he would have been content to stay at home instead of upsetting the world. One of the greatest Nazi crimes was to deprive the French not only of proper nourishment for several years, but of the opportunity to turn food into something approaching ambrosia.

On a farm in Normandy however they prepared as perfect a chicken as I ever ate, but left the head on. All during the meal, while I gnawed cheerfully on a breast, that head regarded me dismally and reproachfully. Not even a couple of husky drinks of Calvados, that sin against humanity, could bring me out of it. Even today I seldom eat chicken without thinking of those empty eye sockets, glaring at me like some reptilian monster from another age.

Never very enthusiastic about wine, I almost acquired the taste in France. Before, I'd been strictly a champagne, Scotch and soda or rum drinker. The champagne of Reims or Epernay, of any of the good brands, is still tops for me, but I've wandered down the wine list a few times, and like enough of them to make me decide it has something after all, this custom of wine with meals.

But it isn't drinking that matters. Eating is the important thing. It was Meredith who said that "Civilized man cannot live without cooks." I agree. Although a C or K ration diet is nothing for a gourmand to go into ecstasies over. But right now what I would like to see is not palm heart salad or bird's nest soup, but a thick steak, about two inches thick, with plenty of butter.

The importance of cooking is overlooked, as I've said. When, during my lecture touring days some lovely creature, ancient dowager or otherwise, invited me for dinner, I always hesitated until I saw her husband. If the husband looked plump and pleasant, I accepted, and the formula may have made me miss some good meals, but those I had were all good, too.

In Shakespeare's play on Julius Caesar, if you'll recall, it wasn't his wife they asked about when he was making quite a stir in Rome. Nor was it his friends, his teachers or his advisers or the books he read. What they asked was, "What meat doth this our Caesar eat that he hath grown so great?"

## From a Sun Porch in Westphalia

June 23, 1945

It is quiet now, and to ride along beside the Main River, winding so peacefully among the high green hills, one would not believe there had been a war. The leaves and the grass are hastily arranging a veil to cover the ugly scars, and the scars upon the people are not yet showing too deeply.

I have never seen a more beautiful river than the Main as it flows, limpid and still, mirroring the tall, slim candles of the poplars, the hills and the old towers; as it turns and bends as though for no other reason than to flow through these tiny villages south from the highway from Frankfort to Wurzburg.

The girls are out in the early evening walking along the road, pretty girls, with full round breasts (Germany will be remembered by every G.I. for this, if nothing else!!) and ready smiles for the Americans. But the trucks roll on and do not stop, and one comes to believe that the conquest of Germany has not been a success for the women. One feels that the policy of non-fraternization, no matter how good, was a distinct disappointment to this land that has known so many wars.

Many conquering armies have passed and each succeeding generation of Germans has inherited something of what the armies left as they passed. The Franks were here long ago, and their land has been passed over in part by Hannibal, a Semitic, and his army, which was a mixture, with many Semitics and many big, black Nubians from the banks of the Nile. Probably, Germany has least right of all the countries in the world to claim racial purity.

Yet it is a lovely land and one wonders, seeing the trees loaded with blossoms, the fields green and beautiful, the once barren soil now dark and rich (I wonder how much blood helped to change the color?) why these people have their drive to war? Is it some urge to annihilation? Some sombre psychological malformation that drives them on to the Valhalla of destruction?

The people are friendly. My first news of the war's end was from the shouted words of a German along the road. The people have seen the end to the war, and already they are trying to be friendly, and so ease the occupation. For a people who stride so heavily when they conquer, they are most obsequious when conquered.

I walked a few days ago, through the amphitheatre at Nurnberg where once Hitler held his reviews and addressed his throngs. The steps where the Nazi leaders sat are marked with zigzag camouflage of red tile, and the seats where the crowds gathered are overgrown with grass. (So many times this spring I have thought of Sandburg's poem "Grass," and the line that goes, I think, "I am the grass, I cover all.") Like white corpuscles in the blood stream, the grass comes in and tries to knit together this blasted land, tries to cover up the scars, heal the wounds. (It will take more than grass to rebuild the cities!)

The war here was ended quietly. I heard no cheers, no shouts. Everyone seemed relieved in a sense, but only news that we were to go home would arouse any enthusiasm. And few of us expect to.

We are living now in the summer home of one of the Nazi leaders. Not of the top flight, yet close. His daughter, an attractive blonde with vacant eyes, was married to a cousin or nephew of Von Papen. The house was quickly and cheaply built but is large, spacious, and comfortable. The furniture is largely hand carved, from China and Java, and there is a wealth of old china in the house. Yet the house is a hodgepodge and not well done for the money spent.

The last town we were in was a village, a quiet little place where after curfew hours the people sat in their open windows and talked across the street. The town before that, we lived in a house filled with clothing looted from five countries. The Germans are today the best dressed people in Europe; and if one looks at the labels, it is easy to see why.

And the town before that was a little town in Lorraine where I saw a girl that wrung a gasp from every G.I. who passed. She had the daintiest and best-shaped figure I've ever seen in lo, these many summers, sang like an angel, played the piano, and if in any place but a jerkwater town in Lorraine with a war just over, would be headed for Hollywood and some training.

It is growing dark now, and the poplars are pointing long fingers of shadow toward the forest beyond the fields, a cuckoo is calling in the lilacs down in the lower garden, and out on the road I see a released German prisoner, bedraggled and beaten, walking toward home. The pride of the Wehrmacht takes the road back.

## *Paris—1945*

October 20, 1945

Strolling along the Champs Elysées, and watching the gay afternoon crowds . . . Paris has changed, of course. It is recovering from the war now, regaining assurance, coming back to itself again as it has many times in the past. It still isn't what it was, but it has come far from the dark, empty streets right after liberation. It was a haunted town then, ghostly in the blackout, with only the phosphorescent wands of the M.P.'s to show a light of any kind.

There are uniforms everywhere now and so many ranks the mind is confused and cannot register them all. WACS, too, and WAAFS and ATS, and girls from every country that has women in uniform, some here for duty, and some for play, but all seeing Paris, gathering memories they will never forget. And there is much to see.

Monique Melinand, French film star whose picture recently graced the pages of *Yank,* looking very chic in a new hat . . . a WAC from a Texas cowtown talking to a French army officer . . . lovely Annie Lacorne, most photographed girl in Paris, walking swiftly along the street, her honey colored hair blowing in the wind . . . the sidewalk tables at Fouquet's, and not one vacant.

The rue Marignan which replaced the winter garden where Beethoven's symphonies were first played in France . . . most of the treasures are on display in the Louvre again . . . and they tell me the Venus de Milo had a 37 inch bust . . . they tell me Jane Russell does as well.

Two husky paratroopers wearing the shoulder patch of the 101st Air Borne . . . another major . . . there must be as many majors in Paris as privates . . . the Cours la Reine where the gallants used to put their horses through their paces to show off for the girls . . . and sometimes the girls' coaches became tangled and then the girls did some showing off too . . . the Cours la Reine dates from 1616 and Marie de Médici, but for many years it was reserved for intimates of the court.

This area where now are many fashionable restaurants was, until 1789, a dairy farm and its pastures . . . the Postage Stamp Exchange, where collectors gather . . . the Place de la Concorde, designed in 1754 by Gabriel, the famous architect of the reign of Louis XV . . . it was here that Louis XVI, Marie Antoinette, Danton, and many others died on the guillotine.

Two G.I.'s taking pictures of the obelisk, its hieroglyphics recounting the accomplishments of the Pharaoh Ramseses II, 1300 years before Christ. That obelisk has seen some strange sights in the hundred years since it was erected.

Walking down the Quai des Tuileries, I glimpsed a dignified gentleman recovering a half smoked American cigarette from the gutter . . . the current price is about 120 francs the packet, black market . . . that amounts to about $2.40, American . . . but prices are often in excess of that . . . crops in France have been hurt by dry weather . . . in some areas there will be no potatoes, no beans . . . the wheat crop is good, but the price will be high, which is very good for the land owners, not so good for the buyers of bread.

The French are always astonished when the Americans like their bread, as so many do . . . they much prefer our white bread, and, in the early days at least, ate it like cake. A few scattered G.I.'s noticing a pretty girl riding by on a bicycle with her skirt blowing about her hips in entire unconcern . . . no Frenchman even turns his head. French bathing suits more abbreviated than ours . . . some of those at home look like Mother Hubbards by comparison . . . and in some places it is not unusual to see girls go in minus a halter . . . bathing caps are very rare.

Endless carnivals along the Avenue de Clichy . . . and the French seem to prefer rides, for there is an unending line of them. Pigalle, the rue Lepic, and the winding streets to the top of Montmartre and the finest view in Paris . . . an American captain with three campaign ribbons, three decorations and a camera. He is getting some good shots, different from the unimaginative thousands who continue to take the Arc de Triomphe and Eiffel Tower, available on any post card . . . while they miss the odd little streets, the quaint old women, the stone paved courts.

The Byzantine dome of the Sacré Coeur reminds me of Fez . . . or Marrakesh . . . a few days ago, two old maps of Paris were given me by the Countess de Felcourt. They were highly interesting. In 1824 Montmartre was still on the outskirts of Paris, and the fashionable shopping center of Champs Elysées was largely open country . . . the Place de la Concorde was the Place de Louis XV, and the Avenue de la Grande Armée was the Route de St. Germain. The avenue now known as the Champs Elysées was the Avenue de Neuilly . . . there have been many changes.

Books secretly published during the occupation are rapidly becoming collector's items.

The Bateau Lavoir where Picasso and his followers once lived . . . when painters went on a spree they usually found their way to the Lapin

Agile or the Place du Tertre . . . Manet, Gauguin, Vincent Van Gogh, and many others went there. The Lapin Agile used to be known as the Cabaret des Assassins . . . on the register there are the names of now famous artists who formerly came to the cabaret.

The Moulin de la Galette still puts on a somewhat risque show, but the Montmartre of the apache is largely a legend . . . but here and there are a few writers and artists even now, walking the streets and sitting in the cafes that knew Verlaine, Berlioz, Baudelaire and Mimi Pinson.

Paris has an atmosphere all its own, but then, so does every city . . . I've often said that if I were suddenly put down in any of the cities I've visited, without warning and without any landmark close by, that I could know the city within a couple of blocks. That is true of Paris, also Budapest, San Francisco, New York or Rio.

## *To Montmartre*

January 5, 1946

There is always something happening in Paris. At the moment it is a lively trade in pistols. GI's on pass with guns brought back from Germany are selling them.

The Lapin Agile, closed for a time, is open again . . . now one can sit at the tables made famous by Manet, Van Gogh and many others. The Bal Tabarin puts on a better show than the Folies Bergère . . . Behind the Lapin Agile is a vineyard, the one remaining vineyard of the many that once covered the slopes of the Montmartre Butte . . . this is the Paris that one reads about and hopes to find, this little corner atop Montmartre.

Coming down the Rue Lepic a GI and his WAC girl friend with cameras . . . certainly this generation of Americans will have its memories . . . the war will pass from mind and the glamour of Paris will creep in and its impressions will stick in their thoughts.

These two looked fresh as the plains of Kansas, and there will not only be Paris to remember, but Cologne, Berlin, Brussels, Liege, Maastricht, Rome, Athens, Teheran . . . this will be the most widely travelled, world-conscious generation of Americans we have ever bred.

Wonder if much French music will return with the GI's? Many are humming or whistling *Petit Vin Blanc,* or other popular and amusing tunes . . . American-held buildings are fewer now, and the Army is drawing closer together . . . soon few will be seen on any of the streets in France.

Walking late on the quais, a man who might have been Gorky's *Chelkash* accosted me for a cigarette, then talked in fairly good English . . . he said he had known Cezanne and Picasso years before . . . and during the occupation had killed three Germans in the darkness along the quais . . . one with a girl. He had served in the army for awhile and had once visited the Salt Mines at Taudeni, in the Sahara . . . once several years before the war I flew there from Marrakesh . . . it is a prison, and a life sentence in those salt mines rarely lasts more than four years.

He was a dry, hard-bitten fellow of perhaps fifty, who might be good for thirty years more of his misspent living. He wore his old hat with a good bit of dash, and his scarf was clean, which is rare among the gentry of the quais. He had been to Istanbul, too, and to Salamis Bay, and knew the little inn on the hillside where I once went to eat fried tuna, purple grapes and one of those long loaves of bread.

He told me of the fights the artists and workers used to have on Montmartre, and of one grand brawl near the Place Emile Goudeau. In those days when any of the poets or artists went on a spree, which was often enough, they usually ended it at the Lapin Agile. After the cigarette he asked me for nothing more but I offered him fifty francs and tactfully suggested that I'd like to buy him a drink, but had so little time. He protested politely, while pocketing the fifty francs, and we left each other mutually pleased.

A most interesting chap. He slept on the quais, ate when possible, and drank when funds permitted, and talked entertainingly of the world and of women. His life was full, even if his stomach wasn't. What more can a man ask than to spend his boyhood on Montmartre, his young manhood in North Africa and the eastern Mediterranean, his fifties on the quais of the Seine? No doubt he will die some day, though it's a pity, and until the last day he will talk shrewdly and well for a glass of wine, and there will be a twinkle in his eye. A wise man who doesn't impart wisdom, but, rather, seems to agree with you on those things which gentlemen of the world understand. It is a curious thing that while many of those in higher places have at times betrayed France, the men of the quais and the gutters never have.

There are things to see in Paris . . . a million things, and a few to do . . . one must, of course, hear the musical coffee pots at Corcellet's . . . and shop in the Palais Royal . . . and visit at least once the Chez Suzy, where Suzy Solidor, descendant of the famous corsair of St. Malo, holds forth. These things are so much more worthwhile than looking at the Eiffel Tower, which is merely a monstrosity and a leftover from the Exposition.

And so back to the jeep at the St. Augustine Casual Officers' Mess, up Malesherbes to Courcelles and down to the Place des Ternes and the Avenue Wagram, then past the Arc and down the Grand Armée, and a right turn on the road to Pontoise, and so through Pontoise and Magny to Rouen and our home for the moment. And no orders to ship out . . . more days of waiting.

## Paris Today, Tomorrow, Home

January 19, 1946

It is cold in Paris now. There are chill winds blowing down those wide streets. The fuel shortage is serious, and will probably continue to be so as transportation is not yet what it should be.

In many of the apartments there is a fire in but one room, and that often enough is supplied from a slender gathering of black market wood. It will take another year for much to be done about this lack of fuel.

Rome is a city to be seen, London to be visited, but Paris is to be lived in. No city in the world has more charming vistas, no city can offer so much to the memory, so much to the living, as Paris. It hasn't been itself since the liberation or during the occupation. Slowly, it is recovering, but the glitter isn't there, and the gaiety is still more of an attempt than a reality. Yet whatever else it may be, it is a city for love, for leisure, for art and imagination.

Vivid with historical background, the city somehow remains modern. It has kept step with the world without losing its beauty or its patina. And it is so easy to forget that Paris has a history. Easy enough when riding along the Rue St. Antoine to forget that where the jeeps and command cars roll now, there were once Roman chariots. A history of the Rue St. Antoine is almost a history of Paris, and yet it is sedate and unhurried now. If there are ghosts there at night they are typically Parisian ghosts, and merely looking for a likely café, and if they go in, instead of frightening the habitués, would probably merely watch the floor show and enjoy apéritifs.

If that blonde with the nice legs thinks of anything, it is marketing, and she isn't giving a thought to the fact that she walks in the footsteps of Madame de Sevigné. Or that Racine, Molière and Corneille knew the Rue St. Antoine as well as she. Yet, being Parisian, she might remember that.

No corner of Paris is without its memories. No doubt even the stones of the Rue St. Honoré recall that it was in a millinery shop just off that street that a certain blonde and lovely salesgirl named Jeanne Becu became Madame Dubarry, mistress of a King and finally a victim of the guillotine.

Paris hasn't yet learned the art of the strip tease. Over there it is definitely strip, but without the tease. The girls are shapely enough, but there isn't a Margie Hart among them.

To see "A Thousand and One Nights" and have seldom heard a more appreciative G.I. audience. Of course, with the girls, it was no wonder, but the kidding by Phil Silver, ending with his little masterpiece on "Frankie Boy" Sinatra, was definitely in the groove. All over Europe one hears the same criticism of American films, that the girls are all alike. And there is truth in it. Very lovely, yes, but too much glamour in many cases, and not enough real ability. And many of those who have real ability don't have a chance to show it. Again and again in speaking of the best American films, they hark back to Garbo in "Anna Christie."

There were underground showings of Chaplin's "The Great Dictator" in Paris during the war, some say with Nazi connivance. Some were willing to go to any lengths to make money before the end came . . . the G.I. crowd in Paris thinning out . . . trouble between civilians and soldiers is exaggerated . . . the little is largely with the waterfront toughs of Marseille, Le Havre, and other ports . . . and of course, most G.I.'s are on edge, eager to get home . . . the present restrictions in sending money home will do much to curb the black market, but is hitting the lads hard who gambled and won.

Howe's excellent study of the Chinese woman on a *Script* cover last October was commented on by a number of people here . . . DeGaulle still stands head and shoulders above all the others in popularity and second is Georges Bidault . . . prices are still very high . . . an evening gown by a good shop might come to $2,500 and an afternoon dress of the sort one might find in New York for $60 sells for around $300. Little wool to be had, and warm clothing is very scarce. Fuel is the principal lack . . . food also, but so far it can be had. Those Americans who got inside French homes mostly found homes for themselves. Certainly, no people could be more hospitable than the French.

## *Thoughts after Paris*

June 8, 1946

Home again from the wars and at work with a good start for the new year of work. Sold seven short stories and a novel since the return, and that's all right.

Albert Camus, young playwright, novelist and editor, is coming over from Paris. One of the real figures in French literature, Camus has power, originality, and courage. The last named is a quality especially to be desired in these days in France when too many writers and political figures are trying to set their sails with the wind.

Camus' play, "Caligula," was the best I saw during my time in Paris, a fine piece of work with a good deal of power and spirit. Incidentally, the young actor who played the title role was the best I saw in Paris . . . and I've forgotten his name.

The best of the younger actresses seen in Paris was Ann Olivier, a honey-haired girl of eighteen with really great dramatic ability. Probably the most photographed girl in Europe, she appeared in *Vogue's* issue for April in two pictures, but has been a regular feature of *L'Officiel* for months.

American films very popular in France, but considerable criticism because of emphasis on glamour and costumes regardless of drama or acting.

The liveliest black marketing in Paris when I left was in guns, preferably American Colts, and they were supposed to be going into Spain. Several cafes in Paris, and especially in the Latin Quarter, were headquarters for agents buying these guns at top prices.

All sorts of contraband was available, but guns were in most demand. The Black Market has been the curse of France in many respects. Begun as a patriotic move when the Germans occupied the country, some minor officials and others grew wealthy through its operation, and still others, who handled the goods, saw no reason to lose a lucrative business when the Allies came in. Hence the Black Market has grown instead of falling into disuse.

To an extent this was aided and abetted by American soldiers with cigarettes, clothing, blankets or food they wanted to sell, either for the easy profit, or merely for good-time money, and around every haunt of the Yanks several Black Market agents could be found, usually willing to buy almost anything.

Paris has long been known as a city of evil . . . a good part of the story originating in the elaborate stories told by G.I.'s of the first World War, few of whom actually plumbed the depths but passed on stories they had themselves heard.

There is plenty of evil in Paris, and more now than at any previous time. Hard times and shortages have led more and more men and women, as well as students of both sexes, to go into illegal lines to make a living. Yet Paris is mild compared to sections of Shanghai or Grant Road in Bombay.

Many of the second- and third-class hotels in Paris rent rooms for an hour at a time to couples who are given the rooms for specified hours. It is never surprising to see a dozen or more couples waiting in the lobbies of these hotels until their time comes. And usually a few luckless odds and ends around who merely want to sleep in the rooms and must wait until the more active business is taken care of.

There is a lively business around many of the Boul' Mich' cafes in cocaine, shoes, cigarettes, clothing, counterfeit gas tickets, and rarely, in tires.

Some alarmists have suggested that the youth of Paris is largely corrupt, but such is far from the truth. Under the noisy surface there is a core of serious, hard-working students busy with medicine, law or other studies who take little part in the illegal activities of the criminal element. It is possibly true that the situation now is in some respects worse than it was before the war, but that is no more than what is to be expected. The students of Paris have always had these elements, and they have been notorious in France since the days of Francois Villon.

The villages and smaller towns throughout France usually have more food and better food than can be found in Paris, and that includes the Black Market cafes of the city.

Whatever else France may have lost, she hasn't lost her appetite for good cooking or the ability to produce food.

Russian and American books are the most popular in France, and a good many are available, yet there should be more. There was, when I left, and still is, according to my brother who is still in France, a good deal of talk of war between the United States and Russia. No one seems to have any reason why the two countries should fight, nor can they think of a good reason. Actually the differences the two nations have are minor and represent no basic conflict. The United States and Russia have never had sympathetic governments, although the two countries have always had interests in common. Among the major powers, Russia is the one country with which we have never had war or danger of war.

## *Russia Included*

June 22, 1946

The greatest danger to world peace now does not lie with Russia. It is with those who persist in pointing their fingers at her and continually holding up the spectre of war with Russia. An alliance, such as suggested by Churchill, of England and the United States, would constitute a threat, and would be the beginning of the end. There should be no alliances, merely a working agreement between the three major powers, the United States, Russia, and Great Britain. The three together can maintain peace for many generations.

Peace, now as always, lies in unity among the three great powers, and a mutual desire to keep that peace. Without it, the world we know cannot possibly survive.

# In Profile: Tracking Down Louis L'Amour

*by Jean Mead*

*The Roundup,* May 1981

SEVERAL years ago, while serving as WWA's publicity director, I conceived the idea of writing a book titled *Maverick Writers,* a candid look at some of the West's best authors. Not long afterward, *Fifty Western Writers* appeared along with a similar book, so I bemoaned my luck and started on another project. Loren Estleman, the sage of Whitmore Lake, was quick to nudge me back into line, and I diffidently dusted off my list of writers and queried some publishers.

Louis L'Amour was among those at the top of the list, because I had just finished reading *Yondering* and had enjoyed it along with his other work. I knew that readers would expect to find him in a book about Western writers. I also knew that arranging an interview with him would not be easy.

A number of letters written to him went unanswered over a long period of time, so I sent him a copy of *Wyoming in Profile,* an interview book I had written about the cowboy state's most colorful characters. That should get his attention, I thought. But there was still no response. I then decided to contact his editor, Irwyn Applebaum, then at Bantam. A couple of months later a letter arrived from Irwyn, stating that L'Amour was a very busy man. But that my letter had been forwarded to him.

I waited.

Contract negotiations had begun last January with Green Hill/Jameson Books. *Maverick* was going to be featured in Kampmann's fall catalog, and I had a May 21 manuscript deadline although I hadn't even finished my list of writers. So I made a last-ditch attempt by writing another letter and enclosing an SASE with L'Amour's 1985 membership card—a rash act, but desperation spawns skulduggery.

A few weeks later my family was transferred back to Wyoming, and in the midst of unpacking a letter arrived from L'Amour, granting me an interview, with the addendum: "I doubt that the interview would be worth the trip down here." Unfortunately, the SASE had been addressed to my former Washington residence, and was ten days in transit. By that time he was at a lodge in Colorado, one day's driving distance from my new home in Laramie. A call to Irwyn in New York got me his vacation phone number, and I put in a call only to find that by that time the L'Amours were leaving for Los Angeles.

I happened to track them down by phone at an art gallery in Durango before they left, and an interview was arranged for the following weekend. Dropping everything, I flew out to my sunny place of birth with a bit of apprehension. This hard-earned interview would probably be a disaster, I thought, remembering how the batteries fell from my tape recorder and rolled under a desk while I was interviewing Curt Gowdy at a cocktail party, and that the Marlboro Man refused to let me tape his interview until I pleaded an arthritic incapacity to handwrite notes. Both those interviews had been hard won. And I heard rumors from envious sources that L'Amour was arrogant and a literary myth.

A longtime friend, Marge Hughes, picked me up at LAX, provided bed and board, and drove me across three crowded freeways to Sunset Boulevard in West Los Angeles where the attractive Spanish-style L'Amour home is located near Bel Air and Beverly Hills. Arriving early we toured the nearby hills where iron-gated, pretentious mansions hide behind manicured jungles, complete with Rolls Royces and guard dogs. The L'Amour home is modest by comparision.

Having just survived a thirty-two-degrees-below-zero morning in Laramie that froze most ungaraged car batteries, I was nearly overwhelmed by the seventy-degree weather, brilliant green grass, and exotic flowers. It seemed as though a hundred years had elapsed since I'd grown up in Southern California, and it was going to be hard to leave.

The interview was scheduled for noon, and we pulled up to the curb at ten minutes till, behind a pickup truck that had seen better days.

"You don't suppose that's his?" Marge asked.

We began reading the cowboy stickers on the well-dented rear bumper.

"Must be," I replied, feeling better. Anyone who drove a battered truck like that couldn't be all bad. But why wasn't it parked in the three-car garage?

About that time a muscular young man walked across the lawn and gathered up some gardening tools from the bed of the pickup. We smiled at him through the windshield and then at each other. He frowned back, probably thinking we were tourists trying to catch a glimpse of L'Amour.

Oh well. By that time it was 11:55 and time for the interview. Marge would take a long walk around the neighborhood, and we joked about her getting arrested as a potential burglar. When she returned, she could read her golf magazine until I reappeared. I ambled up the curved brick walk and knocked on the door. A small square window opened into the violet-colored stained-glass insert, and a voice with a Latin accent asked who I was. The window closed and a few minutes later I was admitted by a petite, dark-haired maid who ushered me into a small room that was furnished with a round, glass-topped table, four chairs, a soft-pillowed couch, and a coffee table loaded with books and magazines, just opposite the entryway.

At precisely twelve noon, L'Amour entered, smiled, and shook my hand. He was slightly shorter and much younger looking than I had expected, and his smile was genuine. Dressed in a new pair of Levi's, dark brown Western shirt, beige cardigan sweater, and white tennis shoes, he looked like my Uncle David, only not as gray and cranky. I liked him immediately, and that fondness grew as the interview progressed. He was soft-spoken and looked away most of the time as though he were shy about being interviewed.

I couldn't help asking him about his mail and how he answered it. He has no secretary, and doesn't want one.

"It would keep me busy finding work for her to do," he said with a half grin.

"Who answers your mail?" I asked, puzzled.

He does, at least some of it. He receives around five thousand letters a year and admits to answering those from children, handicapped people, and selected others.

The interview was scheduled for an hour but it stretched into two. I could have stayed all afternoon but I knew that Marge was baking in her Chevy at the curb. I had ceased to think about her after a series of dove calls punctuated the interview. An aging white dove has been a member of the L'Amour household for the past twelve years, a good-luck mascot who flew into a former residence and was promptly adopted. She would have been killed by blackbirds if they had turned her loose, he said.

Half an hour into the taped session, Angelique L'Amour, his tall, pretty twenty-year-old daughter, came in the front door with her tennis partner. From the smile on her father's face, she was a welcome interruption. Angelique is a budding writer, as is her twenty-three-year-old brother, Beau.

When the interview was finished I was taken on a tour of the library, dining area, and his office. The polished floors of the L'Amour home are partially covered with muted handwoven Indian rugs and books abound in floor-to-ceiling shelves. The dining room, just off the entryway, is furnished with a substantial mahogany table and chairs, softened with blue patterned cushions.

The dining area leads to an addition the L'Amours built not long ago onto their home. The wide hallway leading to his office is filled with colorful kachina dolls, Indian artifacts, awards, keys to various cities, and a huge knife hanging over the door to his office, which he hesitantly admits wrestling from a smuggler who climbed aboard his ship in the Indian Ocean while he was a merchant seaman.

A large Indian rug covers the floor of the hallway and is turned back at one corner to prevent further wear and tear. On either side of the hallway are many small drawers containing maps of every country. He literally has the world at his fingertips, but his grasp of global geography stems mainly from his earlier travels as a seasoned sailor, cowboy, professional boxer, and jack-of-all-trades. His home is a trove of books and maps, and he seldom has to travel for research. His library of thousands of books, many of them rare and out-of-print editions, now allows him to armchair travel.

He's proud of his tremendous book collection, which is so large that he had hinged bookcases installed in his office to store the constant influx. Upon opening one floor-to-ceiling book shelf, another just like it appears from behind.

His large office is even more cluttered than my own, with boxes and boxes of books waiting to be put away, including the latest editions of his leather-bound volumes from the Bantam series. Myriads of research papers, charts, and miscellaneous paper are stacked neatly around his massive desk and high-back leather chair, ready for him to sort through and file away—somewhere. A secretary couldn't do it, he says. Only he knows where to put them.

An IBM Selectric typewriter, still in its box, sat waiting to replace an older model on his desk. The old one will travel with him to his Durango ranch the next time he goes. His two-fingered typing might be enhanced by a word processor, I suggest, but his son has already convinced him that he doesn't need one. WPs are good for quick revisions, he says, but he only writes one draft. The IBM is all he really needs, although he occasionally does some rewriting.

He was currently working on book number ninety-five, and I wondered how he found the time to write his perennial three books a year while conducting his never-ending library and secretarial chores. His thirst for knowledge—incessant daily reading of books, magazines, and newspapers—has more than compensated for his tenth-grade education, but he doesn't appear to be slowing down or resting on his laurels.

This pleasant, easygoing man, whose appearance and enthusiasm belie his age, is refreshingly humble, and I came away a confirmed admirer.

# A Visit with Louis L'Amour

*by Jon Tuska*

from *A Variable Harvest,* 1990

THE GREGG PRESS began a Western-fiction reissue series in cloth-bound editions in 1978. The field editor for this series was Priscilla Oaks, a contributor to *The Encyclopedia of Frontier and Western Fiction,* which I had edited with Vicki Pierkarski. Both Vicki and I were assigned the writing of introductions to various books that were scheduled for reprint. During the final years of its existence, because Priscilla was to spend a year teaching in the People's Republic of China, I took over as field editor of the Gregg series.

Louis L'Amour was very anxious for his fiction to appear in hardbound editions. He had submitted one of his novels to Doubleday, but he refused to revise it as the publisher suggested. The Gregg Press was willing to reprint some of his older titles that had appeared as paperback originals and I was asked to write the introductions to three of them. Of course, I had corresponded with L'Amour when preparing his entry for the *Encyclopedia,* but now I thought a personal interview would perhaps be advisable. Always affable, he acceded to my request.

"The cowards didn't go," L'Amour remarked as we sat across from each other in the summer of 1980 on the patio behind his large, Spanish-style home in the heart of Los Angeles. "It was inevitable that the Indian way of life should cease. And look at what replaced it! Where there was wilderness, there are now hospitals and schools."

"And what of the buffalo?" I asked him.

"They had outlived their usefulness," he replied confidently. "It was necessary that they be killed. Now there are farms throughout that whole area, farms that grow food to feed one-third of the world. It's a matter of progress. The Indians didn't own the lands they occupied. Many of the tribes, in fact, had only recently occupied certain regions before the white man arrived. The Indians took the land from others, the cliff dwellers, for example. And the white man took the land from the Indians. It wasn't the Indians' to claim or to sell. It went to the strongest. The white men were stronger. There's nothing more stupid, in my opinion, than to talk about paying the Indians for the land. It was never theirs to sell."

The garden beyond the patio was neatly manicured, a truly Wordsworthian garden. Nature cut back, trimmed, and controlled. A seemingly endless stream of cars swished past on Sunset and the sky was tinted by a reddish-brown smog. Maybe in this setting, it was easy to believe—as the Germans used to put it—"that world history is the judgment of history."

"My favorite tree," L'Amour continued, "is the white aspen. For me, it is the most beautiful tree in all nature. I saw a terrible thing on a recent trip I took. I climbed to the top of this hill and I could see white aspens covering an adjacent hill. But growing around the bottoms of those white aspens was scrub oak. Scrub oak is short, tough. It will choke the life out of the white aspens. That's the way it is in nature."

L'Amour then took me on a tour of that part of the house in which he worked, the library with its ten thousand volumes stored in gigantic bookcases that could swing out into the room only to reveal built-in bookcases of similar dimensions, all of them filled from top to bottom with books, most of them pertaining to some aspect of the American West.

"I use these books in my research," L'Amour explained. "Every incident in any story I write is authentic and usually based either on something I personally experienced or something that happened in history. And over here," he said, moving toward the map case in the hall way, "are my maps." He pulled open a drawer to show a thick pile of topographical maps. Handing me one to study, he pointed out the extensive detail in the cartography. "When I say there is a rock in the road in one of my books, my readers know that if they go to that spot and look they'll find that rock."

"There is one thing that continues to trouble me about your books," I said.

"And what is that?"

"Well, take *Last Stand at Papago Wells*. After an Indian attack, according to the story, only five characters have been killed, but one of the surviving characters counts six corpses."

"I'll have to go back and count them again," L'Amour said, and smiled. "But you know, I don't think the people who read my books would really care."

It was a curious remark and very much at odds with the impression he had been trying to give me when showing me his library and his detailed maps. Even the way he dressed, with the striped cowboy shirt, the silver belt buckle, the Western boots, and the rawhide neck piece, was intended to give one the impression that he was a man who had stepped out of the last century into this.

"If you want to know about the way the West was, and if you want to know about me," he said with emphasis, "you're going to have to read my books, as many of them as you can. It'll become clearer to you that way, rather than by anything I might tell you here today."

# Lunch With Louis 'n' Me:
# A Few Casuals by Way of Reminiscence

*by Harlan Ellison*

LOUIS L'AMOUR was the kind heart of America. The walking, talking, smiling, and story-telling best of what we like to think we really are. Long after the Olympian virtues about which Louis wrote had been traded in the flea markets of Wall Street, Madison Avenue, the Pentagon, and Hollywood, traded for cultural egomania, dissembling, me-firstism, and Ollie North–style phony patriotism, the rangy cowboy from Jamestown, N.Dak., remained a speaker for courage, ethic, friendship, craft, and independence. You know what Louis had? He had wisdom. Not just seat-of-the-pants common sense, but genuine wisdom, inspired by kindness. Louis was always the model of our better self.

In truth, I'm not even a minor footnote in Louis's life. We were friends who only shared each other's company maybe half a dozen times in the nine years we knew each other personally . . . which happened to be the last nine years of Louis's life, damn it. And if truth be told, I feel extremely awkward writing a memoir about so great and good a man, when I possess such thin credentials, when there are lifelong acquaintances and companion authors, not to mention family and loved ones, whose knowledge of Louis is vast compared to my few puny anecdotes. Yet here I be, doing it; and I confess to pleasure at the odd stroke of chance that allows me to get in on the legend of Louis L'Amour, however bogusly, however minimally. (Because he was the sort of guy whose association made *you* a guy worth knowing. "Do you know Louis L'Amour?" Yeah, sure, Louis and I go and have lunch sometimes. "Jeez, you *really* know Louis L'Amour?" I'm not saying you could run for public office on the strength of having eaten with Louis a few times, but it sure wouldn't have lost you any votes.)

And if there is any value whatever in these casual memories, let it be by way of example: that whoever met Louis and got to chat with him, whoever got a smile or a sweet word from him in passing, whoever was enriched by his fellowship, even for a few minutes, became—like me—

someone who counted; someone a few ounces heftier in the qualities Louis cherished, a layer or two meatier in the stuff that makes life worth living. Let me be representative of all the unknown buyers of this book, of all of Louis's books, who come away from the encounters heftier and meatier and more decently able to face the toxic pool we call modern society.

I don't usually write in such lofty, flag-waving terms. Louis does that to me. Makes me nobler, so I can do no wrong, so I can appear to get away with high-flown verbiage.

I met Louis first in books, of course. Can't even remember which one it was, but I *think* it was the Gold Medal paperback original of *Hondo* in 1953. Maybe it was the Geraldine Page–John Wayne movie, but I don't think so. If it was, it was just about the only good thing John Wayne ever did for me. I'm not too high on the Duke and his legacy of superpatriotic machismo, as you may gather, but if he was the one who "introduced" me to Louis, it does mitigate his crimes somewhat. (Damn it! Never did get around to asking Louis what he really thought of Wayne. Oh well, one day, when Louis and I meet up again . . .)

Read everything I could get my hands on by Louis thereafter. And so, in October of 1979, when I was scheduled to be one of the featured authors at the San Jose, Calif., *Mercury News* "Creative Encounter IV," logged in with Jessamyn West and Paul Erdman and my pal the late Tommy Thompson, I was drooling and anxious to meet, actually and really, one of the other participants, the mythic Louis L'Amour. Because, though Louis and I lived within a mile or so of each other here in Los Angeles—me at the top of Beverly Glen, him down the road below in Holmby Hills—we had never crossed paths. Come 1979, I was twitchy with ready.

I've rummaged through my memories for even a wrack that would remind me if Louis was the man with whom I had a terrific, minutiae-filled conversation about Sarah Winchester and the Winchester Mystery House, up there in San Jose, on the night of October 12. I *think* it was Louis, whom I didn't actually *meet*, formally, till the next day . . . but I can't be sure, because we were being led on a guided tour of that spectacular, wonderful manse (which, in more than small measure, has been the model for my own home) and I was so entranced by what I was seeing that the man behind me—who wasn't the guide—became almost the equivalent of one of those tape decks they give you in museums to inform your observations. But I *think* it was Louis, because he was certainly there later that evening at the dinner party the San Jose *Mercury News* threw for us "celebrities" at the Winchester. He was pointed out to me at another table, but we didn't meet that night.

I remember being impressed with the size of his belt buckle. It was as big as the Ponderosa. Actually, it was the size of Lithuania, but I'm trying desperately to maintain a L'Amouresque idiom, so let it be the Ponderosa. Being from Ohio doesn't help.

Next day, Saturday the thirteenth, we were all herded into the San Jose Center for the Performing Arts, to hear Louis and Mr. Erdman and Ms. West and James Kavanaugh speak. Then, at noon—before the afternoon series of public addressed by me and Tommy and David Horowitz and Elizabeth Hailey—we were all shepherded across the street from the Center for the Performing Arts, to McCabe Hall for a two-hour autographing session.

Tommy and I knew each other pretty well, and I'd met David Horowitz once or twice, but I knew none of the others, and I was nervous about possibly being seated for two hours next to Jessamyn West, who was so damned legendary that I was afraid I'd make my usual blithering idiot of a self; or that I'd get put next to one of the others with whom I had no common ground; so I tried to steer myself alongside Tommy. It never occurred to me that I'd wind up seated next to Louis L'Amour.

That was simply so amazing a possibility that it never got into my forebrain. I was just panicked that Ms. West would have to put up with me.

So naturally, I sat down where they assigned me space, and I started signing books. And about five minutes later, at a stirring to my right, I looked up and found myself staring straight into that enormous belt buckle from the night before, as it lowered past my eyes, appended to the midsection of this guy dropping into the empty chair beside me; and it was Louis goddamn L'Amour, who grinned at me with a grin that had he asked me to schlepp water buckets yoked across my shoulders for him I would have gladly bent forward to let him attach the collar! (You had to see that old man's grin! It was bloody lethal. Could've been used to deflect buzz bombs in the Battle of Britain. It had an effect you couldn't fight; you started turning mushy-mallow somewhere just abaft your spleen, and by the time it conked your brain you were already babbling in tongues. Louis could have been a great scam artist or foreign ambassador, with no greater equipment than that sap-you-silly smile.)

He stuck out his mitt and we shook, and he introduced himself, and I introduced myself, and he said he knew who I was, and I said I knew who he was, and he said he'd been wanting to meet me for a long time, and he said didn't we live near each other in L.A., and I said maybe, where did he live, and he told me, and I said, yeah we do live near each other, and I told him where I lived, and he said we had to get together some day for lunch, that he liked having lunch, and I said yeah that was a good idea, because lunch seemed pretty neat to me, too, and we grinned at each other . . . and we went back to signing books for people, because the lines stretched from the edge of our table to the far side of the moon.

Oh, by the way: he didn't "extend his hand," he *stuck out his mitt* to shake hands. That's the way I thought of it at the time, it's the way I remember it now. L'Amourism strikes agin.

And we worked away, signing and answering dopey questions, for maybe an hour, not exchanging more than a few words, till a moment came when Louis mumbled, "Sometimes I wish I'd only written one book that I hadda sign just one time," because, as it was with me, each person in line had brought four or five of our titles. I can't remember how many books I'd had published at that point in 1979, but it was in excess of thirty (not to mention the hundreds of magazines in which my stories or essays had appeared, also set forth for signing); and I have no idea how many of his 108-plus books were in print at that time, but with more than two hundred and fifty million copies in print worldwide at the moment, it had to have been a refrigerator-car-sized load even then. We were both getting constipation of the writing hand.

And I smiled without looking up, because if you fell behind in signing it was like Charlie Chaplin on the assembly line in *Modern Times,* and I replied with a standard response I'd been using for years. I said, "It could be worse. We could be E. Haldeman-Julius."

And Louis L'Amour gave me a *whoooop!* beside me, and he grabbed me by a shoulder and turned me to him, and his eyes were all snapping and sparkling, and he said something like, "You *know* the Little Blue Books!?!" And I managed to say, "Yeah, sure, I know the Little Blue Books . . . I grew up with 'em . . . got a few of them in my library at home. . . ."

And Louis and I were friends.

I'm not going to go into a history of E. Haldeman-Julius and his astounding library of Little Blue Books (some of which were actually yellow ocher and others of which were a hideous belly-lox pink) that emanated from Girard, Kans., from 1919 till I lost track of them in the middle fifties, save to say that next to pulp magazines and comic books, Haldeman-Julius and his Little Blue Books had a greater hand in educating the self-educated in this country than did the Britannica, McGuffey's primer, the Modern Library, and the Great Books series all rolled together in one heap of fustian. And to anyone who grew up on the road—as did Louis and I, decades apart—the Little Blue Books were pocket stuffing as necessary as nuts and packets of cheese. They were survival for the soul, food for the mind, moveable schoolrooms at ten cents a shot.

That they are now almost totally unknown is a tragedy, and Louis whooped when he found a guy more than twenty-five years his junior who knew the Little Blue Books intimately enough to make a joke about them—see, E. Haldeman-Julius had put out thousands, maybe *millions,* of them, and the gag was that as tough as it was for each of us, with many books written, to sit there and sign and sign, well, it could've been worse, we could've been E. Haldeman-Julius with thousands, maybe *millions,* of books to sign, and—well, maybe you had to be there—and he said that now, for *certain,* we had to have lunch, because we had this unbreakable bond between us.

And that's how it was. Louis called me soon thereafter, and we went to the Hamburger Hamlet in Westwood, and we talked.

And then I called him and we went down to the Valley and had Texas hot links and baby backs at Dr. Hogly Wogly's Tyler Texas Pit Barbeque, and we talked.

And he called me and we went over into Hollywood and ransacked Book City and the Cherokee, and had lunch at Musso & Frank's Grill, and we talked.

And if I'd known that Louis was going to die, and I'd be asked to write something about him, I'd have paid a lot more attention to what we were talking about, and what I learned from him, and how historic it all was.

But the simple truth of it is that I'm not even a footnote in Louis's life. He probably had lunch with a million doting fans and equals till he passed away in 1988, and not one of them was any smarter than I am, not one of them likely jotted down all the good and funny things he said. He was a *funny* guy, did I tell you that? He was; he was truly funny. But I did a much better Yiddish accent.

So irony of all ironies, that I should wind up being one of those who, like you reading this, shared moments with Louis L'Amour, who has come to be asked to *write* about Louis. What I have to say about him is there in the books, all hundred-plus of them, even the potboilers. Nothing new or startling here, nothing the *Sun* or the *Enquirer* would spend a paragraph recalling.

Just that Louis L'Amour was the best of us, with our eyes lifted and our hands ready for work, without meanness in our hearts or laziness in our bones. He was the pencil sketch used to make all those great James Montgomery Flagg posters of the spirit of America, with sleeves rolled up and honesty burning in the eyes.

If I'd known then, sitting and laughing and talking about books, as we wolfed down barbecued beef sandwiches, that one day someone would ask me to write about one of the greatest men I've ever known, I honest to goodness swear I'd have paid much closer attention. But to tell you the truth, I was having too damned good a time.

Maybe you had to be there.

# "L'Amour Receives Congressional Medal"

*Publishers Weekly,* October 14, 1983

THE CONGRESSIONAL Gold Medal, which has been presented to only seventy persons since George Washington received the initial one, has been awarded for the first time to an American novelist, Western writer Louis L'Amour. The only other literary figure ever to receive the award was poet Robert Frost.

President Reagan presented the medal to L'Amour during a White House ceremony September 24 honoring the Professional Rodeo Cowboys Association, whose members gave a special performance, followed by a barbecue on the South Lawn.

The medal, struck by the U.S. Mint, bears L'Amour's likeness on one side and on the other a quote from his 1976 novel, *To the Far Blue Mountains:* "To dream is in the mind, the realization in the hands."

Reagan called L'Amour "an author who has made enormous contributions to Western folklore and our frontier heritage." The author, published by Bantam, has written eighty-seven books, all but one of them Westerns, with total sales of about 140 million copies. But his medal didn't come easily. It requires an act of Congress before the medal can be awarded. L'Amour's chief backer, and avid reader, was former newspaper man Jack Evans, who began a four-year campaign in L'Amour's hometown of Jamestown, N.Dak. Through personal appeals and letter-writing campaigns, Evans was able to persuade enough members of the House and Senate to push through the award. Another backer was Malcolm Baldridge, secretary of commerce and a rodeo participant.

L'Amour was standing among the audience of rodeo participants when President Reagan asked him to step forward, but looked for him in the wrong direction. Turning, Reagan started, and then said, "There you are, you sneaked up on me, just like, you know, Bowdrie." Bowdrie is a Texas Ranger character in several L'Amour novels.

# L'Amour Receives the Medal of Freedom

ON MARCH 26, 1984, Louis L'Amour traveled to the White House for the second time in less than a year to be presented the highest honor awarded to a civilian by the United States government, the Medal of Freedom.

The award ceremony took place on the lawn of the White House where L'Amour was praised by President Reagan for his novels, which "brought the West to people of the East and to people everywhere."

On the platform with L'Amour were the other recipients of the award. They included Senator Howard Baker, Jr.; economist Leo Cherne; heart surgeon, Dr. Denton Cooley; singer Tennessee Ernie Ford; founder of the Mexican-American Equal Rights Organization, Dr. Hector Garcia; former NATO commander, Gen. Andrew Goodpaster; philanthropist Eunice Kennedy Shriver; actor James Cagney; clergyman and author, Dr. Norman Vincent Peale; and ballet director Lincoln Kirstein. Two medals were awarded posthumously—to Egyptian president Anwar Sadat and editor and writer Whittaker Chambers.

After the ceremony, at a reception for the winners held in the White House by the president and first lady, L'Amour was heard to remark that he was thrilled to learn that at least half of the recipients of the award were fans of his work.

# Part 2:
# Before the Novels

The professional skills acquired from the pulp
writing have never left me. Many things one could
get away with but one had to have a *story* and
one had to tell it, not talk about it.

Louis L'Amour in *The Roundup*, September 1983
Reprinted by permission of the Western Writers of America

# Introduction

LOUIS L'AMOUR'S first paperback, *Hondo*, appeared in 1953, when the author was forty-five years old. However, L'Amour sold his first poem twenty-five years earlier, and had been writing nonfiction since the early 1930s. He contributed nearly two hundred short stories to the pulp magazines before the publication of his first book. Many of L'Amour's novels were based on his pulp stories, and all of his short-story paperbacks collect tales written for those magazines. Yet little has been written about L'Amour's writing before he became a novelist. This section of *The Louis L'Amour Companion* corrects this major oversight.

L'Amour's poetry and early writings are covered in the first few pieces. Included with an annotated checklist of his early nonfiction work are several essays by L'Amour on poetry. "The Chap Worth While," L'Amour's first published poem, is reprinted for the first time in a trade book. Also reprinted is L'Amour's article "The Lost Golden City of the Manos," one of his early nonfiction pieces that details L'Amour's own encounter with a possible discoverer of a lost civilization.

A group of articles on the pulp magazines comes next. A short history of the pulps is followed by an excerpt from an article by one of L'Amour's first editors. L'Amour's own feelings on the pulps are discussed in an interview with Lawrence Davidson, Richard Lupoff, and Richard Wolinsky.

"Anything for a Pal," L'Amour's first sale to the pulps, is reprinted. Articles on his adventure stories and mystery fiction fill in information about these forgotten sidelights to L'Amour's career. A checklist of L'Amour's short story collections in paperback leads into a discussion of the controversial Carroll & Graf L'Amour paperbacks, highlighted by a long interview with Kent Carroll.

The section concludes with the most comprehensive annotated checklist ever done of L'Amour's magazine appearances. This listing gives details about several L'Amour series characters, such as Ward McQueen and Kip Morgan, who only appeared in the pulps and whose adventures have not all been collected in paperback. Appending that listing is a separate catalog of the nearly fifty Louis L'Amour stories that have yet to be collected in book form.

# Louis L'Amour and Poetry

> We are not like those dearly beloved souls who would place poetry upon a pedestal and make of it something exalted and vaguely unreal. . . . Poetry as everything else should have its definite place in life, and should not become too esoteric or too far removed from the realities of our mundane existence.
>
> Louis L'Amour, "Poetry and Propaganda"

IN HER introduction to the reissue of Louis L'Amour's book of poetry, *Smoke from This Altar,* his widow, Kathy, stated that the first book Louis bought for his own library was *The Standard Book of British and American Verse.* Poetry was always an extremely important part of Louis L'Amour's life. From the time he was a child in Jamestown, N.Dak., he read and savored verse in all its forms. That love remained with him as he voyaged across the oceans in his "yondering" days.

In *Education of a Wandering Man,* he declared, "Wandering men have always had a love for poetry, perhaps in part because it can be easily memorized and prove company on many a cold and lonely night. . . . Often when standing lookout in the ship's bow, I whiled away the time by repeating poetry that I had learned back along the way or, even more often, trying to compose some of my own."

Later, in that same book, L'Amour mentioned that poems and jingles were among the first pieces of writing he ever sold. The earliest L'Amour poem published was "The Chap Worth While," printed in the *Jamestown Sun* in 1926, when he was eighteen years old. Not included in L'Amour's only book of poetry, it follows this piece.

L'Amour continued to write poetry for the next thirteen years. Most of his verse was printed in newspapers and limited-distribution magazines of the period. In 1939, anxious to have an actual book in print, L'Amour persuaded a small firm in Oklahoma City to publish a collection of his best poetry. *Smoke from This Altar* collected thirty-six poems and was evidently done in an extremely small printing, available only in the area. However, it garnered a number of good reviews locally and helped establish L'Amour as a professional writer.

In the 1930s, Louis wrote two short articles about poetry that appeared in *Four Arts Magazine.* They offer a fascinating glimpse at the author's opinions at the time not only about poetry but about the art writing as well. Both of those pieces are reprinted here for the first time in more than fifty years.

"Poetry and Propaganda" deals with the meaning and purpose of poetry. "A Thread of Realism" examines the work of Walt Whitman, Carl Sandburg, and Robinson Jeffers. It is worth noting that in his memoirs, L'Amour singled out Jeffers as one of his favorite poets.

# The Chap Worth While

*by Louis L'Amour*

When you've walked in the gutters of failure—
Stopped in the fires of defeat.
And you sink down further and further
To the uttermost slime of the street;
Where there's naught but shadow, and you seek the sun—
When there's no one your burdens to share,
And your dreams have fallen one by one
Into the bottomless pits of despair.

When you've known the ache of a cruel heart-break,
And its pain shall never die.
You've shattered your dreams for another's sake
With never a word or a sigh;
When it seems your every hope is lost,
And your every chance is gone;
You wait and hope with fingers crossed
To meet the cold, gray dawn.

There's never a struggle but has an end,
And there's never a trail too long;
If there's a beginning there must be an end,
There are paths for feeble and strong.
Just struggle along and forget to curse,
With ever a laugh or a smile;
Take life as it comes for better or worse,
And you'll be a chap worth while.

# Poetry and Propaganda

by *Louis L'Amour*
*Four Arts Magazine,* September 1934

OF LATE there has been considerable discussion on the part poetry plays in the spreading of propaganda of one sort or another. This discussion has been precipitated, no doubt, by the number of advance-guard reviewers who have been giving space to what is usually designated as proletarian verse, or verse advancing the cause of the working man, and usually with a back-ground in some form of Socialism or Communism. Without entering into any discussion of the merits of either form of government as opposed to the existing form, it would seem a good idea to dissect the problem and discover, if possible, just what part poetry is to play in propaganda.

In the first place it might be well to come to some conclusion as to what constitutes poetry, properly speaking, and to discover just what its place may be in the present scheme of things. To get into this problem at all closely would be entirely too involved, however, and would call for a searching analysis into many aspects of literature and aesthetics. Any definition of poetry must necessarily be open to question, for there have been many theories advanced upon the subject, and no doubt some of them contain some grains of truth.

However, it would be our opinion that poetry as such is a branch of literary art, and of aesthetics, and any propaganda it may dispense must be entirely secondary. In the beginning we understand that poetry was largely narrative in form, a means of relating legends or accounts of travel and hunting, of war and adventure. Such were the first poems of which we know, and if, in the process of their story, these poems express some moral, some idea, or series of ideas, they are entirely secondary to the story, and to the rhetorical effect. Art must not be subjugated to propaganda, for it then ceases to be art, and becomes merely propaganda, and fails in both instances, having neither artistic effect nor success as propaganda.

Much of what is termed proletarian poetry is the merest drivel, and the editors publishing such work would never dream of using any other variety of verse when handled so crudely. We are not like those dearly beloved souls who would place poetry upon a pedestal and make of it something exalted and vaguely unreal.

Too much so-called proletarian verse is merely poorly expressed prose written in verse form, usually of a rather loose variety. Poetry can be propaganda and still remain poetry, but too many zealous young writers forget poetry in obsession with their theme. They subject poetry to base indignities to express some idea extolling the laboring classes, they make art, or the form of expression too subordinate to the subject expressed, and that cannot be done with any form of art.

There are numerous examples of poetry that might be called propaganda for the proletariat, and as three shining examples we could point out Thomas Hood's "Song of the Shirt," Edwin Markham's "Man with the Hoe," and probably Gray's "Elegy in the Country Churchyard."

These three poems are truly poetry, and still might be called propaganda, and they succeed in both purposes.

Poetry as everything else should have its definite place in life, and should not become too esoteric or too far removed from the realities of our mundane existence. Gray, Markham and Hood in the poems mentioned above have achieved the desired effect without sacrificing art to propaganda, and have in fact enhanced the later by the use of the former. When propaganda is offered in a poetical form, yet having neither the merits of prose or poetry, the reader, even if he knows nothing of metrical form, is disturbed by the effect and because of its crudity both poetry and propaganda fail of the desired effect. The three poems above have lived not because they were propaganda, but because they were poetry expressing an idea close to the hearts of the multitude, and because the artistic effect of genuine poetry has assured readability and coherence.

# A Thread of Realism

*by Louis L'Amour*

*Four Arts Magazine,* November 1934

IT IS THE acknowledged duty of every writer of worth to interpret the scene with which he is most familiar. In the past this has not been done in America, for in many cases our writers have made a habit of writing of almost everything but their own particular environment and experience. The scene in which the greater part of their lives have been lived, and with which they are most familiar, seem to have offered them no field for literary endeavor. Of late years, however, this tendency has been eradicated to some extent, and now, as at no previous period, the American writers are directing their talents and time to an interpretation of the American scene, to their own individual profit and to the enrichment of American literature.

In this we hail Walt Whitman as a fore-runner, for it was his polyphonic verse that blazed the trail for the many American authors of today who are writing of their own country. Whitman was the first distinctively American poet, and his work exercised a profound influence upon all of the better poets that were to follow him. Edgar Allen Poe was his contemporary, and his senior by ten years, but although Poe was as distinctive a genius in his way as Whitman was in his, Poe's influence upon posterity has not been as great. Poe was closely related to the European writers, and to the European scene, while Whitman was peculiarly American.

Walt Whitman was born on Long Island in 1819, educated in the public schools of Brooklyn, and learned the trades of carpentry and printing. He taught school for a short period, meanwhile contributing small pieces to the New York papers, largely on nature and wildlife. He read diligently from many authors, both American and European, but was particularly interested in Melville, Dickens and Thoreau. Probably the influence of the later was predominant in his writing, as it is always expressive of a deep feeling for life, and particularly the rough and rugged life of America in the building. His was the voice (although for many years an unappreciated voice) of pioneering America. He cast aside all the restrictions as to form and theme, taking a new tack and blazing a trail for new poets to follow if they could. Whitman was addicted to none of the set forms of verse, and wrote in a free style of a growing nation subjugating a continent to its needs.

In Europe, Whitman was already acknowledged, much to the surprise of the American critics and reviewers, and they turned their attention to him, but with a thinly veiled skepticism that revealed their doubt of his ability. Today, however, his reputation is steadily growing, and is already great. The reason seems obvious enough, for Walt Whitman filled a great vacuum in American Literature, and did in poetry what Mark Twain did in prose, devoting himself to his own people and his own country.

Whitman's verse was alive, vibrant, and filled with the joy of life and a vivid vitality that was inspiring. His rugged individuality and the strength of his smooth flowing lines were typically American, breathing the spirit of the open plains and the rough life close to nature.

His closest follower was Carl Sandburg, a poet who chose to sing in the same free style used by Whitman, and of kindred subjects. Neither Whitman nor Sandburg sang of nightingales, clouds or the loves of other days. They sang of the earth, and of the men who worked with the earth or close to it. They sang of steel mills, of ships and men of spirit. They did not sing their songs of roving galleys, nor of Vikings seeking their prey along the barren shores of the English Isles. They sang of cargo ships carrying freight to all the world; of holds filled with lumber, wheat, coal, and iron ore. Their figures of speech were different, their poetic style was new, but there was a certain hearty cheer and a boisterous charm in their rugged lines. These two, Whitman and Sandburg, are particularly American poets. They could be the poets of no other country but this, either in form or subject matter. They did not look in foreign lands for their subjects, but found them at home close to their own door.

No less an American poet, although somewhat different in general style and temperament, is Robinson Jeffers. Jeffers has written some along tabu themes, but his work is as distinctively American as either Whitman or Sandburg. As Whitman writes of the open roads; as Sandburg sings of men and their work in crowded cities; so Jeffers writes of life along the lonely reaches of the coast. His poetry fairly breathes of the air of lonely places and searches into the inmost secrets of those people who live close to the soil in a land where nature has not yet been reduced to the plow. In his poetry one is always conscious of the unconquerable sea lying ever near, always perceptible even though unseen, the low, monotonous rhythm of its surf stirring one's inmost being with a certain rest-lessness peculiar to itself.

In these three, Whitman, Sandburg and Jeffers, America has three poets who are typical of the country in which they live. They have been true to the tradition of that country, and the spirit of their verse is one with the life, national feeling, and Art of America. There is nothing in any of them that speaks of crowded European countries, and even if one had no idea of their origin, one could never fail to realize that theirs was an environment of youth, strength and conquest. Each of these men is in tune with nature and his times; each has a claim to genius.

# Louis L'Amour's Early Writings:
## An Annotated Checklist

LOUIS L'AMOUR'S earliest sales were a number of poems written in the 1920s and 1930s for newspapers and small-press magazines. In the 1930s, between submitting short stories to mainstream magazines and the pulps, L'Amour wrote a number of nonfiction pieces which he managed to place in several independent publications.

The following checklist, while doubtlessly not complete, is a listing of all those pieces known at present. The articles are indexed by date of appearance. Also included in this listing are the few nonfiction pieces L'Amour wrote after the war, but while he was still primarily a short-story writer. *All of the entries in this list have been verified by actual examination of the magazines in question.* Following the title of each piece is a description of the contents of the article.

I am indebted to the late Bill Clark, for his preliminary work in this area of L'Amour scholarship.

**1.** "Poetry and Propaganda"—*Four Arts Magazine,* September 1934— reprinted in this volume. How poetry can be used to further a cause or idea.

**2.** "A Thread of Realism"—*Four Arts Magazine,* November 1934— reprinted in this volume. Comments on Walt Whitman, Carl Sandburg, and Robinson Jeffers. (L'Amour was also present in this issue with a book review column, which ran in the December 1934 issue as well.)

**3.** "Prophets of Darkness, Baudelaire"—*Four Arts Magazine,* December 1934—First of a series of articles written for this small magazine dealing with writers and artists whose work possessed an element of unreality or "darkness." According to the foreword to this piece, L'Amour planned to cover Verlaine, Beardsley, Goya, Rimbaud, Huysmans, Moreau, Poe, Bierce, and De Quincey in the series.

Of Baudelaire, L'Amour wrote ". . . he was tainted with the decadence of the world, but many beautiful flowers have sprung from forms of decay and all living things have grown over and through the bodies of the dead. Baudelaire knew this, and he sensed more. If he dreamed, his dreams were his own, and all things are but the figment of dreams."

**4.** "Prophets of Darkness, Francois Villon"—*Four Arts Magazine,* January 1935—Second in the Darkness series. L'Amour called Villon the father of French poetry. About him, L'Amour wrote, ". . . he was the spirit of his time, the voice of the scum of Paris. He sang the songs of a people whose life-blood had been drained away in a series of oppressing wars, a people who had seen their heroine burned at the stake . . ."

**5.** "Prophets of Darkness, Aubrey Beardsley"—*Four Arts Magazine,* February 1935—Third in the Darkness series. In discussing the life and work of this British artist, L'Amour stated a basic tenet of his philosophy regarding criticism: "It is difficult, and even futile to attempt a detailed analysis of any work of art. Art was not intended to be analysed, and that is equally true of a poem, a bit of sculpture, a vase, a painting, or whatever it happens to be. Art is meant to be heard, to be sensed, and any attempt at analysis must be irritating and a bore to anyone with a true feeling for art and beauty, for contrary to general opinion, the two are not synonymous."

**6.** "Prophets of Darkness, Paul Verlaine"—*Four Arts Magazine,* March 1935—Fourth in the Darkness series. L'Amour called Verlaine "a brilliant and vacillating lyrical vagabond, haunted by the knowledge that he had failed as a man, and singing out the failure in the pathos of superb poems."

**7.** "Prophets of Darkness, Edgar Allan Poe"—*Four Arts Magazine,* April 1935—The final article in the Darkness series (and evidently the last issue of *Four Arts Magazine*). According to L'Amour, "In all the annals of literature there is no more tragic figure, no single person upon whom the misfortunes of life rested more heavily, and yet there have been none blessed with more of the divine fire than this child of strolling players born one cold January night in 1809 in the city of Boston."

**8.** "Hypnotism and Crime"—*The Occult Digest,* August 1935—L'Amour argues in this short article that the use of hypnotism in both the commission of a crime or in its prosecution is impossible other than helping enlarge upon a recollection of the event.

**9.** "The Lost Golden City of Manos"—*Lands of Romance,* January 1937—reprinted in this volume. A brief history of a famous lost city in South America.

**10.** "The Black King of Haiti"—*Lands of Romance,* April 1937—A sympathetic portrait of "black King Christophe; the dish-washer who became an emperor, the slave who became a master. . . . Upon the ashes of French plantation-houses he welded a kingdom in Haiti with only his own iron will and driving power to give it strength."

**11.** "Children of the Sun"—*Lands of Romance,* September 1937—A study of Peru before Pizarro, speculating on the origins of the Inca civilization and its possible tie-in with other ancient civilizations.

**12.** "Simon Bolivar, the Passionate Rebel"—*Lands of Romance,* November 1937—A portrait of the famous South American rebel, told very much in the style of L'Amour's early short stories. "It must be recognized that Simon Bolivar was undoubtedly one of the great military commanders of all time, and it is doubtful if Napoleon himself could have equalled the Venezuelans' success under the same circumstances and conditions."

**13.** "Old Civilizations in the New World"—*Lands of Romance,* January 1938—Speculation on the various lost civilizations in the New World, with emphasis on the Mayans and the Aztecs. L'Amour mentions the similarities between these cultures and ancient Egypt. He dismisses the notion of Atlantis but refrains from offering any theory of his own.

**14.** "Short Story Materials"—*The Writer,* October 1941—L'Amour begins his article with the following declaration: "A great deal has been written about the technique of writing the short story, and too little about the material that makes up the body of the story. As there are only thirty-six dramatic situations, all stories must depend on their originality upon treatment, and the material used in the development of the story." He then proceeds to offer useful advice in constructing stories based on everyday events, using several of his own works as examples.

**15.** "Where to Find Stories"—*The Writer,* June 1942—More advice from L'Amour on where to find story ideas. "One of the best places to find stories is in the human instincts. If you want to touch people and make them feel, get down to the bedrock emotions, the fundamental instincts we all have, dormant though some of them may be."

**16.** "Stories in Your Newspaper"—*The Writer,* July 1947—L'Amour writes on how to become "story minded." He cites the daily news as one of the best sources for story ideas. According to L'Amour, not only are the news stories good for material, but the advertisements and personal columns offer plenty of possibilities as well.

**17.** "You'd Better Be Right"—*The Writer,* November 1947—L'Amour on accuracy in writing fiction. As an example of poor research, he mentions the numerous inaccuracies in Howard Hughes's film "The Outlaw."

**18.** "How to Plot an Adventure Story"—*Writer's Yearbook,* 1947—L'Amour with more solid advice on how to write short stories, concentrating primarily on plotting.

**19.** "How to Become a Character"—*Writer's Yearbook,* 1949—L'Amour on how to handle characterization in short stories without slowing down the story too much. As with most of his writing articles, L'Amour's advice was directed primarily at writers aiming for the pulp fiction magazines.

**20.** "How Tough Can You Get"—*Saga,* October 1951—An entertaining, fact-filled article on some of the toughest men of the Old West. L'Amour states early in his article: "The history of the West is filled with authentic accounts of men who took five or six shots and continued to fight; of men who absorbed eleven, sixteen, and even larger numbers of lead slugs and not only stayed alive but stayed in action." He goes on to describe in vivid terms some of the most dramatic of these encounters.

Along with these articles, a number of L'Amour's letters were published in *Rob Wagner's Script* between 1938 and 1946. A selection of those letters is reprinted in this volume. L'Amour also was a frequent letter writer to *Thrilling Adventures* magazine, often detailing the background to his pulp story in the issue.

# The Lost Golden City of Manos

by Louis L'Amour

*Lands of Romance,* January 1937

*(During the course of his travels as a young man, Louis L'Amour met a number of memorable characters. Several of these unusual people, from Bill Tilghman to Singapore Charlie, were described in L'Amour's book* Education of a Wandering Man. *It seems likely that many of them made it into his novels in slightly altered form. However, none of them matched the unusual beachcomber L'Amour described in the following article. Published in* Lands of Romance *magazine in 1937, this piece provides a fascinating bit of L'Amour lore available nowhere else.—REW)*

## *Prologue*

Sleepy rivers writhe sinuously between the deep green of tropical undergrowth covering muddy banks. Great trees, giants of the jungle, arch overhead, their thick limbs heavy with foliage. Somewhere downstream, the slimy coils of a giant anaconda, largest of living reptiles, slips into the dark, mysterious waters of the river. A vagrant ray of sunshine picks out a spot between the shadows, and finds a trace of movement, the black and gold body of a jaguar, the tiger of the Amazonian jungles. Without a sound he slinks by, his dappled body blending almost indistinguishably with sunlight and shadow.

This is not the forest. This is something threatening, something evil, something ominous with unknown danger. This is something fever-haunted and poisonous, steaming in the tropical heat of Brazil, a bizarre pageant of exotic beauty suspending a veil over lurking death. This is the jungle. The jungle as it must have been in those dim, prehistoric ages when great reptiles roamed the earth. Here, even now, there is but one law: the bloody rule of claw and fang. It is a court of no appeal. The coils of a great snake, the jaws of a giant saurian whose snout seems no more than the end of a sunken log in the muddy water; the creeping jaguar or the more insidious death of fever, all await the wanderer whose temerity

**100**

leads him to dare these strange wildernesses. Birds of gorgeous plumage flit through the trees overhead, and somewhere off in the distance there is the crashing of a giant tapir as he bolts through the jungle.

Somewhere, in a vast, lonely region of Brazilian jungle, in a curious blend of beauty and sudden death, is a ruined city. The fabulous Golden City of Manos, the lost religious capital of a vanished civilization. Somewhere, a heap of broken idols, fallen columns, vast walls and temples; great masses of sculptured visions dreaming through the centuries of a dead world's beauty, a beauty that still speaks with all the voiceless eloquence of stone. About the name of this fabled city are fashioned legends strange and vague, which in our historic day had their origin with the travels of Columbus.

After Columbus came the conquistadores, those swashbuckling adventurers who thronged to the New World on the heels of the Genoese navigator. With their pointed beards and rapiers, their prancing horses and glittering armor, they rode into the bleak wilderness of unknown lands as though to a knightly tourney. A thousand legends gave them enchanting visions of the vast wealth to be won by valor. Whatever else these adventurers may have had, they did possess all the color and glamour one usually associates with adventure. In Mexico and Peru they destroyed civilizations of greater cultural value than their own, they looted and killed with abandon, and thought of nothing but gold. De Soto and Coronado sought for the legendary Seven Cities of Cibola, Ponce de Leon sought the Fountain of Eternal Youth.

De Soto found a dark grave in the waters of the Mississippi; Coronado found wide, unbroken prairies; Ponce de Leon found misfortune, death, and at last a grave on Puerto Rico. It remained for Cortez and Pizarro alone to find the gold they sought. Cortez, landing on a swampy coast of southern Mexico, found a great civilization with temples and cities, a religion and a court. Like Caesar, the conquistadores came, saw, and conquered, leaving behind them a trail of looted cities drenched with the blood of native peoples. But the stories of the vast wealth they found remained to haunt the imagination of all who still possess a spirit of adventure. Montezuma gave to Cortez, among many other vast treasures, a disk of gold as large as a cartwheel, computed to be worth more than a quarter of a million dollars.

In Peru, Pizarro found even greater treasures, and another civilization, distinct from that of the Aztecs. A civilization ruled by an Inca, where no poverty was known, where they had cities, bridges, and extensive irrigation projects. Pizarro captured the Inca and held him for a ransom that would have caused present day kidnappers to turn as green as corroded gold. Pizarro was offered a room full of gold, a room twenty-two feet long, seventeen feet wide, and filled to a height of nine feet. This vast treasure was estimated at no less than fifteen and a half million dollars!

All of which proves that there was gold in those countries—that great civilization mined and stored that gold, leaving the belief that if such great treasures were freely given, still greater ones remained hidden. And thus is blazed the trail for the story of the lost City of Gold.

The Amazon river flows from the foot of the Andes to empty into the Atlantic on the northeast coast of Brazil, not far from 300-year-old Para, founded by the Portuguese. The river, 180 miles wide at its mouth, drains 4,200,000 square miles of territory, most of it jungle. Of all this vast expanse practically nothing is known. Here and there it has been scratched; there are cities, villages, and plantations. Rubber cruisers have wandered through many miles hitherto unexplored.

Other wanderers have sought in those tangled depths for gold, diamonds, orchids, quinine bark, medicinal herbs, and all of the many things that promise a reward. Yet, despite all this exploration, vast areas exist unknown to any white man. Far to the south of the Amazon lies the Matto Grosso, "the great jungle," and somewhere in the Matto Grosso lie the ruins of the legendary City of Gold. Its location is even more closely gauged than that, for it is believed to lie somewhere in the two-hundred-mile area between the Tapajos and Xingu rivers, large tributaries of the Amazon. Beyond that, little is known.

In 1533, a Portuguese sailor came out of the jungle, half dead from fever and starvation. He told a strange tale of a lost city in the jungle, of a once highly-civilized people now returned to degenerate savagery. He told of a city where gold and silver were almost the only known metals, of huge temples, golden images, of diamonds, rubies, and emeralds. It was a tale that fired the blood of the listeners. It was another such treasure as won by Pizarro, another Ophir. Many lost their lives in a futile search. One who attempted and failed was Cabeza de Vaca, one of the most hardy of early explorers. He had wandered in many other lands seeking the Golden City of Manos, but found it not.

Since then many have tried and failed. Krupp, the German munitions manufacturer, sent one hundred men, heavily armed, into the jungle. Not a man returned. They were swallowed by the jungle, and that was all. One of the best known attempts was made by Colonel Fawcett, a former British colonial officer who had been stationed in India. Colonel Fawcett was a well-known archaeologist, and from one source or another seems to have heard the legend of the Golden City. It has even been said that he deciphered inscriptions telling of the City from the walls of a sacred cavern in India! Anyway, he spent sixteen years in the jungles of South America, learning the people, the country and language. He claimed to have secured evidence of the existence of the city from friendly natives. He went into the jungle, and never returned.

Commander Dyott, of the British Royal Air Force, made several futile attempts to find Fawcett. He flew a plane over much of the jungle in that section, but a plane with a cruising speed of 130 miles per hour, which necessarily prevented any thorough survey of the jungle. In even a short time, the creepers and vines will completely blanket such a ruined city, until an explorer can be right in the midst of the fallen stones before he is aware of it. Like others before him, Dyott failed to find Fawcett, but he did contact natives of the region, which was a great accomplishment. These natives are pygmies, very shy, and naturally very fierce when an outsider enters their country. Dyott claimed to have been satisfied from what he discovered that Fawcett was dead, but the most striking result of his expedition was a stone tablet purported to have been given him by the pygmies and containing inscriptions in ancient Hebraic!

There have long been stories of wanderers who penetrated these jungles, even prior to the time of Columbus. The late Arthur Brisbane wrote several years ago of the discovery of a Phoenician galley embedded in the mud of the Amazon. There is the story of a man who came to Carthage in the day when that city was still the great maritime rival of Rome. This man reported that he came from "the lands in the west" and that he was seeking the home of his ancestors. Carthage had been founded by the Phoenicians, the greatest maritime race of the ancient world. That the City of Gold may have been founded by them is not impossible. They were great wanderers and seamen. Hanno, the Phoenician, sailed a galley completely around Africa almost a thousand years before the same feat was accomplished by Vasco da Gama. The Phoenicians had been many times to the Canary and Azores groups, to England and Ireland.

But there were other theories. It may have been the capital of another people similar to the Incas or Aztecs, a people like the Mayans of Central America and Yucatan, whose cities were covered by jungle. Frank Church-ward, the man responsible for the many books on the lost continent of Mu, believes the city to have been the religious capital of that fabled people who lived on a continent in mid-Pacific. Ruins of temples, remarkably similar in architecture, are found upon many of the islands of the Pacific, such as Tahiti and Raratonga. The huge stone images on Easter Island have also been offered as remains of this vanished continent that disappeared beneath the seas so long ago. The people inhabiting many of these islands are a very high type of native, and seem to have the remnants of a once great culture. Legend has it that when the continent of Mu sank beneath the sea, part of South America was lifted above the water in one of those movements of the earth's crust that have taken place so often in times past. The island that was the site of the Golden City was raised, and is now situated in the remains of a crumbling mountain range in Brazil. Fable or truth, it has become one of the unsolved mysteries of the world. To imagine those vast, steaming jungles without having seen them is impossible. Tropical heat, swamps tangled with underbrush, creepers and vines; it is an unbelievable chaos. Insects as large as birds, jungles where the jaguar reigns supreme; where the great anaconda, largest of reptiles, lives along the streams. The tiny pygmies who inhabit the region of the Matto Grosso slip through the jungle so silently as to be all around before one is aware of it, and they are remarkably expert with their long blow-guns which shoot poisoned darts and whose slightest scratch causes almost instant death.

It is no wonder that expedition after expedition has failed. But when one remembers the great city of Angkhor in French Indo-China, a city once populated by three million people, and how it was discovered and uncovered but a few years ago, one does not wonder that there still are people anxious to attempt the search, so often fruitless.

Many stories are told by men who go down in the sea in ships, and more often than not even the most fantastic are true. It was in Java that the writer first stumbled across rumors of the Golden City. That was in a time when it had not yet begun to figure in the news of the day, and when it was known only to a few. Going ashore in Soerbaia, I stopped in a bar room with another drifting seaman and ordered lunch and a couple of glasses of beer. An old beachcomber, on the shady side of seventy, came in and asked us to buy him a drink. In the few days around port we bought him a number of drinks, and one afternoon, slightly touched with good Dutch lager, he interrupted our talk of Brazil and Peru to tell us his own story of the Golden City.

Some thirty years before he had been living in the jungles of Brazil, living precariously on whatever he could find in the jungle worth selling. He had been there fifteen years at the time of the adventure, and hearing some stories of gold somewhere at the headwaters of the Tapajos, he ventured up that stream. As always, he went alone. Near the headwaters he concealed his boat under the roots of a great tree, and started off inland. For eleven days he made his way through the thick of the Matto Grosso, following game trails or cutting his way. On the eleventh day he was suddenly set upon by natives and taken prisoner so suddenly as to leave him no opportunity for defense.

For several hours they led him through the jungle, and then suddenly they began to climb. In a short time, instead of a native village of grass or palm-leaf huts, he found himself in a narrow canyon containing the ruins of a great city. The air was very hot and very damp. Low clouds hung over the jungle, and he began to realize why he had failed to see these low peaks before, as they were probably concealed in clouds much of the time. Vast broken walls stretched before him, there were heaps of debris, fallen columns, and great, roofless corridors.

During the following two months while he was held a prisoner in the city, he had an opportunity to see inside many of the great buildings, and the caverns behind them. He saw rooms filled with ingots of gold, gold and silver vessels of marvelous workmanship set with gems of great value. Diamonds were plentiful, and the natives said there were large deposits in the neighborhood. Some time later, he managed to escape, but in returning to civilization, nearly died of blackwater fever and in his weakened condition, feared to return to the jungle. He hoped to obtain financial backing and return, but feared to trust anyone with his secret, and finally, drinking, it began to be no more than a dream.

At the time, it seemed merely another seaman's story, but one with perhaps a keen imagination behind it. The man possessed little education, and at the time the story was not widely publicized. Fawcett was not to come into the news for a few months, and the story was new to me. However, there was one part of the story that rang true. He was not vague. Every detail was clearly in his mind, and best of all, being a seaman, he had retained his sextant, and while in the city had one clear morning scaled a pinnacle of rock nearby and taken a shot at the sun. In other words, he had the exact latitude and longitude of the Golden City of Manos! The position he gave me, in return for more drinks, places the city in the district where it is supposed to be, between the Tapajos and Xingu Rivers!

Strange stories come out of the abysmal depths of those Amazonian jungles, stories that add to the legends told by the conquistadores. They found gold in Peru, and they found it in Mexico. Why not in Brazil? Was Fawcett's theory correct? Was the old beachcomber's story true? Under the leaves of the jungle giants the silent rivers sweep onward to the sea, the great Amazon, dark, mysterious, stealing along its muddy trail, carrying the soil of Brazil into the Atlantic. The leaves of the jungle whisper to the rivers, and the rivers murmur reply. Were the stories true? Only the jungle knows, and the jungle does not answer.

# The Pulp Magazines

I wrote pulps for several years and at the end of the time I was making a very good living at it. Then overnight they were gone like snow in the desert.

Louis L'Amour, interviewed by Lawrence Davidson, Richard Lupoff, and Richard Wolinsky, KIOU radio, 1986

LOUIS L'AMOUR began his professional writing career in October 1935 with the publication of his story "Anything for a Pal," a short-short story published in *True Gang Life* magazine. For the next fifteen years, L'Amour was a regular contributor to the pulps. It was in those popular fiction magazines of the decades before and after World War Two that L'Amour first made his mark as a writer of adventure and Western fiction.

Now forgotten, the pulps once served as a major source of reading pleasure for millions of Americans. L'Amour was not the only major writer to emerge from these publications. Erle Stanley Gardner, Dashiell Hammett, Raymond Chandler, Edgar Rice Burroughs, and even Tennessee Williams were among the many hundreds of authors who began their careers in the pulps during the first half of the twentieth century.

In the 1920s, 1930s, and 1940s, pulp magazines satisfied the reading habits of millions of Americans. Hardcover books cost too much for the average buyer. Paperback books did not appear until 1939 and for years afterward primarily featured reprints of novels originally appearing in hardcover form. Original novels in paperback format did not gain widespread acceptance until the early 1950s.

Mainstream magazines published on slick paper (and thus dubbed "slicks") flourished but they rarely printed any genre fiction. It was in the pulps that readers found their favorite Western, mystery, science fiction, sports, and even love stories.

There were pulp magazines catering to every taste in genre fiction. And to every budget. Most publications were issued monthly, but some pulps were so popular they came out weekly. Most magazines were priced at a dime, but some cost a quarter and a few thick annual issues cost fifty cents.

Covers were garish and aimed to appeal to the casual browser. Print was small and a typical issue often published more than a hundred thousand words of new material. Strangely enough, while the pulps are remembered as being aimed mainly at men, the best-selling magazines were the love pulps.

Titles included *Astounding Stories, Adventure Magazine, All-Story Love, Football Stories, Dime Detective, Thrilling Adventures, Weird Tales, Love Story Magazine, Black Mask Magazine, The Shadow Magazine, Horror Stories, Dime Western, Aces High, War Birds,* and even *Zeppelin Stories.* During the height of their popularity, there were over a hundred different pulp titles published every month. More than thirty-five Western magazines and a dozen mystery pulps crowded the newsstand in 1939. In all, well over a thousand different publications appeared.

The pulps were notorious for their low rates for fiction, often paying a cent a word or less for stories. However, they provided a huge market for writers and a number of authors did quite well writing for the pulps. They served as a training ground for many writers who otherwise would never have broken into print. And they published a number of excellent stories. Most of the Louis L'Amour short stories now seeing print for the first time in paperback collections of his work first appeared in the pulps. These include all the stories in the very popular Chick Bowdrie collections and the best-selling hardcover *The Outlaws of Mesquite.*

The pulp magazines were begun by an enterprising publisher named Frank A. Munsey at the turn of the century. Up to that time, most magazines were published on slick paper, featured numerous illustrations, and cost a quarter. Reasoning that people were more interested in the story than the presentation, Munsey published *The Argosy Magazine* on cheap wood-pulp paper (thus the name "pulp magazine") without illustrations and priced at only a dime.

The magazine was a huge success. Munsey followed *The Argosy* with a number of other magazines using the same formula. Within a few years, he was chairman of a huge publishing empire.

As with any business, success brought competition. Other magazine chains started their own pulp magazines. At first, copying the original Munsey concept, these new publications featured a mix of all types of fiction. However, specialization soon followed. The earliest pulp devoted to stories on one subject was *Detective Story Magazine* begun in 1910. As before, imitations quickly filled the marketplace. While general fiction pulps continued to flourish, pulps devoted to one subject soon filled the newsstands.

The first Western pulp was Street and Smith's *Western Story Magazine,* dated September 5, 1919. The magazine was published every other week at the price of ten cents a copy. In less than a year, *Western Story's* circulation grew to over three hundred thousand copies sold per issue. It was put on weekly publication and was issued fifty-two times a year for the next twenty-five years. Needless to say, other publishers soon developed their own Western titles.

---

It seems that in the Western field you could divide the field up into two groupings. People like Louis L'Amour, who came from the West and knew the West and loved the West, and gave detailed information about it in their stories. And writers like me, who lived in New York. Hudson River Cowboys they were called and none of them ever got any closer to the West than the Hudson River. As I say, we got all our material from the library and wrote those stories.

Ryerson Johnson, mystery and Western author,
who contributed several hundred Westerns to the pulps

---

Some of the more popular magazines included *Cowboy Stories, Aces High, Ranch Romances, West, Frontier, Thrilling Western, Texas Rangers,* and *Wild West Weekly.* There was even a short-lived *Lone Ranger* pulp magazine in 1937.

The Western pulps were among the most popular magazines ever published. Zorro, who has become so much a part of our culture that numerous sources describe him as a folk hero, was originally the hero of a pulp story by Johnston McCully and published in 1919. Many of Zorro's later adventures were published in *Western Story Magazine.*

Max Brand, creator of Dr. Kildare, wrote hundreds of Western novels including *Destry Rides Again.* Brand, one of the most prolific writers of all time, sold over forty million words to the pulps in a career that lasted a little more than twenty years. For *Western Story Magazine* alone Brand wrote nearly thirteen million words in thirteen years under eleven different pen names.

Many other greats, near greats, and completely obscure writers worked for the Western pulps. Most of them vanished into the sands of time when the pulps died. A few, like Louis L'Amour, became famous.

---

I have a feeling that Harry S Truman and Al Capone were each on the subscription list at Popular at about the same time, because I remarked to some of our advertisers that we covered the entire gamut from presidents to gangsters. Truman subscribed to one of the detective magazines and Capone subscribed to one of the Western books, although you might have thought it would have been the other way around.

Henry Steeger, president of Popular Publications, the company that published *Dime Western, New Western,* and many other Western pulps, commenting on the popularity of the pulp magazines in an interview in *Xenophile* magazine, 1977

---

President Frank Delano Roosevelt was a subscriber to *Dime Western.* So was Al Capone. They were an integral part of the American popular fiction scene in the first five decades of this century. It was in those magazines that Louis L'Amour first plied his trade and defined his heroes. Any study of his work that ignores his pulp fiction cannot be called complete.

The pulps died a quiet death in the 1950s. World War Two dealt them a mortal blow, but their death came as a result of increased competition from television and paperbacks as well as changing public tastes. Still, for more than fifty years, they provided the American public with the fiction they craved at a price they could afford.

It was in the pulp magazines that Louis L'Amour learned his craft. They formed an integral part of his career. This section dealing with them is the first comprehensive study of L'Amour's contributions to the pulps.

# An Excerpt from "The Blank Page"

*by Kenneth Fowler*

*(The February 1983 issue of* The Roundup, *the official magazine of the Western Writers of America, contained a long article by Western editor and author Kenneth Fowler on his long career in the Western field. One particular section was of great interest to fans of Louis L'Amour. It is reprinted here.)*

A NUMBER of years ago, when I was an editor with Popular Publications in New York, our staff shared the drudgery of wading through what was known as the "slush pile"—a name used by magazine publishers to describe the glut of unsolicited manuscripts that day by day accumulate in their offices.

Wading through the slush was a labor editors dreaded yet undertook in the rarely realized hope that by some kind of miracle something usable might unbelievably turn up.

This story is about one of those days when the miracle happened. It was probably the most bedraggled looking manuscript I had ever seen, and as I plucked it gingerly out of the slush it looked as if even a patch job with Scotch tape couldn't hold it together much longer. Plainly, this one had been in and out of dozens of editorial offices, and now at last it had limped forlornly into ours—obviously ready for the scrap heap to which its author was still stubbornly refusing to consign it.

It was seldom necessary to scan beyond the first page of a slush pile contribution, but hope springs eternal for editors as well as writers, so I began reading anyway.

Then came the shocker. The very first line of the story was an attention-grabber—the so-called "narrative hook" that more often than not the professional uses to magnetize his subject and lure his reader on.

Editors are not easily lured, but in this case I knew very quickly that I had stumbled onto something good—a yarn that had pace, suspense, and a plot line from which my interest never deviated. Could our pulp readers ask for more?

I was convinced they could not, and the instant I'd finished reading I hustled the manuscript in to our chief editor, Mike Tilden, with a recommendation to buy.

We did buy. Neither Mike nor I had ever heard of the writer—then. But the manuscript that had been bounced with such unanimity from pillar to post—or if you prefer, from slush pile to slush pile—had at last fallen into responsive hands, and thanks to its author's pluck, pertinacity, and unwavering faith in himself, would now reach print.

Ah, yes—the byline. The name on that battered dog-eared manuscript seemed an odd one for a writer of Westerns, and I remember thinking at the time that it must be a pseudonym.

But it wasn't, and now you see the name everywhere. In fact, when can you visit a bookstore, supermarket, or newsstand kiosk these days and *not* see the name of Louis L'Amour?

And now a few concluding words of advice before you writers-to-be bid fond farewell to your loved ones and pass sadly from sight into your isolation cells.

Don't expect to get rich overnight. In fact, don't expect to get rich— period. But *do* expect a need for filthy lucre while you're still in training, so be sure to have a supply stashed away in a handy place in case of emergency.

Sinclair Lewis wrote on this subject, too, in his "Breaking Into Print" article. "Not for gold," advised Lewis, "would I recommend writing as a career to anyone who cares a hoot about the rewards, or for anything at all save the secret pleasure of sitting in a frowzy dressing gown before a typewriter, exulting in the small number of hours when the words come invigoratingly, the phone doesn't ring, and lunch can go to the devil."

So exult, as Lewis exulted—if you can afford it. Or if, as was the case with Louis L'Amour, you have plenty of postage for your manuscripts, and a grim determination to keep mailing them out even after all seems lost and there appears no place left for them to go.

Just remember: there may *always* be one last place—as L'Amour found out.

# Louis L'Amour on the Pulps—
# An Interview

*(The following is part of a long interview with Louis L'Amour conducted by Lawrence Davidson, Richard Lupoff, and Richard Wolinsky for KIOU radio in San Francisco in 1986. In this portion of the interview, L'Amour discussed his days working for the pulp magazines. It was one of the few times L'Amour spoke about his pulp career with people familiar with the magazines and the editors who worked for them.)*

**LAWRENCE DAVIDSON:**   Harold Keith, in a profile of you, said that it was Leo Margulies who first urged you to write Westerns. I was wondering if you could elaborate on that a little bit.

**LOUIS L'AMOUR:**   Yes, it was. Leo was editor for a whole string of pulp magazines and a very, very good man and a very good editor. I had been writing—my first story that I sold him was for a magazine called *Thrilling Adventures,* and it was a story about the Far East. I wrote a whole series of stories about Indonesia where I had spent some time. In those days, it was called the East Indies. Some called it the China Coast. I wrote some boxing stories for him. I wrote a couple of football stories and a couple of air stories, and he wanted some Westerns. He talked to me a bit, so he knew I knew the field. So finally I wrote some.

**LD:**   Had you been reading Westerns before that?

**LL:**   Oh yes. I'd read Westerns a good deal. I read Zane Grey as all kids did and Clarence Mulford wrote the Hopalong Cassidy stories, the original ones, not the Bill Boyd Hopalong Cassidy stories. There was a vast difference. But I was reading everything in those days. All kinds of magazines, all kinds of books.

**LD:**   You ended up writing some Hopalong Cassidy as Tex Burns.

**LL:**   I never used the name Tex Burns in my life. I did write four Hopalong Cassidy books and the Tex Burns name belonged to them and the books belong to them. I have no connection with them whatsoever. They weren't written the way I wanted. I just sort of edited them is all. So don't credit them to me.

**LD:** Okay.

**RICHARD LUPOFF:** Could you give us a little bit on who actually did write those, because the standard bibliographies say Louis L'Amour wrote these books. Can you straighten that out?

**LL:** I know, I know. It says that. But my contract with the publishing firm said that my name was not to be used in connection with them at all. Of course, at that time, Louis L'Amour meant nothing whatsoever. As to Tex Burns, there was no such person, it was a house name. The original deal that I made with them, I was to write four Hopalong Cassidy stories using the old, original Hopalong. I insisted upon that. The original Hopalong was a red-headed, tobacco-chewing, dry-whiskey-drinking cowboy, who had a limp because he was shot in the knee. That's why they called him "Hopalong." Then after I had gotten some of the money and spent some of the money, they switched on me. It had to be the Bill Boyd character. I would not do it, so they did it. I mean, I wrote some of the stories but the Bill Boyd character was put in, much else was changed. So the stories are in no way mine. I would not sign one of those books or anything at that time. I have nothing to do with them.

**RL:** I'm glad you got that straight because all of the bibliographies say Tex Burns wrote them.

**LD:** Another pseudonym that you are connected with is Jim Mayo.

**LL:** That's right. That was mine.

**LD:** So, all of the stories you see with Jim Mayo on them are your stories.

**LL:** They are legitimate. However, not James Mayo, it has to be Jim Mayo, because there was a writer who wrote for a while called James Mayo. That happened because I had an editor back in those days who said nobody would ever buy a Western by a guy named Louis L'Amour. [much laughter] Obviously, this man was a genius. Anyway, he insisted that I use another name. I had written a number of these Indonesian stories about a captain of a tramp freighter, whose name was Ponga Jim Mayo. I couldn't think of a name offhand so I just said Jim Mayo.

**LD:** Now, did you know Margulies before you came out of the service?

**LL:** Yes, I did. Yes, I knew him before I came out of the service. I had sold him some stories before I was in the service.

**LD:** One thing I would like to get cleared up a little bit is if you could tell me a little bit about what you did in the service and where you were stationed.

**LL:** I was a tank destroyer officer, but I came in as an enlisted man. Buck private. I took basic training at Camp Romison. I went to officers candidate school at Camp Wood, Tex. Came through there, began training troops and was in Michigan for a while. Then I went overseas. I spent four years in the army. Two years here, two years overseas. Virtually had to start a new career when I came home, because everybody had forgotten.

**LD:** Was that the Indonesia and China Coast?

**LL:** No. That was all done before the war. In the war I was always in the ETO. I had something to do with every major operation in northern Europe except the Battle of the Bulge. I was uninvolved in that. I was involved in all the other campaigns in northern Europe. Not Italy, not southern France.

**LD:** Were you involved in the D-Day operation?

**LL:** Yes.

**LD:** Normandy? The whole . . . ?

**LL:** I didn't go in on D-Day. But I was involved in it on the English side. I made a comment I was there. They were asking me about that on the "Today Show" just a couple of days ago. They were doing a show on it and asked me about it. I told them that I wanted to go in. I wanted to go in the first day very badly. In fact, I even tried to sneak in on my own. Because I wanted to be there on the landing. But I didn't make it.

**RL:** What kind of life did you, you know. . . . How successful was it being a writer for the pulps? I mean, was it a comfortable living?

**LL:** I can't tell you just that. I've got to go back a little ways. I never intended to write for the pulps. I intended to write another sort of thing and I was working at that but I couldn't make any money on it. I did sell a story here and there and I sold a few. A few editors from publishing houses were beginning to write to me and suggest I send them books. Then the war came and I was out of it for four years. When I came out of the army, it was January 6, 1946. I remember the day very, very well. It was one of the few days in my life I remember. I got a call from Leo Margulies. He was having a party in New York. He invited me over there and at the party he asked me what I was going to do and I said, "Well, I have to make some kind of living." He said, "Why don't you write me some Western stories? I need Westerns in the worst way." He had talked to me about it and knew I knew the field, you know. So I did and here I am.

**LD:** It's real curious that a lot of science-fiction people, when they talk about Margulies, seem not to like him very much. They talk about him as if he were somebody who gave them a hard time. The Western writers talk about him as this wonderful guy who loved Westerns.

**LL:** I can't imagine any writer in his right mind not liking Leo Margulies.

I wrote pulps for several years and at the end of the time I was making a very good living at it. Then overnight they were gone like snow in the desert. But there was one reason I stayed with the pulps as long as I did—I could have been selling to *Post*, I could have been selling to *Colliers*, as I did later—I could have been selling to a lot of other magazines. The thing about Leo that made him so great for writers was you sent in a story, you got a check. If he bought it, he didn't fool around. He sent you the money right away.

**LD:** He didn't fool with your copy or anything like that?

**LL:** Well, he never fooled with the copy very much. But the point was you got your check right away. With a lot of these magazines, you could send a story off and it would be sixty to ninety days before you heard from them. The guy who was making a living couldn't do that. You got a check back from Margulies in ten or eleven days. Never missed.

**RL:** That's wonderful.

**LL:** It sure was. It sure was. It was a godsend for me because I was eating from check to check. And if the check didn't come on time, I didn't eat for a while.

**RL:** Where did you live then?

**LL:** I was living in Oklahoma when I started.

**LD:** So all the tougher. You couldn't go and pound on a door if you had any problems.

**LL:** That's right, that's right.

**LD:** You had to have someone you could rely on.

**LL:** You bet. He told me later, "You know, I did you a very serious disservice. I bought many stories from you and they should have been in the *Post*." I said, "Yeah, but you gave me the checks right away. I didn't have to wait six weeks or two months for them."

**LD:** Yeah. It's odd. The same thing seems to happen with Donald Wollheim. The science-fiction writers have a very different view of Wollheim than the Western writers do.

**LL:** That could be. I don't know. I never did much business with him. A little bit.

**RL:** Four books, I think?

**LL:** Well, I've forgotten who I did that business with.

**RL:** I remember that there were three or four of your early books that were Ace paperbacks.

**LL:** Yes. Four of them actually. Margulies was a great guy as far as I'm concerned.

# Anything for a Pal

*by Louis L'Amour*
*True Gang Life*, October 1935

TONY KINSELLA looked at his platinum wrist-watch. Ten more minutes. Just ten minutes to go. It was all set. In ten minutes a man would be standing on that corner under the street light. A green kid. Doreen would come up, speak to him, and then step into the drug store. The kid would wait, and then, after Doreen had put the finger on him, the car would slide up, and he, Tony Kinsella, Boss Cardoza's ace killer, would send a stream of steel-jacketed bullets into the kid's body. It would be all over then, and Tony Kinsella would have saved a pal from the chair, and paid another debt.

He looked up to the driver's seat where "Gloves" McFadden slouched carelessly, waiting. He noted the thick neck, and heavy, prizefighter's shoulders. In the other front seat "Dopey" Wentz puffed feverishly at a cigarette. Kinsella didn't like that. He didn't like to work with guys that were jerky, and any guy on the weed was undependable. Kinsella shrugged, and inhaled deeply.

This kid, Bunny Robbins he was going to knock-off. He'd seen Corney Watson pull that Baronski job. Tomorrow he was to identify Corney in court. To put the finger on him. Corney Watson had sprung Kinsella out of a Western pen one time, and they were pals. And Kinsella, whatever his failing, had one boast: he'd do anything for a pal. All around town they knew that. They used to say in the pool rooms when he was a kid: "That guy, Kinsella, he'd do anything for a pal!" Tony was proud of that. He was a right guy.

But that was only one of the two things he was proud of. The other the boys didn't know about except in a vague way. It was his kid brother, George. Their name wasn't Kinsella, and George had no idea that such a name even existed. Their real name was Bretherton, but when Kinsella had been arrested the first time, he gave his name as Kinsella, and so it had been for a dozen years now. But Tony was proud of George. George was ten years the youngest, and had no idea that his idolized big brother was a gangster, a killer. George was a star half-back on the team. Tony hadn't seen him in years, but he'd paid his way through college, and into a classy set of people. Tony smiled into the darkness. George Bretherton: now wasn't that a classy name? Maybe, when he'd put a few grand more in his sock he'd chuck the rackets and take George off to Europe. Then he'd be Anthony Bretherton, wealthy and respected.

Kinsella leaned back against the cushions. It was all set. This was one job he was pulling for nothing. Just for a pal. Corney had bumped "Baron" Baronski, and this kid had seen it. How he happened to be there, nobody knew or cared. Tomorrow he was going to testify in court, and that meant the chair for Corney unless Tony came through tonight, but Tony, who never failed a pal, would come through.

They had located Robbins' hang-out at a downtown hotel, a classy joint. Cardoza had sent Doreen over there, and she got acquainted. Doreen was a swell kid, wore her clothes like a million, and she was wise. She'd put the finger on more than one guy. Now this Robbins fellow. He wasn't one of Baronski's guns, so how had he been there at the time? Tony shrugged. Just one of those things.

Why didn't George write, he wondered? He was working in a law office out West somewhere. Maybe he'd be the mouth-piece for some big corporation and make plenty of dough. That was the racket! No danger of gang guns or coppers in that line, a safe thing.

Tony wondered what Corney was doing. Probably lying on his back in his cell hoping that Kinsella would come through. Well, Tony smiled with satisfaction; he'd never botched a job yet, and tonight he'd turn the heat on this Robbins guy and Corney would be in the clear. Why not? Wasn't Corney his pal? And Tony's motto was, "Anything for a pal."

Suddenly Dopey hissed: "Okay, Tony, there's the guy!"

"When you see Doreen comin', let me know. I'm not interested in this mug."

He suddenly found himself wishing it was over. He always felt like this at the last minute. Sort of jumpy. Prizefighters felt that way before the bell. Tense, nervous. But when the gun started to jump with the recoil he was all right. All of his nervousness streamed away with the steel-jacketed bullets. He caressed his gun lovingly.

"Get set, Tony, here she comes!" The powerful motor came to life suddenly, purring softly.

Kinsella sat up and rolled down the window. The cool evening air breathed softly across his face. He looked up at the stars, and then glanced both ways, up and down the street. It was all clear.

A tall, broad-shouldered fellow stood on the corner. Tony could see Doreen coming. She was walking fast. Probably she was nervous too. That big guy. That would be him. Tony licked his lips and lifted the ugly black muzzle of the submachine gun. Its cold nose peered over the edge of the window. The motor purred softly. He saw a man walk out of the drug store, light a cigar, and stroll off up the street. Tony almost laughed as he thought how funny it would be if he were to start shooting then, how startled that man would be!

There! Doreen was talking to the man on the corner. Had one hand on his sleeve. Smiling at him!

God! Dames were cold-blooded! In a couple of minutes that guy would be kicking in his own gore, and she was putting him on the spot and smiling at him!

Suddenly she turned away and started for the drug store on some excuse or other. As she passed through the door she was almost running. The car was moving swiftly now and Tony Kinsella smiled into the darkness. The car glided toward the curb, the man looked up, and the gun spouted fire and steel-jacketed bullets. The man threw up his arms oddly, jerked sharply, and fell head-long. McFadden wheeled the car and they drove back, the machine gun spouting fire again. The body, like a sack of old clothes, jerked as the bullets struck.


The next morning Tony lay on his back staring at the ceiling. He wondered where Doreen was. Probably the papers were full of the Robbins killing. Slowly he crawled out of bed, drew on his robe, and retrieved the morning paper from his apartment door. His eyes sought the headlines, blaring across the top in bold type:

GANG GUNS SLAY FEDERAL OPERATIVE. MACHINE GUNS GET WATSON WITNESS.

Tony's eyes narrowed. A federal man, eh? That wasn't so good. Who would have thought Robbins was a federal man? Still, they were never where you expected them to be. Probably, he'd been working on the Baronski case when Corney bumped the Baron. That would be it.

His eyes skimmed the brief account of the killing. It was as usual. They had no adequate description of either Doreen or the car. Then eyes glimpsed a word in the last paragraph that gripped his attention. His face tense, he read on.

Slowly, he looked up. His eyes were strange. His face looked old and strained. Walking across to the table he picked up his heavy automatic, slipped back the safety, and still staring blankly before him, put the muzzle in his mouth and pulled the trigger.

His body toppled across the table, the blood slowly staining the crumpled paper and almost obliterating the account of the Robbins killing. The final words of the account were barely visible as the spreading stain wiped it out:

A fact unknown until the killing was that Bunny Robbins, witness for the prosecution in the Baronski killing, was in reality George Bretherton, young Federal operative recently arrived from the Pacific Coast and working on his first case. He is survived by a brother whose present whereabouts are unknown.

# Men of Action: Louis L'Amour's Stories in *Thrilling Adventures*

"THE RADIO announcer's voice sounded clearly in the silent room, and 'Deke' Hayes scowled as he listened."

Thus began Louis L'Amour's second professional sale to the pulp magazines—a boxing story entitled "Gloves for a Tiger," published in the January 1938 issue of *Thrilling Adventures* magazine. It was the beginning of an association that would last for the next six years, until the magazine's unexpected cancellation at the beginning of 1944. It was in the pages of *Thrilling Adventures* that L'Amour scored his earliest successes, and where he refined the writing techniques that he would employ for the rest of his career.

One of the earliest members of the Standard chain of magazines, *Thrilling Adventures* started in December 1931. Obviously patterned after Ridgeway Publications' highly successful pulp *Adventure,* the new magazine featured tales of action and intrigue from all over the world. "Legion Steel," a tale of the French foreign legion in Africa, was the cover story. Other stories took place in "Red" Russia, Madagascar, India, Morocco, and Central America. Most of the stories were by minor writers for the pulps. It was priced at ten cents.

With the second issue, an editorial and letter column combined in one appeared. Titled "The Globe Trotter," it often featured letters from authors with stories in that issue, giving further details on their pieces. Oftentimes, the letters were more interesting than the stories themselves.

The contents remained much the same throughout the 1930s. Stories were fast-paced, action oriented, and primarily took place in the present. Authors were pulp professionals, but usually not the top writers in the field. *Argosy, Adventure,* and *Blue Book* all paid higher rates than *Thrilling Adventures,* and those magazines attracted the big names. The second-stringers worked for the Standard chain. Still, writers like Jack D'Arcy, Anthony Rud, Arthur J. Burks, and Harold Cruickshank always delivered a good story.

Louis L'Amour sold seventeen stories to *Thrilling Adventures.* It was his most important market during the early stages of his career. Working for the magazine, he developed techniques and theories that carried over to much of his later work.

"It is essential the adventure story begins with action or the events immediately preceding action," L'Amour wrote in an article for *Writer's Yearbook* in the late 1940s. One way to insure a fast beginning to every story was to start in the middle and fill in the background with flashbacks.

That was what L'Amour did with "Gloves for a Tiger," the story of a mysterious boxer seeking revenge against the world heavyweight champion. Not until halfway through the story and several boxing matches did the reader learn the truth about Bart Malone, the "Tiger," and why he was stalking Deke Hayes.

"Get into your story, keep it moving in every line, and never let your reader's interest wane," L'Amour told *Writer's Yearbook*. "You must bring your story to a smashing climax, so be careful to build gradually toward that climax."

"Gloves for a Tiger" focuses on Bart Malone's relentless pursuit of the man who stole his girl and left him for dead. Except for several flashbacks, the story moves from one action scene to another. Though the reader knows the inevitable ending (as is always the case in pulp stories), L'Amour does a fine job of building up the suspense leading to the final confrontation between hero and villain.

L'Amour's second sale to *Thrilling Adventures* was "East of Gorontalo," the first of his Ponga Jim Mayo stories. Ponga Jim was a sailing soldier of fortune, owner of the tramp freighter *Semiramis*. During the course of his adventures, he battled gunrunners, pirates, and hordes of Nazi and Axis agents. While a vast majority of his adventures took place in the Far East, one short novel placed him in the Red Sea and his last adventure took place in the jungles of Brazil.

Ponga Jim was the prototype for most of L'Amour's future heroes. Tall and well-muscled, he was fast with his fists and his mind. Like all of Louis's pulp protagonists, he was a man of action. Jim's solution to most problems was to barge ahead and count on his physical prowess to keep him alive.

Such is the case in "East of Gorontalo." Suspecting some villains of smuggling, Jim stows away on their ship to find out the truth. Most of the story is spent with Jim moving from hiding place to hiding place, one step ahead of his enemies. The adventure ends in a flurry of action, with Jim and a friend mopping up a boatful of criminals.

"In politics you can fool some of the people some of the time," L'Amour stated in a 1941 article for *The Writer*, "but not in fiction. Men and women from all walks of life are reading what you write, and you can be sure that no matter what line you take, there are some of those in your audience who know what you're talking about."

As an example, L'Amour discusses writing "East of Gorontalo." He describes Jim's escapades on the tramp freighter, then states, "To accomplish that, both Ponga Jim and the author had to know not only ship construction but the way of life aboard ship."

From the beginning of his career in the pulps until his death fifty years later, L'Amour stressed authenticity in his stories. L'Amour knew ships and he knew the South Seas, and his Ponga Jim stories reflected both.

"From Here to Banggai" follows much the same trail as the first adventure. Ponga Jim is hired by a group of Germans to transport some "farm equipment" to a far island. Shortly after the voyage begins, Jim discovers that the farm equipment consists of contraband weapons and ammunition. Again, the plot is minimal, but the action nonstop.

By the time the third Ponga Jim story appears, in the October 1940 issue, a pattern is emerging. Ponga Jim again helps British intelligence track down a group of foreign agents sinking ships in the South Seas. The plot is secondary to the action. The good guys are easily identifiable, as are the villains. There is no attempt at mystery. The story revolves around the action. And the fights.

L'Amour's Ponga Jim stories for *Thrilling Adventures* always ended with the hero facing the villain for one last showdown. As often as not, that battle was man to man, fist against fist. It was a formula that L'Amour brought with him into his novels. While many of Louis's Westerns end with a blaze of gunfire, a goodly number climax with a rough-and-tumble fistfight. *Flint*, for example, considered by most critics to be one of L'Amour's finest novels, ends in that manner. As does Lando. And many others.

In "On the Road to Amurang," Jim's nemesis is Job Dussel, a huge brute of a man. According to L'Amour, "enormous bulges of muscle hung over his arms and shoulders. His torso was like the trunk of a vast tree!" Jim defeats Dussel in a slugfest on the deck of a sinking ship that takes up most of a page.

L'Amour's villains leapt straight from the pulps into his novels. They are tough, powerful men, not the least bit ashamed to bloody their hands in battle. Shrewd and unscrupulous, they allow nothing to stand in their way. While motivated by greed or ambition, they often have a personal score to settle with the hero. In most respects, Job Dussel is not very different than Porter Baldwin, the chief heavy in *Flint*.

In all, L'Amour wrote nine Ponga Jim Mayo tales for *Thrilling Adventures*. They were all formula action stories, but each one read a little better than the last. Seven of the tales were collected in *West from Singapore*. Only missing were two short novels, "Voyage to Tobalai" and "Wings over Brazil."

"Wings over Brazil," the last of the Ponga Jim stories, was probably the best. It featured Jim in Brazil, fighting a Nazi plot to take over the country. As usual, the climax of the story featured Jim in a dramatic fistfight with Hugo Busch. Disdaining to use the gun in his pocket, Mayo instead stands toe-to-toe with the German, "[who] had been for a time the best heavyweight in the world."

"Pirates of the Sky" introduced Turk Madden to the readers of *Thrilling Adventures* in February 1941. A group of New York gangsters take over the small island of Eromanga in the South Seas. They plan to board and take over a passenger liner passing close by the island. Only Turk Madden, aviator and soldier of fortune, can stop them.

Turk is as tough as they come. He's described as a little over six feet tall with powerful shoulders and arms. In most respects, he could have been Ponga Jim's brother, although Turk doesn't use his fists as often. He is, though, a man of action.

In a welcome change of pace, the Turk Madden stories do not end in hand to hand combat with the chief villain. Turk believes in the destructive power of hardware. At the end of his first adventure, he rakes the deck of the criminals' yacht with tommy-gun fire. It proves quite bloody and very effective. The one gangster who avoids the carnage Turk shoots with a handy Luger.

"Coast Patrol," a short story printed in January 1943, was Turk's only other appearance in *Thrilling Adventures*. With the war going on, Turk was no longer working on his own. Instead, he was flying for the Russians. Encountering Japanese spies trying to pirate an American ship, Turk treated them to a dose of lead justice. Villains rarely survived encounters with the ruthless airman.

Turk then moved on to the pages of *Sky Fighters* for another seven exploits. Oddly enough, both Turk and Ponga Jim starred in nine stories for the Standard magazines.

Along with his series stories, L'Amour also wrote several nonseries stories for *Thrilling Adventures*. Typical of them was "Mission to Siberut," in which tramp flyer Steve Cowan destroys a boat-load of Messerschmitt pursuit planes headed for Japan. Change the hero's name and the story could have been about Turk Madden or Ponga Jim.

"Gold Is How You Keep It," printed in July 1941 (extensively revised when reprinted as "The Dancing Kate" in *Yondering*), features treasure hunter Rafe Morgan marooned on a tiny reef in the midst of the South Pacific. Rafe's wife is pregnant and he's anxious to return to his plantation, especially after finding gold on the reef. First, though, he has to deal with Bloody Jack Randal, piratical captain of *The Dancing Kate*. Needless to say, Morgan does so with usual L'Amour ruthlessness.

As in L'Amour's series stories for the magazine, it was business as usual for the good guys. They took their lumps, engaged in some fistfights with the nasties, and in the end triumphed over all adversity. The plots were minimal, but the action was fast and continued from beginning to end.

The winter 1943–44 issue of *Thrilling Adventures* featuring the last Ponga Jim Mayo story was also the final issue of the magazine. During the war years, pulp publishers had to cut back on the size of their magazines and the number of titles published. *Thrilling Adventures* was one of the casualties of the war. Ponga Jim and Turk Madden could vanquish Nazis without taking a deep breath, but neither man could defeat a paper shortage.

Louis L'Amour's adventure tales were typical of the work being done for the pulps in the early 1940s. They depended more on setting and action than on plot or characterization. Still, the stories are fun reading even now. And they served as a necessary first step in L'Amour's long climb to success.

# Death in Cold, Hard Light:
# The Mystery Fiction of Louis L'Amour

*by Robert Sampson*

---

Suspense that the reader feels clear down to his guts is
the most important word in the writer's book.

Louis L'Amour in "Louis L'Amour: Man of the West"
by Harold Keith, *The Roundup*, January 1976.
Reprinted by permission of the Western Writers of America

---

"THE DETECTIVE protagonist," Louis L'Amour wrote, "does not usually
come to fear the land as much as the characters in a frontier story. . . . In
detective stories, the characters come to fear the people they have to
associate with in the city."

As well they might. The city stands in a glow of light, its towers
transparent, its women beautiful, its streets fragrant with money. But let a
detective lift any part of that luminous surface and out writhes a disgust-
ing swarm—thugs and sluggers, drug addicts, psychopaths and tawdry
ladies, professional killers.

They have eyes hard as metal and ice pellets for hearts. Treachery
and brutality are the small coins of their lives, and murder is their natural
response to any problem. But they are not the worst the city offers.
Behind them, manipulating them, looms a more terrible figure.

It is the figure of a powerful man, big, thick of chest and neck, slabbed
with muscle, relentless as a force of nature. Alert, intelligent, quick to
strike, he radiates violence the way molten metal radiates heat.

In one guise or other, this figure stands at the core of L'Amour's mystery fiction. Like the devil at the core of hell, he is the cause of all the

trouble, the menace whose dreadful vitality puts a shiver of suspense into the adventure. Before any story can end, he must be dragged foaming and snarling into the light.

In L'Amour's frontier stories, such struggles usually climax in a stutter of gunfire. In L'Amour's mysteries, gunfire is distributed in satisfying amounts all through the action; but when the final struggle takes place, it is not with gun but with fist. The detective must whip that muscular menace in a free-for-all brawl. Even for L'Amour's rock-hard detectives, the process is an ordeal.

L'Amour wrote about fifteen stories of hard-action mystery fiction. Most of these appeared in the detective pulp magazines between 1946 and 1950. (Single stories published in 1938 and 1952 serve as a prelude and coda to this effort.)

By the mid-1940s, L'Amour had already published a hefty body of work. He had written adventure stories for *Thrilling Adventures* magazine, air war stories for *Sky Fighters,* and a number of Westerns for *Dime Western, Thrilling Western,* and others. Some stories got written simultaneously. As he remarked, ". . . I might be working on a detective story in the morning and a Western story in the afternoon. . . ."

All stories share a clear, direct prose. The action line rushes from danger to danger, hot with excitement. The scene is vividly drawn, bright with authentic detail. Few of the characters are less than tough. They slug and shoot each other with slit-eyed indifference.

L'Amour's detective fiction grew seamlessly from his prior fiction. "Good storytelling," he wrote, "can be applied to any area at any time." He applied techniques devised for his adventure and Western stories to create a sense of place, generate conflict between the characters, and keep suspense singing like wind on a tight wire.

His mystery stories also incorporate important elements of the hard-boiled style of writing. Like any competent craftsman, L'Amour wrote for a market, and the detective-fiction market of the time strongly favored the hard-boiled story form. As employed by Hammett, Nebel, Chandler, Davis, and a dozen or so others, the hard-boiled style was a lethal instrument, polished and edged. Often written in the first person, it was contemporary, slangy, full of color and vitality, as pungent as black radish sauce.

It was also disrespectful of authority, cynical of human behavior, sardonic about love. It was lowbrow and unsentimental, and behind its usual view of a society gone corrupt in every cell lay a grim melancholy that the world should be so.

In its classic form, the hard-boiled story concentrated on character as revealed by action. That was harder to do than it looked. In the 1940s, a lot of good hard-boiled material was still being written. But over the years less able imitators of the style deemphasized character in favor of pure action, one bloody event chasing another, a drumroll of violence. Scattered through this savage emptiness were the mannerisms, situations, and character types of the hard-boiled school.

While L'Amour accepted the hard-boiled conventions, he was not content to recycle old bones. To the story form he brought a rather different view of the detective. And from his astoundingly varied background, he brought the freshness of personally observed detail.

First of all, his lead character was a fighting man. Somewhat secondly, he was a detective. With minor variations, this figure appeared in most of L'Amour's short mystery fiction under various names—Kip Morgan, Neil Shannon, Bruce Blake. When presented as a police detective, his name was Joe Ragan. Each man is slightly different. Slightly. You wouldn't be fool enough to kick sand on any one of them.

Collectively, they are six-footers in their late twenties, with a boxer's build and a boxer's agility and speed. All know what hard, manual labor is. They have poured out their sweat on shipboard, on the waterfront, as circus roustabouts, cowboys, sailors, or hard-rock miners.

Grinding work with the hands hasn't slowed their minds. Each has a glib tongue and an agile intelligence. Each can think while looking down a gun muzzle. That is often necessary.

Kip(ling) Morgan for example. (His mother developed a fondness for the writings of Rudyard Kipling and named her son after him.) Kip, a powerful young man, was formerly a light-heavyweight boxer. He retired from the ring, brain undamaged.

As any ex-boxer, Kip has a strong aggressive streak. He wants to sail right in and clean things up. And he doesn't like to be told to back off. During his boxing years, he met both police and underworld figures. As a private investigator, he gets help from these people—particularly from Mooney of the police, who provides official information or sends a squad around when needed.

"Dead Man's Trail" (*Thrilling Detective*, August 1947) is Kip's first case. It is a sort of prototype for stories to come. The problem is to find evidence that a widow's husband was victim, not murderer. Kip baits a trap with a newspaper ad, ends up slugged unconscious. Kidnapped by two thugs, he whips them in a wild, free-for-all fight. Immediately afterward, he is nearly shot dead by the murderer but escapes by a spur-of-the-moment trick. Although he is much battered, Kip stops the murderer from killing the widow and hands him, a little shot up, to the police.

The story ends with a faint suggestion of romance between Kip and the widow. It is a suggestion only, used by L'Amour to give this story—and others—an upbeat ending. To judge from these endings, nothing stirs a woman more deeply than a man whose face has been beaten to hamburger—providing he got that way while detecting for her.

The next published story, "The Sucker Switch" (*Thrilling Detective*, December 1947), contains a lot more mystery elements, and a far more violent story line. It features Neil Shannon, operative for an unnamed agency. Shannon wears a trench coat, carries a .380 Colt automatic, and uses chewing gum three sticks at a time. Like Kip Morgan, Shannon is quick-witted and handy with his fists.

Furs have been stolen from an impregnable warehouse, the watchman murdered. The theft seems completely impossible, and the most probable crooks have an unbreakable alibi. But now Shannon scratches up some strange clues: threads of sharkskin material, a few damp tarpaulins, dry dirt under a tire track. Before you know it, "Things began to click into place, and when I started back, I knew I was going to bust this wide open. Only a few loose ends remained."

At this point, the story is half over. From here to the end, it is action, action, gasping action. Shannon bluffs his way into the crime boss's office, resulting in a fine shooting match. With two crooks down, Neil takes on the big tough hard powerful boss in a bare-knuckle slugfest. Following this excitement, the cops pile in, just in time to be too late. Neil then reveals the name of the mastermind behind the fur robberies. The narrator of this first-person piece (Neil Shannon), forgot to tell the reader that he found a loose wallet at the looted warehouse and hunted up the owner and discovered that the wallet owner had witnessed the whole blessed robbery. These last-minute revelations are necessary because all the racing around, fighting, and shooting failed to develop any solid evidence connecting the mastermind to the crime.

Such barefaced dealing from the bottom of the deck is not usual in these stories. Not often. Not so boldly. Although it's true that in "Under the Hanging Wall," the detective uncovers information explaining the crime's motive and entirely neglects to mention it till the end of the story. And in "The Vanished Blonde," another Shannon case, most of the clues remain invisible to the reader.

To resolve a story by a mass of withheld information shows a certain casualness in narrative management. For subsequent stories, L'Amour devised a more sophisticated, and technically more difficult, way of telling the concealed story that constitutes the mystery. This story he allowed to come out, piece by piece, between flares of action. The narrative flow is never interrupted for long. And the traditional static explanation scene at the end is either omitted or drastically shortened—greatly improving the pacing. The increased clarity and polish of stories published during 1948 and 1949 show how completely this approach succeeded.

"With Death in His Corner" was published by *Thrilling Detective* (December 1948) and reprinted in the spring 1953 issue of *Five Detective Novels*. In this first-person story Morgan is searching the fringe of the underworld for an old sparring pal. At last he finds his friend. Murdered. From here the story explodes. Four separate fights are described in loving detail. Again Kip is slugged unconscious and carried off by killers. But they don't manage to keep him long and presently the police cart away stacks of well-battered thugs.

Scattered through the action are familiar images from earlier hard-boiled fiction: The aging blonde with an alcohol problem. The detective at the bar seeking information. (His drink is bourbon and water, although none of L'Amour's detectives are very much interested in alcohol.) And the customary description of the detective's clothing: ". . . I changed into a navy blue gabardine suit and a blue and gray striped tie. . . ."

The action flows through nightclubs, garish with lights, where cold faces watch from the shadows, to tenements smelling of dirt and roaches, to decrepit garages, back alleys, and hotels. Kip finds violence in them all. The prose moves with force, clarity, and even an occasional touch of humor.

"The Hills of Homicide" (*Detective Tales*, May 1949), also a first-person story, is told by an unnamed operative working out of a Los Angeles agency. He is a right tough fellow, a two-hundred-pounder with a .45, who has worked lumber camps and waterfronts, speaks Malayan, and studies criminal methods from all over the world. He is also expert at the kick, stomp, thumb-in-your-eye, knee-to-your-crotch slugfest.

Lucky he knows how to fight. He meets one of L'Amour's tougher villains. The fight, which continues for pages, reads like the battle for Hamburger Hill.

Before that, the detective meets two women, one of them treacherous, gets taken for a ride, and has a fine shoot-out with a pair of thugs. All this occurs in a small Nevada town. The detective has been hired to investigate an impossible murder in a house on an isolated butte to which only one path gives access. No one could use that path without detection. The solution isn't hard—provided you know how thieves scale walls in India.

"Under the Hanging Wall" (*Thrilling Detective,* June 1949) is a fine action adventure set in a played out Arizona mining town. Ex-miner Bruce Blake is the detective, with all the usual fighting skills. Blake's job is to look into a murder case to make sure the police have the right murderer. They don't. A lot of peculiar clues jump up—the imprint of a body in the dust under the bed of a sexy lady; an alarm clock that didn't go off; a new .38 that is unfired; and a crumpled-up magazine. The deputy sheriff is tougher than a bag of black walnuts and has things to hide. The murdered man's wife has melting eyes and perfectly round heels.

It's complicated. But, as Blake remarks, "There's no such thing as a perfect crime, there are just imperfect investigators."

Blake and the deputy sheriff get trapped in a collapsing mine. After a fistfight of great violence, they get together and drill an escape passage through yards of rock. Specific details pepper the story—from the description of the rotten stone in a mine roof (the hanging wall) to the techniques of hard-rock blasting and elements of mining geology.

L'Amour's next stories turn from private investigators to ex-boxer and homicide detective Joe Ragan. He appears in "I Hate to Tell His Widow" (*Detective Tales,* July 1949) and "Collect from a Corpse" (*Black Mask,* September 1949). Although Ragan is an official detective, he is not much for team activities. He operates on his own as much as any private operative.

"Widow" involves the murder of Ragan's oldest friend on the force; "Corpse" offers a series of crimes with faked modus operandi, causing innocent crooks great embarrassment. In both cases, important physical evidence is generated by the criminal's unconscious habits, such as crushing a paper cup or splitting a paper match with the fingernail.

These stories would never be mistaken for police procedurals; they are action stories involving policemen. These police grate on each other's nerves and have jurisdictional disputes, and now and again the stink of interoffice politics drifts through. But the cases flow smoothly to logical climaxes. There is a minor reduction in freestyle shooting and punching.

And once more, friendship leads the detective into violent events—L'Amour's detectives are constantly doing favors for friends or avenging their murders.

The final stories published in *Detective Tales* are in L'Amour's mature hard-boiled style. Across the action falls a cold, hard light. The scenes, reeking with fear and danger, are crisp, urgent, often brutal, full of guns and criminals as deadly as adders. Kip Morgan is the detective. In the first-person "Stay Out of My Nightmare!" (November 1949), he tries to locate a friend and finds, instead, the usual whirlwind of murder. He gets himself trapped in a seaside room about to be flooded by the tide, and escapes, barely, after physical exertions that would startle Superman. Helped by Mooney, an undercover police woman, and a lot of bullets, he cleans up the matter—a systematic defrauding of veterans.

The following story, "The Street of Lost Corpses" (January 1950), is told in the third person. It is novelette-length, filled with harsh incident, and the crooks capture Kip rather often as he untangles a complicated insurance swindle.

Neil Shannon returned in the December 1950 issue of *Thrilling Detective*. During the events of "The Vanished Blonde," his investigation moves from California to Arizona. There the killer corners the girl on a cliff over a box canyon. Shannon arrives in time and the killer gets clobbered. Most of the clues appear out of thin air, after Shannon decides to tell how he detected who was behind it all.

More than a year later, *Popular Detective* published "Unguarded Moment" (March 1952), an unusual story lacking a formal detective. Arthur Fordyce, a decent, average man, finds a money-stuffed wallet dropped by a friend. In a moment of weakness, he keeps the wallet, but is seen and blackmailed by a cheap grifter.

The story theme is that an incautious act may instantly throw your life out of control. Fortunately for Fordyce, he thinks faster, is bolder, bluffs better than any average man you ever met. Fairly soon, he has accidentally killed the blackmailer. But now he is blackmailed by the crook's wife. After tracking her down by clever detective work, he bluffs her (and another small-time crook) into dropping the matter. Whereupon he anonymously returns the money.

An interesting story. All characters are intelligent, physical violence is at a minimum, and the world of petty chiselers, angling for a quick dollar, is nicely drawn. As is Fordyce's distress as his single transgression drags him inexorably deeper into a morass of criminality.

With this taut story, L'Amour's mystery fiction ends. It is a distinct loss, apparently a consequence of his commitment to Western fiction and the collapse of the pulp detectives magazines by mid-1953.

His contributions to the hard-boiled detective story are continuously interesting. Arriving late in the field, he devised fresh variations to a story form encrusted with mannerisms. The energy of his mysteries brought vividly to life that dangerous world on the crummy side of town—that world of hard men and strutting toughs, where a chance meeting may balloon to insane violence, where there is always a friend or a widow to be helped, and where a detective with a healthy punch can always find danger and enough exhilarating fistfights to whet his fighting edge.

# L'Amour's Short Story Collections: A Checklist

THROUGH May of 1991, the following collections of Louis L'Amour short stories had been published by Bantam Books. This checklist records the contents of those books.

Approximately forty L'Amour pulp stories have not been collected in book form and probably consist of enough material for another four or five volumes.

Books are listed in chronological order of publication.

**1.** *War Party*—originally published by Bantam Books in February 1975.

Contents: Trap of Gold; One for the Pot; War Party; Get Out of Town; Booty for a Badman; The Gift of Cochise; A Mule for Santa Fe; Alkali Basin; Men to Match the Hills; The Defense of Sentinel

**2.** *The Strong Shall Live*—originally published by Bantam Books in January 1980.

Contents: The Strong Shall Live; One Night Stand; Trail to Squaw Springs; Merrano of the Dry Country; The Romance of Piute Bill; Hattan's Castle; Duffy's Man; Big Man; The Marshal of Sentinel; Bluff Creek Station

**3.** *Yondering*—originally published by Bantam Books in June 1980.

Contents: Where There's Fighting; The Dancing Kate; Glorious! Glorious!; Dead End Drift; Old Doc Yak; Survival; Thicker Than Blood; The Admiral; Shanghai Not without Gestures; The Man Who Stole Shakespeare; A Friend of the General; Author's Tea; A Moon of the Trees Broken by Snow: A Christmas Story; Let Me Forget. . . . (poem)

In November 1989, Bantam Books published a revised edition of *Yondering,* edited by L'Amour's son, Beau. The story "A Moon of the Trees Broken by Snow" was dropped. Added to the revised edition were "By the Ruins of El Walarieh," "And Proudly Die," and "Show Me the Way to Go Home." Also included was the article "So You Want Adventure, Do You?" from *Rob Wagner's Script.*

**4.** *Buckskin Run*—originally published by Bantam Books in November 1981.

Contents: The Ghosts of Buckskin Run; No Trouble for the Cactus Kid; Horse Heaven; The Squatters on the Lonetree; Jackson of Horntown; There's Always a Trail; Down the Pogonip Trail; What Gold Does to a Man

**5.** *Bowdrie*—originally published by Bantam Books in March 1983.
Contents: Bowdrie Rides a Coyote Trail; A Job for a Ranger; Bowdrie Follows a Cold Trail; Bowdrie Passes Through; A Trail to the West; More Brains Than Bullets; Too Tough to Brand; The Killer from the Pecos

**6.** *Law of the Desert Born*—originally published by Bantam Books, August 1983.
Contents: Law of the Desert Born; Riding On; The Black Rock Coffin Makers; Desert Death Songs; Ride, You Tonto Raiders!; One Last Gun Notch; Death Song of the Sombrero; The Guns Talk Loud; Grub Line Rider; The Marshal of Painted Rock; Trap of Gold

**7.** *The Hills of Homicide*—published by Bantam Books, August 1983.
Contents: The Hills of Homicide; Unguarded Moment; Dead Man's Trail; With Death in His Corner; The Street of Lost Corpses; Stay Out of My Nightmare!; Collect from a Corpse; I Hate to Tell His Widow

**8.** *Bowdrie's Law*—published by Bantam Books, December 1984.
Contents: McNelly Knows a Ranger; Where Buzzards Fly; Case Closed—No Prisoners; Down Sonora Way; The Road to Casa Piedras; A Ranger Rides to Town; South of Deadwood; The Outlaws of Poplar Creek; Rain on the Mountain Fork; Strange Pursuit

**9.** *Dutchman's Flat*—published by Bantam Books, March 1986.
Contents: Dutchman's Flat; Keep Travelin', Rider; Trail to Pie Town; Mistakes Can Kill You; Big Medicine; Man from Battle Flat; West of the Tularosas; McQueen of the Tumbling K; One for the Mohave Kid; Lion Hunter and the Lady; A Gun for Kilkenny

**10.** *Riding for the Brand*—published by Bantam Books, March 1986.
Contents: Riding for the Brand; Four Card Draw; His Brother's Debt; Strong Land Growing; The Turkeyfeather Riders; Lit a Shuck for Texas; The Nester and the Piute; Barney Takes a Hand; Man Riding West; Fork Your Own Broncs; Home in the Valley; West Is Where the Heart Is

**11.** *The Trail to Crazy Man*—published by Bantam Books, September 1986.
Contents: The Trail to Crazy Man; Riders of the Dawn; Showdown on the Hogback

**12.** *The Rider of the Ruby Hills*—published by Bantam Books, September 1986.

Contents: The Rider of the Ruby Hills; Showdown Trail; A Man Called Trent; The Trail to Peach Meadow Canyon

**13.** *Night over the Solomons*—published by Bantam Books, October 1986.

Contents: Night over the Solomons; Mission to Siberut; Pirates with Wings; Tailwind to Tibet; The Goose Flies South; Wings over Khabarovsk

**14.** *West from Singapore*—published by Bantam Books, April 1987.

Contents: East of Gorontalo; On the Road to Amurang; From Here to Banggai; The House of Qasavara; Well of Unholy Light; West from Singapore; South of Suez

**15.** *Lonigan*—published by Bantam Books, October 1988.

Contents: Lonigan; Regan of the Slash B; Heritage of Hate; Rowdy Rides for Glory; Partner From the Rio; Bill Carey Rides West

**16.** *Long Ride Home*—published by Bantam Books, October 1989.

Contents: The Cactus Kid Pays a Debt; Bad Place to Die; That Triggernometry Tenderfoot; The Town No Guns Could Tame; Shandy Takes the Hook; No Man's Man; Ride or Start Shootin'; Long Ride Home

**17.** *The Outlaws of Mesquite*—published by Bantam Books, June 1990.

Contents: The Outlaws of Mesquite; Love and the Cactus Kid; The Ghost Maker; The Drift; No Rest for the Wicked; That Packsaddle Affair; Showdown on the Tumbling T; The Sixth Shotgun

The following collections were published by Carroll & Graf Books. The entire story of Carroll & Graf versus Louis L'Amour and Bantam Books follows this checklist:

**1.** *Law of the Desert Born*—published in hardcover and paperback in August 1983.

Contents: Law of the Desert Born; Ride, You Tonto Raiders!; The Black Rock Coffin Makers; Desert Death Songs; Trap of Gold

**2.** *The Hills of Homicide*—published in paperback in August 1983.

Contents: The Hills of Homicide; I Hate to Tell His Widow; Collect from a Corpse; Stay Out of My Nightmare!; The Street of Lost Corpses

**3.** *Man Riding West* (later reprinted as *Dutchman's Flat*)—published in paperback in March 1986.

Contents: Big Medicine; Man Riding West; His Brother's Debt; Four Card Draw; Keep Travelin', Rider; Dutchman's Flat; Trail to Peach Meadow Canyon

**4.** *Riding for the Brand*—published in paperback in March 1986.

Contents: Riding for the Brand; Lit a Shuck For Texas; Mistakes Can Kill You; The Nester and the Piute; Trail to Pie Town; The Turkeyfeather Riders; McQueen of the Tumbling K

# Writing for the Brand—
# An Interview with Kent Carroll

*by Stefan Dziemianowicz*

WHILE there has been no lack of fiction by Louis L'Amour available for the last thirty years, in 1983 L'Amour readers had more than the usual abundance of riches to choose from: two different publishers both issued two collections of L'Amour short fiction, each bearing the titles *The Hills of Homicide* and *Law of the Desert Born*. Behind this peculiar incident is a little-known story of publishing ethics and practices that began when fledgling publisher Carroll & Graf tried to issue mass-market paperbacks of L'Amour stories that had fallen out of copyright. L'Amour and his longtime publisher Bantam Books sued Carroll & Graf, claiming a living writer's prerogative to decide how his work will be presented to the public. For their defense, Carroll & Graf invoked the letter of the copyright law. The media described the ensuing court battle in terms more appropriate for the gunfight at the O.K. Corral.

Although the matter was eventually settled out of court with Carroll & Graf exonerated and allowed to publish the books, Bantam surprised everyone by bringing out simultaneous "authorized" editions under the same titles. In addition to extra stories and author notes, the Bantam editions carried forewords in which L'Amour recounted the issues raised during the trial. Readers can find L'Amour and Bantam's view of the episode expressed in these volumes as well as two 1986 collections, *Dutchman's Flat* and *Riding for the Brand*. The following interview with Carroll & Graf publisher Kent Carroll presents the other side of the argument.

**STEFAN DZIEMIANOWICZ:**   How did the project that produced the two Louis L'Amour books *The Hills of Homicide* and *Law of the Desert Born* come to Carroll & Graf?
**KENT CARROLL:**   It was brought to us by a collector of pulp magazines who quite literally asked, "How would you like to publish some stories by Louis L'Amour?" At first, my reaction was neutral because I wasn't too sure who Louis L'Amour was. I knew he wrote Westerns, but I

had always assumed that the name was a pseudonym. I really wasn't cognizant of his popularity, although my partner, Herman Graf, was.

So we said, "Okay, this interests us, but how do we go about doing this? He's a living author, and he's published by Bantam." And this person said, "Yes, that's true, but the stories I have are all in the public domain." So we read the stories, and found them more than up to the standard. They were his early stories, but they weren't throwaways.

**SD:**  They were good pulp fiction?

**KC:**  Excellent pulp fiction. So the next thing we did was have a lawyer in Washington check with the Library of Congress, and, indeed, all of these stories were in the public domain. So we had a perfect right to publish them, and decided to publish them in mass-market paperbacks.

We also thought at the time that because L'Amour was a living author the only fair and honorable thing to do was to inform him that we wanted to publish these stories and offer him the same royalty he would have received from Bantam for a paperback. We also gave him the opportunity to write an introduction, if he so chose, to put the stories in context.

We acted appropriately. But the response on the part of L'Amour and Bantam was unexpected, to say the least. We did not understand or anticipate how important L'Amour was to Bantam. It quickly became apparent that L'Amour and his books were virtually a profit center for Bantam, and Bantam wanted to protect that. Also, from everything that came out later, it seems that L'Amour was furious that anybody would attempt to publish his work without his consent.

**SD:**  Do you think L'Amour put pressure on Bantam to take action, or was it the other way around?

**KC:**  Oh, it was clearly both.

**SD:**  Articles in *Publishers Weekly* reported L'Amour finding out about the Carroll & Graf project at that year's American Booksellers Association convention.

**KC:**  We did not disguise what we were doing. We never thought of printing up the books and shipping them out to people without announcing it. We listed them as forthcoming titles in our catalog. And Bantam sued us and took us to federal court.

There were a couple of interesting things about the lawsuit. We literally had certificates from the Library of Congress certifying that all the stories were in the public domain. So Bantam sued us on the grounds that the name Louis L'Amour was a trademark, and thus using the name without his authority was a violation of the trademark.

They also claimed that these stories were inferior to the fiction he was now writing, and therefore this violated a commercial code that prevents pawning off inferior goods as superior goods. It's very ironic that they made this argument, because immediately thereafter they published the same stories in their books, and resurrected a half dozen more.

They tried to claim that the L'Amour books used a typeface that could be considered a Western typeface, and that the use of this typeface was not allowed because only Louis L'Amour could use it. They also tried to claim that you couldn't use a Western scene for a cover that was reminiscent of anything on any Louis L'Amour book.

One thing that they claimed was quite clever, and had to do with the way books are put into mass-market paperback racks. The author's name always goes on top, so it can be seen. But Bantam claimed that only they could put L'Amour's name at the top of one of his books. So what it came down to was, if we were going to publish these books as Carroll & Graf titles, one, we had to put L'Amour's name at the bottom; two, we couldn't use the Western typeface; and three, we couldn't use a Western scene to illustrate the story. All of which was ludicrous, clearly.

But we had some difficulties in court, and one of the biggest came about four or five days into the trial when the judge actually said, "I still don't understand how somebody can publish the work of a living author if that author doesn't agree to it."

**SD:**   So the judge knew nothing about copyright law?

**KC:**   Nothing.

**SD:**   Could you describe the copyright law as it has bearing on this case?

**KC:**   At the time, the copyright law said that anything put into copyright—in this case stories in a magazine—is protected for twenty-eight years, after which the copyright can be renewed for another twenty-eight years. So that equals fifty-six years from the time of publication. If the copyright is not renewed the stories go out of copyright. And there's no such thing as retroactive renewal. In this particular case, all of these stories were published in magazines, and it was the magazine issues themselves that were copyrighted, not the individual stories. So when the magazine copyright lapsed, all the material inside lapsed. L'Amour could have taken the stories and copyrighted them individually, but that was never done.

Something that frequently gets lost in public debate about the copyright law is one of the reasons for the law's existence. Copyright laws do not exist just to protect authors. The reason why copyrights expire has to do with the free use and transmission of information. The idea of "public domain" tells you something—it says that the creator should enjoy the privileges and earnings that come from this work for a period of time, but that at some juncture this work should be enjoyed by everybody. A great value of a democratic society is its free flow of information. The benefits to society at large should not be limited by the dictates of a single individual, even if the individual created the works in question.

**SD:** Why do you think L'Amour and Bantam were so adamant about the suit? Do you think L'Amour was just trying to put his pulp writing days behind him?

**KC:** Perhaps, in part. L'Amour wrote a lot, and Bantam probably figured that one new book a year, or one new book a season, whatever they were publishing, was the maximum that should be done. Bantam probably decided that the novels sold a lot better than the story collections, and therefore they wanted to publish the novels.

In point of fact, the stories are every bit as good as the stuff L'Amour wrote later. Essentially, L'Amour is a good storyteller. I think he had that ability for most of his professional life. It's not as though he became a great stylist, or deepened his themes and ideas as he developed. His work is all pretty much the same thing right from the beginning. I think he just forgot about these stories. Bantam may not even have known the things existed. It shouldn't have taken a great deal of thought, though, because L'Amour wrote an awful lot.

**SD:** What was it like going up against Bantam and L'Amour in court?

**KC:** Bantam used the law firm Debevoise and Plimpton, which had James Goodall as lead attorney. Goodall had been the corporate attorney for the *New York Times* for many years. They had as their principal litigator a woman who had been a Manhattan district attorney for a number of years and had just gone into private practice. We had one lawyer! We would go into court and there would be eight or nine lawyers, all the backup from Bantam. They would have something like fifteen people on their side. And Herman and I would be there with our one lawyer.

**SD:** It sounds like they were counting on intimidation.

**KC:** Well, they were counting on two things, which they in effect said. Early on, in the exchanges that went back and forth, they said things like, "We're going to crush you," and, "You're never going to be able to do this again. You're going to be out of business." They felt that they could make it so expensive and so difficult that we would desist.

The second thing they were hoping to do—and this is just a surmise—

was delay us. We found out in the course of the trial that Bantam kept insisting the judge had to show them the stories. They wouldn't accept the certification from the Library of Congress. They said L'Amour had to read the stories to prove that they were actually his. And the judge agreed, until we said no, they can't do that, because we had an idea they would do exactly what they did do, or what it appears they did. By the time the trial was over, they somehow found out which stories we were using in our books and published competing editions.

Bantam's problem was finding out what the stories were. We assumed that they and L'Amour had no idea which stories we wanted to publish— the names of them, where they came from, nothing. Had they known something about them they would have renewed the copyright long before. But a company like Bantam has the resources and the leverage to print and bind a book quickly. Producing the book wasn't their biggest problem. Their biggest problem was finding out what the stories were.

**SD:**   Initially, the Carroll & Graf editions were promoted under the titles *Homicide Street* and *Rawhide Range,* which were fairly generic names. But you were asked to change the titles of them to those of stories that appeared in the books, "The Hills of Homicide" and "Law of the Desert Born." That gave Bantam the right to bring its competing editions out under the same titles, since they were taken from stories in the public domain.

**KC:**   Yes, that was a very clever thing for them to do that we didn't understand at the time. They said we had to use a title from one of the stories in the book. And by agreeing to do that we gave away the identity of at least two of the stories and also gave them the opportunity to use the same titles on their books. That was just a very clever legal maneuver on their part.

Really, the court fight didn't have anything to do with whether or not we had the right to publish these stories, or whether or not the stories were really in the public domain. It all had to do with Bantam's attempt to interfere with our doing business—publishing these books, distributing them, and selling them. The suit gave Bantam the time to find out what the stories were so they could produce their competing editions.

**SD:**   Bantam reproduced the same stories that appeared in the Carroll & Graf editions but added another two or three. Do you have any idea how they acquired their information about the contents of the Carroll & Graf books?

**KC:**   We don't know for sure, except that they went to great lengths to find out what these stories were. We assume that at some point they didn't know which stories we had chosen, but the similarity of their editions to ours indicates they must have found out. It was a clever move on their part to add the extra stories so their editions were superior.

I also think that from the beginning they understood better than we did—probably because they had the manpower and the time and the resources—that this was a publicity battle. The letter that L'Amour put on the back of the Bantam editions telling readers to buy only the "authorized" versions wasn't thought up the night before they went to press. It was part of their whole calculated tactic to discredit what we were doing by appealing to the loyalty of L'Amour fans. I think they did that quite effectively.

**SD:** Did the Carroll & Graf editions appear simultaneously with the Bantam editions?

**KC:** Well, they were simultaneous in that both appeared right after the court battle ended. We won the case in the sense that we had all the bogus charges against us dismissed and were still able to publish the books. We tried to make a charge to the court, and I still believe it's true, that Bantam was using the court to do business. It was obvious, because none of their accusations had any merit whatsoever.

**SD:** According to news reports, when you found out Bantam was preparing to bring out competing editions you tried to get an injunction to prevent them, and before the injunction could be ruled on you settled out of court.

**KC:** We settled for two reasons. First, although our legal advice was to prevent Bantam from publishing their editions, we realized we were sort of contradicting our own basic argument about why *we* should be allowed to publish *our* editions. Secondly, even though we had made an arrangement with our attorney to pay him a percentage of the book royalty if we won, the case was disrupting our business. At the time, it was only our second year of business, Herman and I and one other person were about the entire staff, and it just wasn't worth my time, Herman's time, and the amount of our energies it was absorbing. We just decided that it was best to end it.

**SD:** Did Bantam and L'Amour make any stipulations in the settlement regarding future Carroll & Graf editions of Louis L'Amour stories? Surely they must have realized there were more stories out there that you or another publisher could put into print.

**KC:** There were several things that we agreed to, largely because we never intended to do them in the first place. We agreed to some terms about not reprinting the books after a certain amount of time had elapsed. But these were not things we felt handicapped by.

You have to remember that when we got into this tangle, first we didn't really know who Louis L'Amour was, second we wanted to be friendly, and third we thought we were doing a pretty good thing for L'Amour. Here we were resurrecting these stories that he probably didn't remember existed. We didn't think we were going to sell a million copies of them or anything of that sort. Our expectations were such that we were able to make these agreements to end this lunacy without any disappointments. We ended up selling 100,000 or 125,000 copies, something like that, which was more than we had initially imagined from the start.

**SD:**   After all, all you wanted was to publish the book.

**KC:**   Correct. Now, what we caused to happen—it's something Bantam has never given us credit for, but while we sold 125,000 copies or so of our books, they sold half a million or more of theirs. They then proceeded to publish another six or eight volumes of these older stories, each of which was very successful. So in fact, we helped Bantam to publish more Louis L'Amour volumes, which means that Bantam ended up, because of our efforts, pocketing at least half a million dollars, and L'Amour ended up with another half a million dollars in royalties. And I'm very disappointed that we haven't gotten thank-you notes from either one.

**SD:**   Bantam published another volume of L'Amour stories in 1986 entitled *Dutchman's Flat,* and L'Amour warned readers in his introduction to the book that a publisher was trying again to bring out unauthorized collections of his stories.

**KC:**   Yes, that was us.

**SD:**   And once again, Bantam brought out editions simultaneous with the Carroll & Graf volumes, entitled *Dutchman's Flat* and *Riding for the Brand.* At the last minute, though, you changed the title of the first to *Man Riding West* and added another story. And once again, you wound up in Manhattan federal court. Why did you get into this situation again, knowing the trouble you had the first time?

**KC:**   It was for several reasons. After we settled out of court in the initial suit, L'Amour and Bantam said things about us to the papers that were rather unkind.

Bantam thought they had really outsmarted us, and thought that they were so clever. But it seems to me that if you're willing to spend nearly half a million dollars for high-priced legal talent, and put your entire staff to work to find out what stories a rival publisher is going to publish, and send people all over the country to tell bookstores not to buy Carroll & Graf Louis L'Amour books, and, in some cases, *any* Carroll & Graf books—if you're willing to spend that amount of money, or if you've got that kind of manpower and financial and business resources, well that's not clever.

For all the time and money Bantam spent, we pretty much did what we wanted to do. We made money, and because we didn't have to pay Louis L'Amour royalties, our profits were bigger. We sold a lot more books than we intended to. It seems to me that if Bantam and L'Amour came to us and said, "Look guys, you're enterprising, and this is a clever idea, but we don't want you to do it. And we don't want you to do it for these reasons. So here's twenty-five thousand dollars. Go home," we probably would have accepted that, even if it wasn't twenty-five thousand dollars, which is a lot less than we would have made by publishing the books. It would have squared with our intentions in the first place, which was to do something straightforward and not something sneaky, or surreptitious, or underhanded.

**SD:** Dare I ask at this point if you have any intentions of bringing out any more Louis L'Amour titles? Technically, a lot more of his work is in the public domain.

**KC:** Well, I was told that Bantam had L'Amour make minor changes in the stories in their editions. They're just corrections, but the stories get recopyrighted as new work. So you have to be real careful about reprinting so-called public domain stories from the Bantam editions. You have to go back to the original sources. But I think people should do it.

The only other thing we ever thought of doing—and we didn't think about it too long—was when somebody came to us later and said they wanted to bring out a series of gay Westerns, under the general title of "L'Amour the Merrier." We flirted with the idea of not actually doing the book, but advertising it in the catalog. But then we decided it wasn't worth the hassle.

**SD:** An article concerning the lawsuit in the *New York Times Book Review* seemed to imply that this was a landmark case because it established a precedent for authors, giving them some say in how their work would be presented and distributed to the public, even if they no longer owned the rights to it. In general, a picture was presented of the victimized author being protected from predatory publishers.

**KC:** There was absolutely no way in which the writer was victimized in this case. Generally, when you talk about the victimized writer, what you really mean is somebody's publishing this book and not paying him for it. Well, L'Amour got royalties from the Bantam editions, and would have gotten royalties from ours. A writer also is victimized if his work is distorted somehow. Say he's written a novel and somebody comes in, cuts it in half, and publishes it without his permission. That wasn't the case here. In no way were we going to change his work from the way he wrote it. Indeed, we offered him the opportunity to enhance it, at least by writing an introduction, to put it into whatever context he wanted. The only people who were not going to get their fair share of another Louis L'Amour success was Bantam. The notion that somehow L'Amour's rights were being violated is nonsense.

At one point, L'Amour said, "Well, I should have the right to choose my publisher." That's also nonsense. In most cases, authors don't choose their publishers. Your agent gets you the best deal he can, that's the route they take. In most cases when authors have their books reprinted in paperback after they were originally published in hardcover, they don't choose who does it. It's the agent or some other deal maker who chooses it. The whole case was nutty. L'Amour and Bantam raised a lot of unimportant side issues to camouflage what the case was really about. And that was money. Nothing other than money.

# L'Amour's Short Stories:
# An Annotated Checklist

THE FOLLOWING checklist is the most comprehensive ever published of Louis L'Amour's short fiction. Unfortunately, there are no checklists of the thousands of Western pulp magazines published during the first half of this century. Holdings at the Library of Congress are quite small when compared to the actual number of issues published. Most of the research done on this and similiar pulp checklists has been done utilizing private collections of L'Amour materials.

While Louis L'Amour claimed to have written over four hundred short stories, the actual number of tales published appears to be slightly under half of that. This checklist is arranged in chronological order. The title of the story is given first, then the name of the magazine publishing it, and the date. Titles are precisely as they appeared in the magazines, and may vary from those later used in short-story collections; substantive title changes are noted. If a pen name was used by L'Amour, this name is given next. Reprint information, including both other magazine appearances and short-story collections, follows. Finally, a brief description of the story concludes the listing, oftentimes using some of the original blurbs for the work.

Included at the end of the checklist are the titles of the few stories for which titles are known, but no other publication information could be found.

"Anything for a Pal"
*True Gang Life*, October 1935
Gangland killer Tony Kinsella, whose motto is "anything for a pal," murders the wrong man in L'Amour's first short story sold to a professional magazine.

"Gloves for a Tiger"
*Thrilling Adventures*, January 1938
Deke Hayes, world heavyweight champion, is challenged by the mysterious "Tiger Man," a powerful contender whose background is a mystery.

Louis L'Amour on the range. (Copyright © John Hamilton)

The October 1935 issue of *True Gang Life*,
containing L'Amour's first professional short story.

10 CENTS

# Rob Wagner's Script

| Vol. III | Beverly Hills, California, February 15, 1930 | No. 53 |

## BIG First Anniversary *Number*

### Mary Pickford Has Nothing to Wear

### "Beverly Hills," a New Song by the "Oh, Susanna!" Boys

### Notes of a Dead Scenario Writer
dug up *by* FLORENCE RYERSON *and* COLIN CLEMENTS

### Greetings to *The Script* from *Everybody!*

| Comment | — | Gossip | — | Fiction | — | News |
| Society | — | Business | — | Gags | — | Reviews |

A typical issue of *Rob Wagner's Script* magazine, which published numerous L'Amour letters during World War II.

L'Amour outdoors. (Copyright © John Hamilton)

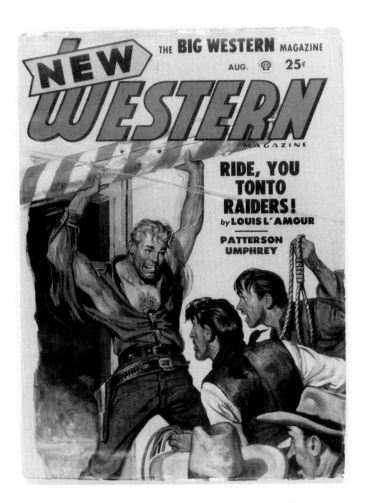

The August 1949 issue of the pulp magazine *New Western,*
with L'Amour's story "Ride, You Tonto Raiders!"
(Copyright © 1949 by Popular Publications.
Reprinted by permission of Blazing Publications.)

The Winter 1949 issue of the pulp *Sky Fighters,* with a Turk Madden story by L'Amour. (Copyright © 1948 by Better Publications.)

The February 1953 issue of the pulp *Western Short Stories,*
with "Lonigan" by "Jim Mayo."

L'Amour and unidentified friend. (Copyright © John Hamilton)

A first edition of *Hondo*, L'Amour's first U.S. paperback, with the famous quote by John Wayne on the front and back covers. (Copyright © 1953 by Gold Medal Books. Reprinted by permission of Ballantine Books.)

First edition of L'Amour's early novel *Utah Blaine,*
by "Jim Mayo." (Copyright © 1953 by Ace Books.
Reprinted by permission of Ace Books.)

First edition of L'Amour's early novel *Crossfire Trail,* mentioning his best-seller *Hondo.* (Copyright © 1954 by Ace Books. Reprinted by permission of Ace Books.)

Louis L'Amour in his library. (Copyright © John Hamilton)

*Trap of Gold and Other Great Adventure Stories*—an extremely rare
L'Amour collectible. (Copyright © 1952 by Popular Publications.
Reprinted by permission of Blazing Publications.)

*Rawhide Range*, the original cover proof for the Carroll & Graf paperback
that resulted in the famous L'Amour suit against that company.
The book was later published as *Law of the Desert Born*. (Copyright © 1983
by Carroll & Graf. Reprinted by permission of the publisher.)

*Homicide Street,* the original cover proof for the Carroll & Graf paperback that resulted in the famous L'Amour suit against that company. The book was later published as *The Hills of Homicide.* (Copyright © 1983 by Carroll & Graf. Reprinted by permission of the publisher.)

A typical L'Amour publicity pose. (Copyright © John Hamilton)

Only Hayes knows that the Tiger is actually his old friend, Bart Malone, whom he abandoned on Tiger Island six years earlier.

"The Admiral"
*Story Magazine,* March 1938
Paperback: *Yondering*
One of L'Amour's stories about Shanghai. The crew of a U.S. boat tries to build a sampan for a Chinese family, whose youngest child, a five-year-old boy, the crew nicknames "The Admiral."

"Too Tough to Kill"
*Detective Short Stories,* October 1938
Just married, Pat Collins witnesses three men kill Little Augie Petrone. Instead of going on his honeymoon, Pat must stay around as a witness when the gangsters are caught. But the criminals have other ideas, and plan to murder the only witness to their crime. But Pat Collins is a lot tougher than they imagine.

"It's Your Move"
*Tanager,* February 1939
A short-short story of two longshoremen who take their game of checkers very seriously.

"Survival"
*Tanager,* April 1939
Paperback: *Yondering*
When the ship *Raratonga* goes down, Tex Worden finds himself the only seaman in a lifeboat filled with helpless passengers. At an inquiry back on shore, he is forced to defend his actions to a hostile board.

"Shanghai, Not without Gestures"
*Rob Wagner's Script,* May 13, 1939
Paperback: *Yondering*
A character study of a young woman in Shanghai.

"Author's Tea"
*Rob Wagner's Script,* August 26, 1939
Paperback: *Yondering*
A brief fragment about an author signing.

"Thicker Than Blood"
*Rob Wagner's Script,* October 14, 1939
Paperback: *Yondering*

Bilge water, they say, is thicker than blood, and once men have been shipmates, no matter how much they hate each other's guts, they stand together against the world.

"Glorious! Glorious!"
*Tanager,* December 1939
Paperback: *Yondering*
Four desperate men are the only ones left alive after the Riffs attack a North African outpost.

"East of Gorontalo"
*Thrilling Adventures,* January 1940
Paperback: *West from Singapore*
The first adventure of Ponga Jim Mayo. Introduces the tough two-fisted sea captain and his friend, Major William Arnold of British intelligence. In this story, Ponga Jim is without a ship of his own.

"There Are People Like That"
*Rob Wagner's Script,* February 17, 1940
Moody was a strange looking character who could only put up with so much joking about his ugliness, as the crew of the SS *Iron Worker* discovered one voyage.

"The Town No Guns Could Tame"
*New Western,* March 1940
Paperback: *Long Ride Home*
L'Amour's first published Western. When the city fathers of Basin City hire a miner named Perry to be town marshal, they had no idea that Perry was actually the notorious gunman Clip Haynes.

"From Here to Banggai"
*Thrilling Adventures,* June 1940
Paperback: *West from Singapore*
The second Ponga Jim Mayo South Seas adventure. Ponga Jim now is master of his own ship, the *Semiramis.* More adventures with Nazi spies.

"Dead End Drift"
*New Mexico Quarterly,* August 1940
Paperback: *Yondering*
A group of miners is trapped in a cave-in. While waiting for rescue, they decide to try to dig their way out.

"On the Road to Amurang"
*Thrilling Adventures*, October 1940
Paperback: *West from Singapore*
Ponga Jim Mayo fighting Nazi spies trying to paralyze trading among the South Seas islands. Ponga Jim goes head to head against a brutish fighter named Dussel.

"The House of Qasavara"
*Thrilling Adventures*, December 1940
Paperback: *West from Singapore*
Ponga Jim Mayo fighting a Nazi plot to overrun New Guinea.

"Show Me the Way to Go Home"
*Rob Wagner's Script*, January 4, 1941
Paperback: *Yondering* (revised edition)
A short romantic piece about a sailor meeting a girl, with his ship leaving the next morning.

"Pirates of the Sky"
*Thrilling Adventures*, February 1941
The first Turk Madden story. Madden, a tough aviator, fights a band of New York gangsters who have taken over a small South Seas island. They plan to rob the passengers of a passenger liner that will pass close by.

"The Man Who Stole Shakespeare"
*Rob Wagner's Script*, March 8, 1941
Paperback: *Yondering*
The nameless narrator discovers a man stealing a book in a used book shop in Shanghai. When he trails the culprit home, he discovers that it is an old man who loves books. Only later does the hero discover the old man's secret.

"Gold is How You Keep It"
*Thrilling Adventures*, July 1941
Paperback: *Yondering* (rewritten and retitled "The Dancing Kate")
Dugan finds gold on a deserted atoll in the South Seas after being shipwrecked there, but he has to battle a shipful of tough customers when they rescue him.

"Old Doc Yak"
*New Mexico Quarterly*, August 1941
Paperback: *Yondering*

A character study of a solitary, proud man living with a band of poor sailors searching for work.

"Well of the Unholy Light"
*Thrilling Adventures*, September 1941
Paperback: *West from Singapore*
A Ponga Jim Mayo story. Jim and his friend Arnold of the British secret service battle both Nazis and Japanese at the edge of a volcano in Indonesia.

"Where There's Fighting"
*Thrilling Adventures*, January 1942
Paperback: *Yondering*
Four men fight the Germans in the hills of central Greece.

"The Phantom Fighter"
*Thrilling Sports*, January 1942
Kip Morgan, a young fighter, dreams how to win his biggest matches. His subconscious mind provides the information he needs to win. When Kip is faced with his greatest challenge, his manager uses Kip's dreams to help him become world champion. L'Amour's first sports story, he referred to this work in articles as "The Ghost Fighter."

"The Rounds Don't Matter"
*Thrilling Adventures*, February 1942
Paddy Brennan, a tough young boxer, is threatened by mobster Vino Cortina,who wants him to throw the big fight. But Paddy has plans of his own.

"South of Suez"
*Thrilling Adventures*, March 1942
Paperback: *West from Singapore*
Ponga Jim Mayo at the Red Sea, searching for a secret Nazi base from which they are raiding shipping important to the Allied cause.

"One Last Gun Notch"
*.44 Western*, May 1942
Paperback: *Law of the Desert Born*
Morgan Clyde, a gunfighter and killer, finally decides to break with his crooked companions. But there is always one last gunfight that has to be fought.

"West from Singapore"
*Thrilling Adventures*, May 1942
Paperback: *West from Singapore*
A Ponga Jim Mayo adventure. Ponga Jim battles the Nazis in the South
Seas.

"Voyage to Tobalai"
*Thrilling Adventures*, July 1942
When treachery threatens the U.S. Navy, Ponga Jim goes into action to
protect a precious cargo of airplanes. Instead of Nazis, he battles Japanese
agents.

"Mission to Siberut"
*Thrilling Adventures*, October 1942
Paperback: *Night over the Solomons*
Tramp flier Steve Cowan destroys a boat filled with Messerschmitt pursuit
planes being shipped to Japan.

"Coast Patrol"
*Thrilling Adventures*, January 1943
The second Turk Madden story. Turk is flying for the Russian army. When
he finds a group of Japanese spies trying to take over an American ship
with precious war supplies, he gives them a taste of American gun justice.

"Night over the Solomons"
*Thrilling Adventures*, July 1943
Paperback: *Night over the Solomons*
Mike Thorne, the only survivor of a supply ship blown out of the water
near Kolombangara Island, discovers the Japanese constructing a secret
base to attack the Allies on Guadalcanal. With the help of beautiful Jerry
Brandon, Mike succeeds in bringing American paratroopers to the island
where they wipe out the enemy forces.

"Flight to the North"
*Sky Fighters*, September 1943
Turk Madden moves to a new magazine, but continues his airborne
exploits flying for the Russians as they battle the Japanese in World War
Two. Turk Madden takes a routine job—but won't accept being pushed
around and double-crossed as part of the routine.

"Wings over Brazil"
*Thrilling Adventures*, November 1943

The final Ponga Jim Mayo story, and his longest adventure, a short novel. Ponga Jim is in Brazil where he fights a Nazi plan to take over the country.

"Wings over Khabarovsk"
*Sky Fighters,* January 1944
Paperback: *Night over the Solomons*
Turk Madden discovers a plot to invade Russia by the Japanese, masterminded by a member of his own base of operations.

"Down Pooguemene Way"
*Sky Fighters,* March 1944
Fighting against desperate odds, flier Steve Cowan (the hero of "Mission to Siberut") battles a half-caste Japanese crew to foil a plot against an American convoy and save a beautiful American actress.

"Flight to Enbetu"
*Sky Fighters,* Summer 1945
Turk Madden cleans up against the remnants of the Japanese air force in the Pacific.

"Law of the Desert Born"
*Dime Western,* April 1946
Paperback: *Law of the Desert Born*
Shad Marone crosses the desert to escape a posse after him for killing a sheriff's brother in a fair fight.

"Fighters Don't Dive"
*Popular Sports,* Summer 1946
When "Soldier" Barney tries to quit during a crucial boxing match, it's up to middleweight fighter Flash Moran to keep him on his feet. Otherwise the D.A. would suspect that the fight was fixed, which could cause irreparable damage to the boxing game in New York. Flash Moran was a name favored by L'Amour; he used the same name in "Moran of the Tigers," though the characters are not the same.

"Barney Takes a Hand"
*Thrilling Western,* October 1946
Paperback: *Riding for the Brand*
Harrington and Clyde want Tess Bayeux's land. But she refuses to move, hoping that Rex Tilden will come to her rescue. Instead, a stranger named Barney Shaw, walking out from the desert, proves to be her salvation.

"A Job for a Ranger"
*Popular Western,* December 1946
Paperback: *Bowdrie*
The first Chick Bowdrie Texas Ranger adventure. Bowdrie hunts for the mastermind of a bank robbery and a killing.

"McNelly Knows a Ranger"
*Popular Western,* February 1947
Reprinted in *Treasury of Great Western Stories #8, 1972*
Paperback: *Bowdrie's Law*
A Chick Bowdrie Texas Ranger story. When a friend is killed, Chick Bowdrie finds he must take on the notorious Ballard gang.

"Jackson of Horntown" by "Jim Mayo"
*Texas Rangers,* March 1947
Paperback: *Buckskin Run*
Matt Ben Jackson the Younger, the last of the tough Jackson clan, returns to Horntown where his father and his brothers once lived. Both the law and the outlaws worry about Matt Ben's motives for return to the town.

"Bowdrie Rides a Coyote Trail"
*Popular Western,* April 1947
Paperback: *Bowdrie*
A Chick Bowdrie Texas Ranger adventure. A dead man leads the Ranger on the trail of a dangerous killer.

"The Guns Talk Loud"
*Fifteen Western Tales,* April 1947
Reprinted in *Zane Grey Western Magazine,* March 1970
Paperback: *Law of the Desert Born*
Dan Ketrel wants to help Ruthie Belton against Harvey Kinsella and Bill Riding, two wealthy men after her ranch. But to do so he has to confront the mysterious stranger known only as Sonora.

"Death Song of the Sombrero"
*New Western,* April 1947
Paperback: *Law of the Desert Born*
Six-foot-five Stretch Magoon is fired by beautiful Kelly Jarvis, new to the West, for killing the foreman of her ranch, even though the man had been rustling cattle from her. Fortunately, Stretch stays around to rescue Kelly from the outlaws intent on taking over her spread.

"The Rider of Lost Creek" by "Jim Mayo"
*West,* April 1947
Paperback: *The Rider of Lost Creek* (novel)
When the Live Oak Country is rife with feuds, killings, wire-cuttings and rustlings, the call goes out for the gun help of the deadly young gunfighter Lance Kilkenny. The first of the Kilkenny series.

"Fork Your Own Broncs" by "Jim Mayo"
*Thrilling Ranch Stories,* May 1947
Paperback: *Riding for the Brand*
Trapped in an underground watercourse, Mac Marcy finds a man's solution to his problem—with Sally Kenyon as his prize.

"That Triggernometry Tenderfoot"
*Ace-High Western,* May 1947
Paperback: *Long Ride Home*
Schoolteacher Van Brady's class expanded to include all of Willow Creek when he started to teach, instead of the three R's, the three S's of Shootin', stompin', and stayin' alive.

"West of the Pilot Range" by "Jim Mayo"
*Texas Rangers,* May 1947
Reprinted in *Exciting Western* (British), June 1955
The setup looked square enough on the surface, but Ward McQueen suspected that there was something funny going on with Ruth Kermitt's herd. And he intended to find out exactly what, even if it meant taking on two of the toughest outlaws in the West. First of the four Ward McQueen stories published under the Jim Mayo pen name. The other three are "West of the Tularosas," "McQueen of the Tumbling K," and "Roundup in Texas."

"Bowdrie Trails West"
*Popular Western,* June 1947
Paperback: *Bowdrie* (retitled "A Trail to the West")
A Chick Bowdrie Texas Ranger story. The Ranger dares death in an attempt to save a girl from desperadoes.

"Murphy Plays His Hand"
*15 Western Tales,* June 1947
Reprinted in *Treasury of Great Western Stories #6,* 1970
Murphy finds that card playing and gun justice often go hand in hand.

"The Goose Flies South"
*Sky Fighters,* Summer 1947
Reprinted in *American Eagles* (British), 1947
Paperback: *Night over the Solomons*
Turk Madden in South America, flying in the wildest parts of Chile and
Argentina, discovers a plot by spies to steal America's atomic secrets.

"Bill Carey Rides West" by "Jim Mayo"
*West,* July 1947
Paperback: *Lonigan*
Bill Carey, a bank robber, comes across Jane Conway, a young woman
who lives in fear of outlaw Tabat Ryerson. Carey, who was driven to
robbery by the foreclosure of his ranch, finds that he cannot leave Jane to
her fate, and takes on Ryerson and his gang of bandits.

"The Romance of Piute Bill"
*Thrilling Ranch Stories,* July 1947
Paperback: *The Strong Shall Live*
Tom Galway and Piute Bill go after the men who stole Galway's horses.
When they kill several of the outlaws in a gunfight, the two men are
confronted by the wife of one of the dead men. It's Galway who suggests
she come away with them, but it's Piute Bill she marries.

"Heritage of Hate" by "Jim Mayo"
*Texas Rangers,* July 1947
Paperback: *Lonigan*
Facing the tough gun-throwing crews of two ranches, Con Fargo swings
into a desperate, last-ditch battle in order to save his dead partner's range.

"The Outlaws of Poplar Creek"
*Popular Western,* August 1947
Paperback: *Bowdrie's Law*
A Chick Bowdrie Texas Ranger story. Crack Ranger Chick Bowdrie pits
himself against bandit chief Shad Tucker.

"Dead Man's Trail"
*Thrilling Detective,* August 1947
Paperback: *The Hills of Homicide*
Kip Morgan's first case. Kip struggles to find evidence to prove that a dead
man was actually a victim and not a killer. It is not clear if this Kip Morgan
(who was once a boxer) is the same character who appeared in "The
Phantom Fighter."

"Bowdrie Hits a Cold Trail"
*Popular Western,* October 1947
Paperback: *Bowdrie* (retitled "Bowdrie Follows a Cold Trail")
A Chick Bowdrie Texas Ranger story. Bowdrie rides up like a Nemesis to avenge a sixteen-year-old crime.

"The Sucker Switch"
*Thrilling Detective,* December 1947
Working to recover a truckload of stolen furs leads private detective Neil Shannon into a melange of murder and gunplay.

"No Trouble for the Cactus Kid"
*Texas Rangers,* December 1947
Paperback: *Buckskin Run*
The first of four Cactus Kid stories. The Cactus Kid is in love. When he rides to town for some calico, he swears not to drink or get into trouble. But trouble is something that seems to follow the Kid wherever he goes.

"Right Hand Crazy"
*Popular Sports,* December 1947
They said McGraw couldn't fight—but then a lovely girl and a murder case came along, and a brand-new round in his career started.

"McQueen of the Tumbling K" by "Jim Mayo"
*Thrilling Western,* December 1947
Reprinted in *Thrilling Western* (British), 1948
Paperback: *Dutchman's Flat*
A fighting foreman faces three-to-one odds when he puts up a grim scrap against desperate enemies in order to protect his lady boss. One of the four Ward McQueen stories published under the Jim Mayo pen name. The others are "West of the Tularosas," "West of the Pilot Range," and "Roundup in Texas."

"A Man Called Trent" by "Jim Mayo"
*West,* December 1947
Paperback: *The Rider of the Ruby Hills*
The second adventure of Lance Kilkenny. More adventures of one of the fastest gunfighters alive. This story was rewritten as *The Mountain Valley War.*

"Backfield Battering Ram"
*Popular Football,* Winter 1947
When Coach Temple's football team bogs down, he uses a lot more than

horse sense to pull it out of the rut. With the help of Socks Barnaby, "Hoss" Temple and his big Polish halfback, Muggs Kolowski, turn in the biggest upset of the football season.

"Big Medicine" by "Jim Mayo"
*Thrilling Western,* January 1948
Paperback: *Dutchman's Flat*
Grizzled prospector Billy Dunbar pays a debt to the wily Apaches. And tricks the Indians into thinking he is a medicine man who can change into a wolf.

"Trail to Pie Town" by "Jim Mayo"
*West,* February 1948
Paperback: *Dutchman's Flat*
Dusty Barron finds you cannot talk peace to men who only understand force. But the outlaws soon discover that they should have listened to Dusty instead of challenging his lightning-fast guns.

"More Brains Than Bullets"
*Popular Western,* February 1948
Paperback: *Bowdrie*
A Chick Bowdrie Texas Ranger story. Ranger Bowdrie waits for his clues— and then moves fast.

"Keep Travelin', Rider" by "Jim Mayo"
*Thrilling Western,* March 1948
Paperback: *Dutchman's Flat*
Tack Gentry returns to his uncle's spread after a year in Texas to find the old man dead, supposedly killed in a gunfight. But Tack knows that his Uncle John was a Quaker and would never have drawn a gun in anger. When he discovers other ranchers have been driven off their range as well, he knows that only gun justice will solve his problems.

"The Road to Casa Piedras"
*Popular Western,* April 1948
Paperback: *Bowdrie's Law*
A Chick Bowdrie Texas Ranger story. A few marks on the ground tell plenty to Ranger Bowdrie.

"The Ghosts of Buckskin Run" by "Jim Mayo"
*Thrilling Ranch Stories,* May 1948
Reprinted in *Top Western Fiction Annual Vol 2 #1,* 1953

Paperback: *Buckskin Run*
Everyone, including the girl he loved, suspected that Rod Morgan was a killer. But he refused to leave the haunted canyon until he could find the real murderer and the buried treasure in Buckskin Run.

"Corpse on the Carpet"
*Popular Detective*, May 1948
She was a honey of a gal and her jewels had plenty of sparkle. But when detective Kip Morgan followed her out of that bar, grim Death tagged along. The second Kip Morgan detective story.

"Lit a Shuck for Texas"
*Thrilling Western*, May 1948
Paperback: *Riding for the Brand*
A rebel steer runs the Sandy Kid into a roaring rapid-fire fracas. But when the smoke clears, the Kid finds he wasn't ready to settle down with beautiful Betty Kurland.

"Where Buzzards Fly"
*Popular Western*, June 1948
Paperback: *Bowdrie's Law*
A Chick Bowdrie Texas Ranger story. Ranger Bowdrie lifts the veil of secrecy from a mystery ranch.

"The Trail to Crazy Man" by "Jim Mayo"
*West*, July 1948
Paperback: *The Trail to Crazy Man*
Shanghaied, Rafe Cardec makes his escape only to ride pell-mell into a roaring melee of gunpowder trouble and flaming danger. In honoring the request of a dying seaman, Rafe finds himself involved in a deadly rangeland justice campaign. This story was rewritten as *Crossfire Trail*.

"The Nester and the Piute"
*Exciting Western*, July 1948
Reprinted in *Exciting Western* (British), August 1954
Paperback: *Riding for the Brand*
Bin Morely goes after a Piute half-breed that has stolen something very precious from him. And, in the meanwhile, manages to save the unnamed narrator's girlfriend.

"There's Always a Trail" by "Jim Mayo"
*Exciting Western*, July 1948
Reprinted in *Exciting Western* (British), August 1954

Paperback: *Buckskin Run*
When Bill Leeds is killed, the fifteen thousand dollars he had with him taken, four ranchers in Pagosa are sure they have lost their fortunes. That is, until a stranger who calls himself Handy proves that no matter what, there is always a trail to be found.

"The Outlaws of Mesquite" by "Jim Mayo"
*Masked Rider Western*, August 1948
Paperback: *The Outlaws of Mesquite*
Surrounded by enemies, Milt Cogar had just one slender chance of escape. But he wasn't planning to run while Jennie Lewis was in danger.

"Merrano of the Dry Country"
*Thrilling Western*, August 1948
Reprinted in *Triple Western*, February 1953
Paperback: *The Strong Shall Live*
They hated him in Mirror Valley—but their hate could not scare Merrano out as he struggled against both man and nature in a land hit by drought.

"Chick Bowdrie Passes Through"
*Popular Western*, August 1948
Paperback: *Bowdrie*
A Chick Bowdrie Texas Ranger story. When Bowdrie discovers Josh Pettibone in jail on trumped up charges, he takes on the whole Tatum outfit and a crooked judge to prove his friend innocent.

"Riding for the Brand" by "Jim Mayo"
*Thrilling Western*, September 1948
Reprinted in *Triple Western*, Spring 1954
Paperback: *Riding for the Brand*
Taking advantage of a dead man was one thing, but it was quite a different matter when the subject was a live and very lovely girl. For the first time in his life, loner Jed Asbury was forced to take a stand.

"Dutchman's Flat"
*Giant Western*, Fall 1948
Reprinted in *1955 Top Western Annual*, 1955
Reprinted in *Treasury of Great Western Stories #2*, 1966
Paperback: *Dutchman's Flat*
Six grim and purposeful men follow the telltale tracks on a lynch trail. But, after being led on a wild chase by Chat Lock, the posse finds itself wondering if it is doing the right thing after all.

"South of Deadwood"
*Popular Western,* October 1948
Paperback: *Bowdrie's Law*
A Chick Bowdrie Texas Ranger adventure. Bowdrie, on the way to pick up a murderer, encounters a girl who wants to question the man as well, on the faint hope his testimony might save the life of her brother. But Curly Starr has no desire to help anyone but himself. Or so it seems until his life is on the line.

"The Unexpected Corpse"
*G-Men Detective,* November 1948
"I didn't kill Larry Craine," said Sue Shannon, but was she putting on an act? Private Detective Jim Cash had to find out the truth—before it killed him.

"With Death in His Corner"
*Thrilling Detective,* December 1948
Reprinted in *5 Detective Novels,* Spring 1953
Paperback: *The Hills of Homicide*
Kip Morgan wades through a battle of fists and knives when he sets out to deliver a hard-hitting knockout to his criminal foes. The third Kip Morgan detective story.

"Take It the Hard Way"
*Exciting Sports,* December 1948
Middleweight Finn Downey was plenty sore at himself. So he went into the ring ready to fight for more than a win.

"Showdown Trail" by "Jim Mayo"
*Giant Western,* Winter 1948
Paperback: *The Rider of the Ruby Hills*
Rock Bannon's warnings of peril fell on deaf ears as the settlers forged onward, lured by the glowing vision of a rangeland paradise. Into the peaceful-looking valley rumbles the wagon train, heedless of lurking Indians and renegades in its path. This story was rewritten as *The Tall Stranger.*

"Tailwind to Tibet"
*Sky Fighters,* Winter 1948
Paperback: *Night over the Solomons*
Hired by lovely film actress Raemy Doone to find her lost aviator brother,

Turk Madden, the daring pilot of the *Goose,* heads his plane into deep mountain fastness where grim and deadly perils lurk. This story is wrongly attributed to Joe Archibald on the contents page.

"Roundup in Texas" by "Jim Mayo"
*Thrilling Western,* January 1949
Ward McQueen, gunfighting foreman, uses guns and fists and brains to solve the baffling mystery of a thousand missing head of cattle. Third of the Ward McQueen stories, the others being "West of the Pilot Range," "McQueen of the Tumbling K," and "West of the Tularosas."

"Too Tough to Brand"
*Popular Western,* February 1949
Paperback: *Bowdrie*
A Chick Bowdrie Texas Ranger story. When Ranger Chick Bowdrie puts his sign on a case, it stays branded.

"Fighters Should Be Hungry"
*Popular Sports,* February 1949
Boxing is a tough game. And only the strong survive. Strong both physically and mentally.

"Rowdy Rides to Glory" by "Jim Mayo"
*Rodeo Romances,* April 1949
Paperback: *Lonigan*
Rowdy Horn needs money to marry Jenny Welman. The only way to obtain the funds is at the rodeo at the Stockman's Show held once a year. But Rowdy didn't have a horse worth riding. Trying to obtain one, he learns more than he wants about Jenny. But the beautiful Vaho Rainey more than makes up for the loss of Rowdy's first love.

"The Turkeyfeather Riders" by "Jim Mayo"
*West,* May 1949
Paperback: *Riding for the Brand*
When the Bar S schemers finished with Jim Sandifer, they thought he was a goner. But he came back fighting mad and ready for blazing gunfire battle.

"Pogonip Trail" by "Jim Mayo"
*Exciting Western,* May 1949
Paperback: *Buckskin Run* (retitled "Down the Pogonip Trail")
Jeff Kurland is determined to find Ross Stiber and claim the five thou-

sand dollars reward on the outlaw. But that was before the pogonip—the dreaded fog that covered everything on the mountain with a sheet of ice—hit.

"The Hills of Homicide"
*Detective Tales*, May 1949
Paperback: *The Hills of Homicide*
A nameless detective investigates an impossible murder taking place in a house on an isolated butte with only one path leading to it.

"Under the Hanging Wall"
*Thrilling Detective*, June 1949
Private eye Bruce Blake pursues a clue deep in the heart of a mine where an elusive killer stalks—ready to deal death. Not even a cave-in can stop Bruce from solving a murder.

"Waltz Him around Again, Shadow"
*Rodeo Romances*, June 1949
Dike Murphy, stock wrangler for the Stockman's Rodeo in Bluff Springs, had never been in love before. So when he fell hard for Carol Bell, the girl with Bill Bly, the rodeo's star, he wasn't sure how to act.

"In Victorio's Country"
*Giant Western*, June 1949
Reprinted in *Top Western Fiction Annual Vol 3 #1*, 1956
Reprinted in *Ranch Romances*, August 1960
Reprinted in *Treasury of Great Western Stories #1*, 1965
Four hard-bitten outlaws brave savage fury in a stronghold of hate. This short story served as the basis for the novel, *High Lonesome*.

"I Hate to Tell His Widow!"
*Detective Tales*, July 1949
Paperback: *The Hills of Homicide*
It's mighty hard to hide a secret that every police radio in town is scream-ing—"Cop killer wanted!" And Joe Ragan was the one stuck with the dirty job of telling Ollie Burns's wife.

"Showdown on the Tumbling T" by "Jim Mayo"
*Thrilling Western*, July 1949
Paperback: *The Outlaws of Mesquite*
Wat Bell, on the run from the law for a crime he didn't commit, finds himself in gun trouble in central Arizona. A man is killed and his friends

believe Bell is the killer. And the one man Bell thought he could trust might be the one who framed him for murder.

"Ride, You Tonto Raiders!"
*New Western*, August 1949
Paperback: *Law of the Desert Born*
When Matt Sabre had killed Billy Curtin in a fair fight, he had no idea the trouble he was getting into. Because, he promised a dying Curtin he would help his wife, Jenny. And Jenny was involved in a land feud that would need all of Sabre's gun skill to solve.

"Home in the Valley" by "Jim Mayo"
*Rio Kid Western*, August 1949
Paperback: *Riding for the Brand*
Steve Mehan, fighting rancher on horseback, covered plenty of territory, driving his herd of cattle from Nevada to California in the dead of winter.

"Collect from a Corpse"
*Black Mask*, September 1949
Paperback: *The Hills of Homicide*
Joe Ragan, the detective of "I Hate to Tell His Widow," investigates a series of crimes with fake clues left to frame innocent men.

"The Rider of the Ruby Hills" by "Jim Mayo"
*West*, September 1949
Paperback: *The Rider of the Ruby Hills*
Equipped with magical six-gun speed and nerves of iron, Ross Haney embarks on a daring campaign for range justice—and braves jeopardy with a smile. This story was rewritten as *Where the Long Grass Grows*.

"Pardner from the Rio" by "Jim Mayo"
*Thrilling Western*, September 1949
Paperback: *Lonigan*
Tandy Thayer comes looking for Jim Drew's ranch but finds nothing there. Determined to find out what happened to his friend, Tandy hires on with a local outfit. And finds himself involved in a daring plot to swindle a big rancher out of his land. Thayer uses a unique card-shooting trick in this story.

"The Trail to Peach Meadow Canyon" by "Jim Mayo"
*Giant Western*, October 1949
Reprinted in *Triple Western*, Fall 1956

Paperback: *The Rider of the Ruby Hills*
Mike Bastian, son of the wilderness, raised as an outlaw, could trust only his lightning guns and keen wits when he found himself at a fork in the road of life. It was then that he had to choose between riding the outlaw trail and honesty, love, and loneliness. This story was rewritten as *Son of a Wanted Man.*

"Alkali Basin"
*Range Riders Western,* October 1949
Paperback: *War Party*
Price Macomber, vice president of the Overland Stage Company, heads west on an inspection tour. With him go his niece and the district superintendent. Macomber has definite ideas on how to save money for the line. But all that changes when he stops at the station at Alkali Basin.

"Case Closed—No Prisoners"
*Popular Western,* October 1949
Paperback: *Bowdrie's Law*
A Chick Bowdrie Texas Ranger story. When fighting Ranger Chick Bowdrie finds the original thread—he battles against all odds to unravel a ribbon of range lawlessness.

"Regan of the Slash B" by "Jim Mayo"
*Thrilling Western,* October 1949
Paperback: *Lonigan*
When rustlers bluff a once-mighty ranch, a lion hunter takes a hand. Dan Regan uses both his guns and his fists to show Burr Fulton the error of his ways. And win a stake for him and the beautiful Jenny Meadows.

"Secret of Silver Springs" by "Jim Mayo"
*Range Riders Western,* November 1949
"Dud" Shafter and his partners discover how to take the right turn at the right time. And how to find gold hidden in a secret death trap.

"Stay Out of My Nightmare!"
*Detective Tales,* November 1949
Paperback: *The Hills of Homicide*
Pat Muldrennan was straight out of Kip Morgan's dreams. But the gun in her hand and her friends—Pete Merrano and his menagerie of murderers—would make even a nightmare look good. The fourth Kip Morgan detective story.

"The Marshal of Yellowjacket"
*Golden West Romances*, December 1949
Paperback: *The Strong Shall Live* (retitled "Trail to Squaw Springs")
Jim Bostwick heads into Yellowjacket aiming to file a claim on the land at Squaw Springs. But when he gets there, he discovers that a young girl and her grandfather planned to file a claim as well. And that Cap Pennock, the crooked marshal of the town, desires both the land and the girl.

"Pirates with Wings"
*Sky Fighters*, Winter 1949
Reprinted in *American Eagles* (British), Summer 1949
Paperback: *Night over the Solomons*
When Turk Madden flew across the Amazon jungle hunting for oil, he expected to meet trouble. But he didn't expect to encounter so much, so often, or so deadly.

"Moran of the Tigers"
*Thrilling Football*, Winter 1949
Old Pop Dolan learns that real loyalty can outlast luck. Flash Moran of the Rangers gets help in the big football game from all of Pop's old players who have returned to save the old man's job.

"Man Riding West" by "Jim Mayo"
*West*, January 1950
Paperback: *Riding for the Brand*
Trailhead ghosts dog Jim Gary halfway across cow country until he finally puts them all to rout in a heavy cloud of powder smoke.

"The Street of Lost Corpses"
*Detective Tales*, January 1950
Paperback: *The Hills of Homicide*
Kip Morgan untangles a complicated insurance scam in the longest and last of the five Kip Morgan stories.

"The Killer from Pecos"
*Popular Western*, February 1950
Paperback: *Bowdrie*
A Chick Bowdrie Texas Ranger story. Fighting Ranger Chick Bowdrie tames a lawless town in order to clear the way for himself when he embarks on a dangerous manhunt.

"Desert Death Song"
*Dime Western*, February 1950

Paperback: *Law of the Desert Born*
Nat Bodine is accused of bank robbery by Pete Daley. When the sheriff breaks up their fight, he is shot by Daley but Bodine is accused of that crime as well. Hunted by a posse, Nat heads for the desert, hoping to stay alive long enough to see justice done.

"The Black Rock Coffin Makers"
*.44 Western*, February 1950
Paperback: *Law of the Desert Born*
Jim Walker didn't belong on that northern range. But how could he return to Texas—when he was dead?

"The Ghost Maker"
*Rodeo Romances*, Spring 1950
Paperback: *The Outlaws of Mesquite*
They called Marty Mahan yellow for his fear of the killer horse, but he showed them his true colors.

"Horse Heaven" by "Jim Mayo"
*Rio Kid Western*, April 1950
Paperback: *Buckskin Run*
To deliver justice, Jim Locklin took the long, dusty trail to Toiyabe. But the murder of his brother demanded revenge. Even if it meant taking on a whole town.

"His Brother's Debt" by "Jim Mayo"
*Giant Western*, April 1950
Paperback: *Riding for the Brand*
When bully Ben Kerr challenges young Rock Cassidy to a gunfight, Cassidy panics and runs away. From that time on, he considers himself a coward and a failure. But when he hires on with the Three Spoke Wheel outfit, he finds that he suddenly has to stand up for his friends or be on the run for the rest of his life.

"Red Butte Showdown"
*Texas Rangers*, April 1950
Gunthorp was not a fast man with a gun, but he was ready to defend two youngsters from Kelman and his crew.

"Ride or Start Shootin'" by "Jim Mayo"
*Thrilling Western*, July 1950
Paperback: *Long Ride Home*

When wealthy cattleman Art Tollefson learns that newcomer Tandy Meadows has a quarter horse he intends to race against Tollefson's Lady Luck, he foolishly bets his ranch against the stranger. He has no idea that Tandy Meadows has returned to the range with plans to wipe out Tollefson's ill-gained empire.

"Showdown on the Hogback" by "Jim Mayo"
*Giant Western*, August 1950
Paperback: *The Trail to Crazy Man*
If he wanted to protect his own hide, troubleshooter Tom Kedrick had to be as changeable as a chameleon when he hired out his guns and turned his fighting fury against the land baron of Mustang town. This story was rewritten as *Showdown at Yellow Butte*.

"A Ranger Rides to Town"
*Rio Kid Western*, September 1950
Paperback: *Bowdrie's Law*
A Chick Bowdrie Texas Ranger story. Bowdrie stops a bank robbery and then solves a murder that took place inside the bank while the robbery was in progress.

"Guns of the Timberlands" by "Jim Mayo"
*West*, September 1950
Paperback: *Guns of the Timberlands* (novel)
Clay Bell and Jud Devitt, two tough, ruthless men, battle over timberland.

"Love and the Cactus Kid"
*Thrilling Ranch Stories*, Fall 1950
Reprinted in *Thrilling Ranch Stories* (British), April 1951
Paperback: *The Outlaws of Mesquite*
The Cactus Kid goes to get his girl, Jenny, some fresh flowers and as usual finds himself in more trouble than any two ordinary cowpokes could handle. The second of four Cactus Kid stories.

"Rustlers of West Fork" by "Tex Burns"
*Hopalong Cassidy's Western Magazine*, Fall 1950
The first Hopalong Cassidy novel, written by L'Amour as a work-for-hire novel for Doubleday Books. This story was revised and printed in hardcover as *Rustlers of West Fork*.

"The Crime, the Place, and the Girl"
*G-Men Detective*, Fall 1950

More hard-boiled detective action as motive, opportunity, and chance all add up to a lethal combination.

"Mistakes Can Kill You" by "Jim Mayo"
*Exciting Western,* November 1950
Paperback: *Dutchman's Flat*
Johnny O'Day teaches a gunhand that there are times when error is fatal.

"The Vanished Blonde"
*Thrilling Detective,* December 1950
Was that beautiful girl dead, or worse than dead? Detective Neil Shannon wanted to know—and a ruthless killer gave him the answer. The second Shannon story.

"Shandy Takes the Hook" by "Jim Mayo"
*Texas Rangers,* February 1951
Paperback: *Long Ride Home*
Tinhorn Kotch thought cheating Shandy on the price of his cattle would be easy pickings. After all, Shandy was only seventeen. But in the West, age didn't make a man. Shandy was smarter than he looked and a lot tougher than anyone ever imagined.

"Four Card Draw" by "Jim Mayo"
*Giant Western,* February 1951
Paperback: *Riding for the Brand*
Allen Ring wins a small cabin in a card game with Ben Taylor. But when he moves in, he discovers that other people in the valley have a claim on the cabin as well. Soon, he finds himself in the midst of a hunt for an important tally book that could begin—or end—a range war.

"West of the Tularosas" by "Jim Mayo"
*West,* March 1951
Reprinted in *Top Western Fiction Annual Vol 3 #1,* 1956
Paperback: *Dutchman's Flat*
Ward McQueen, ramrod for the lady boss of the Tumbling K, accepts the gunsmoke challenge of hired range killers—and gives renegades and land grabbers a hot time on the Firebox ranch. The fourth Ward McQueen story. The other three are "West of the Pilot Range," "McQueen of the Tumbling K," and "Roundup in Texas."

"Rain on the Mountain Fork"
*Rio Kid Western,* March 1951
Paperback: *Bowdrie's Law*

A Chick Bowdrie Texas Ranger story. Bowdrie comes riding in during a terrible storm to a stagecoach station where a mixed group of people waits for the stage. Bowdrie is hunting a killer who he knows must be one of the people at the lodge, but he doesn't know which one.

"West Is Where the Heart Is"
*Popular Western,* April 1951
Paperback: *Riding for the Brand*
Jim Loudon is returning home to his wife out West in a wagon train after the Civil War. When the wagons are attacked by Indians, only Jim and a little girl, Betty Jane, survive. Together, despite the doubts of others, they make it back to Jim's home where they find his wife and son waiting for him to return.

"We Shaped the Land with Our Guns"
*Texas Rangers,* April 1951
"Get out or die!" was the order—but Rye Tyler and his partner stayed. Only a few people knew that Rye was the Laredo Kid. Until the day when he fought Jerito Juarez and Chet Bayless to save the life of Betty Lucas.

"The Blood of Ryan"
*Thrilling Western,* May 1951
Reprinted in *Top Western Fiction Annual Vol 3 #2,* 1957
Paperback: *The Strong Shall Live* (rewritten and retitled "Bluff Creek Station")
The dying station hostler had to stay alive—just long enough to save the lives of the passengers of the stage coach due in his station.

"Riders of the Dawn"
*Giant Western,* June 1951
Paperback: *The Trail to Crazy Man*
Matt Sabre, the hero of "Ride, You Tonto Raiders!" is made partner in a ranch by a dying man. To keep his land, he has to prove that he did not murder the old-timer. Sabre was renamed Brennan when this story was rewritten as *Silver Canyon.*

"Duffy's Man"
*Texas Rangers,* June 1951
Paperback: *The Strong Shall Live*
Duffy owned the livery stable in a small town. When Clip Hart, the notorious outlaw, wants to leave seven horses in the stable, Duffy knows the

bandit is planning some trouble. But Duffy is an old man. It is up to his hired hand, a young man who is not a gunfighter, to stop the outlaws. Which he does in a methodical if unorthodox manner.

"Grub Line Rider" by "Jim Mayo"
*Triple Western,* June 1951
Paperback: *Law of the Desert Born*
Kim Sartain, a tough cowboy who's fast with a gun, finds himself in the thick of a range war between cattle king Jim Targ and his hired guns, and Tom Monaghan and his smaller outfit. The fact that Monaghan has a beautiful daughter named Rusty has little to do with it—at first. Sartain also appeared in the Ward McQueen series.

"Trap of Gold"
*Argosy,* August 1951
Paperback: *War Party and Law of the Desert Born*
Wetherton, searching for gold in the desert, finds a vein of quartz laced with pure ore. However, the vein is inside a shattered cliff where the wrong move could mean death by avalanche. Wetherton has to fight the rock and his own greed to bring home the treasure to his wife and son.

"The Lion Hunter and the Lady" by "Jim Mayo"
*Giant Western,* August 1951
Paperback: *Dutchman's Flat*
Cat Morgan and Lone John Williams are lion hunters. When Karl Dorfman tries to lynch him for stealing horses, Cat knocks the rancher senseless. Later, when Cat's away, Dorfman kills Lone John. But no one crosses a man who hunts and catches mountain lions for a living.

"Riding On" by "Jim Mayo"
*Exciting Western,* November 1951
Reprinted in *Exciting Western* (British), June 1952
Paperback: *Law of the Desert Born*
Reb Farrell is foreman for Nathan Embree's ranch. When rustlers strike, Reb goes hunting the outlaws. But he never expected one of his bullets to kill his own father. Or to have Nathan Embree accuse him of being in league with the rustlers. It doesn't take long for Reb to discover that he's been framed, and his father was the innocent victim of the same plot. With all hands raised against him, Reb knows the only way to clear his name is through gun justice.

"Down Sonora Way"
*5 Western Novels Magazine,* December 1951
Paperback: *Bowdrie's Law*
A Chick Bowdrie Texas Ranger short story. A tenderhearted hard case lends Bowdrie a helping hand.

"Long Ride Home"
*Best Western,* December 1951
Paperback: *Long Ride Home*
Tensleep Mooney has killed seven men in a feud, and now has the Rangers on his trail. So he heads south through the desert for Mexico. Three days on the trail he finds an Indian girl and a badly wounded old man. The rich Don Pedro is out to kill the pair, but Tensleep has little respect for wealthy landowners who think they can push people around. And Tensleep is willing to let his six-gun do his talking. Or his bowie knife!

"Trail to Seven Pines" by "Tex Burns"
*Hopalong Cassidy's Western Magazine,* Winter 1951
The second Hopalong Cassidy novel, this was written by L'Amour as a work-for-hire novel for Doubleday Books. This story was revised and published in hardcover as *Trail to Seven Pines.*

"Gold Does to a Man"
*Thrilling Western,* January 1952
Paperback: *Buckskin Run* (retitled "What Gold Does to a Man")
Pike Downe and his miner friends learn what gold does to a man. The deadly danger starts after the gold is found, not hunting for it or battling Indians. Greed is the killer.

"The Man from Battle Flat" by "Jim Mayo"
*Rio Kid Western,* January 1952
Paperback: *Dutchman's Flat*
When they called cowboy Krag Moran a turncoat, he answered with the only argument bullies could savvy—roaring six-guns.

"Sixgun Stampede" by "Jim Mayo"
*Western Short Stories,* March 1952
Sometimes the only law out on the prairie came from a gun. And a man strong enough to hold his herd together no matter how hard he was pushed.

"Unguarded Moment"
*Popular Detective,* March 1952
Paperback: *The Hills of Homicide*

It seemed like a harmless little theft—but the murder that came on its heels wasn't so harmless.

"That Slash Seven Kid" by "Jim Mayo"
*Rio Kid Western,* March 1952
They tagged Johnny Lyle a tenderfoot, but they were wrong. He was the one man in the Slash Seven outfit who could stand up to Hook Lacey, the fastest gun in the country since *Billy the Kid.*

"Strange Pursuit"
*Texas Rangers,* April 1952
Reprinted in *Treasury of Great Western Stories #4,* 1968
Paperback: *Bowdrie's Law*
A Chick Bowdrie Texas Ranger story. Bowdrie has to find Charlie Venk. Even if it first means rescuing the outlaw from a band of savage Apaches.

"The Cactus Kid Pays a Debt"
*The Rio Kid Western,* May 1952
Paperback: *Long Ride Home*
Drawn into a cutthroat game, The Cactus Kid tries some fancy dealing of his own. And three sharp card sharks discover that even an ordinary-looking cowboy might be a lot smarter than he appears. The third of four Cactus Kid stories.

"That Packsaddle Affair" by "Jim Mayo"
*Texas Rangers,* June 1952
Paperback: *The Outlaws of Mesquite*
Red Clanahan, wanted in Texas and many other points as well, comes upon the stagecoach station at Packsaddle. Red senses something odd is taking place and soon discovers a plot by several outlaws to cheat a young girl arriving by stage out of her inheritance. Red might be an outlaw, but like most men of the West, he refuses to stand by when a woman is in peril. But Red also sees a chance to make a bit of loose change in the deal. And does so.

"Men to Match the Hills"
*Triple Western,* June 1952
Paperback: *War Party*
Jim Bostwick looked like another sitting duck to this hired killer named Cap Moffit who had no conscience. The trouble was, Jim didn't sit long in one place. But Cap Moffit was tough as nails—and so was Jim. This story is a sequel to "The Marshal of Yellowjacket."

"Squatters on the Lonetree"
*Texas Rangers,* July 1952
Paperback: *Buckskin Run*
Wiley Dunn wants the squatter named Morgan Tanner off his range. But every time he sends his outfit to do the job, Tanner manages to elude its trap and come out the winner. Dunn is too stubborn to let Tanner stay, until he realizes that Tanner is the man once called the Lowry Kid.

"Crash Landing"
*Male,* July 1952
A plane crashes in the mountains, killing the crew and most of the passengers. Only the stewardess, a mysterious man named Dyea, and six others remain alive. One of them is a young girl trapped in her seat. Carefully, Dyea guides the others who can move out, aware that one wrong move will send the precariously balanced plane tumbling off the cliff. Then, alone, he goes back for the girl.

"The Gift of Cochise"
*Colliers,* July 5, 1952
Reprinted in *Zane Grey Western Magazine,* June 1970
Paperback: *War Party*
L'Amour's most famous short story and the one that made him a success. Angie Lowe lives in Apache country, with her son, waiting for her husband, Ed, to return from El Paso. What she doesn't know is that Ed is dead, killed in a gunfight between Ches Lane and the Tolliver brothers. When Ches rides out to tell Angie what has taken place, Cochise and his warriors assume that he is the man Angie has been waiting for. This short story was expanded into *Hondo.*

"No Man's Mesa" by "Jim Mayo"
*Western Novels and Short Stories,* August 1952
The whole range was against him, but Matt Calou still wanted to make Black Mesa his home.

"No Rest for the Wicked" by "Jim Mayo"
*Giant Western,* October 1952
Paperback: *The Outlaws of Mesquite*
The whole town turned against Marshal Morgan when he tried to save them from a swindle. Larik Feist claimed to have found the Lost Village Diggings, where a treasure in gold was hidden, and only Morgan knew that he lied.

"The Defense of Sentinel"
*5 Western Novels Magazine,* October 1952
Paperback: *War Party*
Finn McGraw, the town drunk of Sentinel, wakes one morning to find the town deserted. It doesn't take Finn long to figure out that the townspeople left fearing an Indian raid. On his own, he decides to defend the town, using all of the weapons he finds in the general store.

"Unwritten Chapter"
*Giant Western,* December 1952
Paperback: *The Strong Shall Live* (retitled "Hattan's Castle")
Bon Caddo wouldn't knuckle under to town boss John Daniel—and then Cherry Creslin, John Daniel's woman, entered the picture.

"Lonigan" by "Jim Mayo"
*Western Short Stories,* February 1953
Paperback: *Lonigan*
What could one man do against heat and dust and distance, against storms and rustler raids? Everyone was betting that Lonigan would never be able to take the herd through.

"The Marshal of Painted Rock" by "Jim Mayo"
*Triple Western,* February 1953
Paperback: *Law of the Desert Born*
The third Matt Sabre story. The other two are "Ride, You Tonto Raiders!" and "Riders of the Dawn." Sabre has just been appointed the town marshal of Painted Rock. And his first job is to make sure that killer Rafe Berry is hung. And Sabre means to do it in a town filled with Berry's friends and fellow outlaws.

"Big Man"
*Giant Western,* April 1953
Reprinted in *Top Western Stories, 1964*
Paperback: *The Strong Shall Live*
Cherry Noble had read his Bible. So he knew that Ruth had to go wherever he went.

"The Cactus Kid Goes A-Courting"
*Two-Gun Western,* August 1953
The Kid never hoped to meet a more beautiful señorita. And right off, she tells him to go at once, to ride away. The fourth and last of the Cactus Kid stories.

"One for the Pot"
*Giant Western*, October 1953
Reprinted in *Ranch Romances*, May 1959
Paperback: *War Party*
Laurie knew she wasn't made for life on the frontier. That was why she was leaving her husband Steve. At least, that was what she told herself until she met the old stranger who knew more about her husband than she did. And discovered that despite all the gun trouble, she had to stand by her man.

"Lost Mountain"
*Texas Rangers*, December 1953
Reprinted in *Top Western Fiction Annual Vol 3 #3*, 1958
The Wild Bunch gave young Riley Branam a chance to get out of the game, but an outlaw past casts a long shadow. And Riley was always loyal to his friends, no matter what they had done. This story was rewritten as the novel *Dark Canyon*.

"When a Texan Takes Over"
*Two-Gun Western*, February 1954
There was a six-shooter in his belt and a Winchester in his saddle boot—yet the stranger wanted no part of any gun ruckus. But Matt Ryan wasn't one to walk away from a fight when accused of being a rustler.

"The Drift"
*Western Short Stories*, March 1954
Paperback: *The Outlaws of Mesquite*
Johnny Garrett had never known the hell of a cattle drift. But then he'd never met a gent as tough as his foreman either—nor a girl as pretty as Betty Garvin.

"The One for the Mohave Kid"
*Western Short Stories*, September 1954
Paperback: *Dutchman's Flat*
The Mojave Kid was born with a streak of viciousness and cruelty that no kindness could eradicate. It was up to his cousin Ab Kale to bring him to justice. But Ab knew that the Kid was faster than him. Still, for every outlaw, there seemed to be a lawman born to be his nemesis.

"A Strong Land Growing"
*Texas Rangers*, January 1955

Paperback: *Riding for the Brand*
Marshal Fitz Moore knows that the Fred Henry gang is planning to raid the bank at Sentinel. And every time the gang strikes a town, they kill the marshal. Meanwhile, the sister of a man he killed by accident is in town. Can the marshal stop the raiders and show the angry young woman how in the heat of battle her brother died in error all in the same morning? This story was rewritten as "The Marshal of Sentinel."

"No Man's Land"
*Texas Rangers,* February 1955
Reprinted in *Texas Rangers* (British), September 1955
Reprinted in *Treasury of Great Western Stories #7,* 1971
Paperback: *Long Ride Home*
They could hire Lou Morgan's guns—but they couldn't buy his sense of fair play when a girl was involved.

"A Mule for Santa Fe"
*Star Weekly* (Canadian), March 1955
Paperback: *War Party*
Scott Miles, a widower with a young son, wants to join the wagon train. Unlike the others involved, though, he wants to use mules instead of horses or oxen. However, he needs one more mule for a team, and his time is running out. To get it, he is even willing to deal with a beautiful widow who makes him nervous every time he looks at her.

"The Burning Hills"
*Saturday Evening Post,* in five parts—November 26, 1955; December 3, 1955; December 10, 1955; December 17, 1955; December 24, 1955
Paperback: *The Burning Hills* (novel)
Trace Jordan tracks down and kills the murderer of his partner. The dead man's relatives relentlessly pursue Trace. However, using his knowledge of the mountains, he manages to kill off most of his enemies until he can persuade the last of them of his innocence.

"Bad Place to Die"
*Best Western,* December 1955
Paperback: *Long Ride Home*
The killers had young Johnny Farrow dead to rights, no question of that. Twenty-five yards and with rifles. They shouldn't have left that identification card on the kid, though.

"Gila Crossing"
*Complete Western Book Magazine,* September 1956
Nobody ever won an all-out cattle war. But maybe this wasn't the ranchers against the nesters. Maybe this was a personal fight over a woman.

"Get Out of Town"
*Saturday Evening Post,* May 16, 1959
Reprinted in *Saturday Evening Post,* September 1983
Paperback: *War Party*
A young boy comes to town to hire a cowboy to help him and his widowed mother with their ranch. The boy, Tom, hires a determined-looking stranger instead of one of the usual town loafers. Though the man, Riley, turns out to have just gotten out of jail, he is exactly the right man for the job.

"War Party"
*Saturday Evening Post,* June 13, 1959
Paperback: *War Party*
A young boy, Bud, his sister, and his parents are members of a wagon train heading West. When Bud's father is killed in an Indian raid, the other members of the wagon train assume that Bud's mother will want to turn back. But she is a strong woman and one of many hidden talents. Not only does she continue on, but after several disagreements with the leader of the train, branches out from the original group to found her own settlement. This story was rewritten to form the beginning of the novel *Bendigo Shafter.*

"Booty for a Badman"
*Saturday Evening Post,* July 30, 1960
Reprinted in *Saturday Evening Post,* September 1980, October 1980 (two-part serial)
Paperback: *War Party*
Tell Sackett is a young man hunting for gold without much luck. A group of miners asks him to take their gold to Hardyville through the outlaw gangs on the trail. Two men before him who had tried were both killed by the Cooper gang. But Tell was willing to take a chance in order to earn the hundred dollars offered for the job. That was, until he met the girl waiting by the side of the trail.

"One Night Stand"
*TWA Ambassador Magazine,* October 1976
Paperback: *The Strong Shall Live*

Frank Mason wants Emmett Brady's land. The Pioche Kid, a ruthless killer, is a friend of Mason and plans to kill Brady. The only man deadly enough to stop the Kid is Wild Bill Hickok, an old buddy of Mason's. But Wild Bill is hundreds of miles away. Hearing about Mason's problem, Stephen Malone, an out-of-work actor, offers to impersonate Hickok and scare the kid away, for a price.

"A Moon of the Trees Broken by Snow"
*The American Way Magazine*, December 1977
Paperback: *Yondering*
An unusual Christmas story with fantastic elements about the cliff dwellers.

"The Strong Shall Live"
*Far West*, March 1978
Paperback: *The Strong Shall Live*
Cavagan, a tough Irishman, has been a thorn in wealthy rancher John Sutton's side for too long. When Sutton and his men finally capture Cavagan, they take him to the desert, sixty miles from water, and abandon him there. But, as before, Sutton has underestimated Cavagan's will and desire for revenge.

"The Marshal of Sentinel"
*Far West*, September 1978
Paperback: *The Strong Shall Live*
This story was a slightly revised version of "A Strong Land Growing."

## *Publication Dates Unknown*

The following stories were published in L'Amour paperbacks but their original publication dates are unknown. It is possible that several of them were unpublished stories never printed until their appearance in paperback.

"A Friend of the General"
Place and date of original publication unknown
Paperback: *Yondering*
One of L'Amour's Shanghai stories. A complicated story of arms dealing told by the mysterious general to a young serviceman.

"By the Ruins of El Walarieh"
Place and date of original publication unknown
Paperback: *Yondering* (revised edition)
A fragment of conversation between the narrator and a native boy.

"And Proudly Die"
Place and date of original publication unknown
Paperback: *Yondering* (revised edition)
A character study of a seaman named Snipe who was afraid of everything, but most of all, afraid of dying.

"A Gun for Kilkenny"
Published in *Impact Magazine,* date unknown
Paperback: *Dutchman's Flat*
Montana Croft, a two-bit gunman, is mistaken for Kilkenny by the citizens of a small Western town. Capitalizing on the fabled gunfighter's reputation, Croft terrorizes the town for weeks. Then the real Kilkenny comes riding in.

"The Man in the Seersucker Suit"
Place and date of publication unknown
In "Where to Find Stories," published in *The Writer* of June 1942, L'Amour described this story. Several unrelated tragic accidents when viewed in the proper sequence tell the story of a murder. It is not clear whether or not this story ever saw professional publication.

"The Sixth Shotgun"
Place and date of publication unknown
Reprinted in *Treasury of Great Western Stories #3,* 1952
Paperback: *The Outlaws of Mesquite*
Leo Carver is scheduled to be hung for the murder of Mitch Williams, the stagecoach guard, who has been killed by a shotgun blast in a holdup. However, no one saw Leo actually kill Mitch, and all of the evidence is circumstantial. Little by little, the townspeople realize that Leo couldn't have committed the crime. But they decide to have a hanging nonetheless.

(193 stories)

## *Title Changes*

"The Dancing Kate"—see "Gold is How You Keep It"

"Trail to Squaw Springs"—see "The Marshal of Yellowjacket"

"Bluff Creek Station"—see "The Blood of Ryan"

"Hattan's Castle"—see "Unwritten Chapter"

"The Marshal of Sentinel"—see "A Strong Land Growing"

# L'Amour's Uncollected Stories: A Checklist

THE FOLLOWING Louis L'Amour stories have not been reprinted in any of the seventeen collections of short stories published through June 1991. Entries are listed in chronological order of publication.

"Anything for a Pal"
*True Gang Life*, October 1935

"Gloves for a Tiger"
*Thrilling Adventures*, January 1938

"Too Tough to Kill"
*Detective Short Stories*, October 1938

"It's Your Move"
*Tanager*, February 1939

"The Man in the Seersucker Suit"
Place and date of publication unknown

"There Are People Like That"
*Rob Wagner's Script*, February 17, 1940

"Pirates of the Sky"
*Thrilling Adventures*, February 1941

"The Phantom Fighter"
*Thrilling Sports*, January 1942

"The Rounds Don't Matter"
*Thrilling Adventures*, February 1942

"Voyage to Tobalai"
*Thrilling Adventures*, July 1942

"Coast Patrol"
*Thrilling Adventures*, January 1943

"Flight to the North"
*Sky Fighters*, September 1943

"Wings over Brazil"
*Thrilling Adventures*, November 1943

"Down Pooguemene Way"
*Sky Fighters*, March 1944

"Flight to Enbetu"
*Sky Fighters*, Summer 1945

"Fighters Don't Dive"
*Popular Sports*, Summer 1946

"West of the Pilot Range" by "Jim Mayo"
*Texas Rangers*, May 1947
Reprinted in *Exciting Western* (British), June 1955

"Murphy Plays His Hand"
*15 Western Tales*, June 1947
Reprinted in *Treasury of Great Western Stories #6*, 1970

"The Sucker Switch"
*Thrilling Detective*, December 1947

"Right Hand Crazy"
*Popular Sports*, December 1947

"Backfield Battering Ram"
*Popular Football*, Winter 1947

"Corpse on the Carpet"
*Popular Detective*, May 1948

"The Unexpected Corpse"
*G-Men Detective*, November 1948

"Take It the Hard Way"
*Exciting Sports*, December 1948

"Roundup in Texas" by "Jim Mayo"
*Thrilling Western*, January 1949

"Fighters Should Be Hungry"
*Popular Sports*, February 1949

"Under the Hanging Wall"
*Thrilling Detective*, June 1949

"Waltz Him around Again, Shadow"
*Rodeo Romances*, June 1949

"In Victorio's Country"
*Giant Western*, June 1949
Reprinted in *Top Western Fiction Annual Vol 3 #1*, 1956
Reprinted in *Ranch Romances*, August 1960
Reprinted in *Treasury of Great Western Stories #1*, 1965

"Secret of Silver Springs" by "Jim Mayo"
*Range Riders Western*, November 1949

"Moran of the Tigers"
*Thrilling Football*, Winter 1949

"Red Butte Showdown"
*Texas Rangers*, April 1950

"The Crime, the Place, and the Girl"
*G-Men Detective*, Fall 1950

"The Vanished Blonde"
*Thrilling Detective*, December 1950

"We Shaped the Land with Our Guns"
*Texas Rangers*, April 1951

"Sixgun Stampede" by "Jim Mayo"
*Western Short Stories*, March 1952

"That Slash Seven Kid" by "Jim Mayo"
*Rio Kid Western*, March 1952

"Crash Landing"
*Male*, July 1952

"No Man's Mesa" by "Jim Mayo"
*Western Novels and Short Stories*, August 1952

"The Cactus Kid Goes A-Courting"
*Two-Gun Western*, August 1953

"Lost Mountain"
*Texas Rangers*, December 1953
Reprinted in *Top Western Fiction Annual Vol 3 #3*, 1958

"When a Texan Takes Over"
*Two-Gun Western*, February 1954

"Gila Crossing"
*Complete Western Book Magazine*, September 1956

(43 stories)

# Part 3:
# The Novelist

I do not distinguish Westerns at all from other kinds of novels. If you are going to characterize my stories I would prefer to have them called stories of the frontier.

Louis L'Amour in *Publishers Weekly,* October 8, 1973

# Introduction

THIS THIRD section of *The Louis L'Amour Companion* deals with L'Amour the novelist. The lead article deals with L'Amour's incredible success and tries to analyze how he became the best-selling Western author of all time.

The section features four annotated checklists to L'Amour's novels, grouped by decade. There is a short piece on L'Amour's three nonfiction books. Articles by Bernard Drew and Jon Tuska delve into the truth behind L'Amour's association with Hopalong Cassidy. Tuska and Scott Cupp write about L'Amour's most famous novel, *Hondo*. Ed Gorman deals with L'Amour's work for Gold Medal Books, focusing on *Last Stand at Papago Wells*. R. Jeff Banks presents a fascinating look at L'Amour's crossover novels. And noted historical writer Judith Tarr examines *The Walking Drum*.

Along with these new pieces, there are several in-depth interviews with L'Amour concentrating on his career as a novelist. The section is rounded out by several short pieces on the author and his work, including a reprint of a spirited defense by L'Amour of his novel *Shalako*.

# The Best-Selling
# Western Author of All Time

THE NUMBERS are incredible. As of mid-1991, sales of Louis L'Amour books were over two hundred and thirty million copies. Each year, millions more paperbacks are added to that total. By the middle of the decade, more L'Amour books will have been sold than there are people living in the United States. According to an enthusiastic Bantam Books publicity release, if L'Amour's books were stacked end to end they would stretch around the circumference of the Earth.

L'Amour's sales are even more incredible when matched against other Western writers. His novels have sold more copies than the combined numbers of Max Brand and Zane Grey, the second and third best-selling Western writers of all time. And both Brand and Grey already had novels in print when L'Amour was still a child.

One of the most common misconceptions about L'Amour's staggering sales figures is that they are the result of a flood of titles. While L'Amour was a prolific writer, his output never matched that of many other authors. Frederick Faust, whose most famous of nineteen pen names was Max Brand, authored over three hundred Western novels. In his twenty-five-year career, Faust wrote nearly thirty million words. That averaged out to over a million words, or nearly twenty novels, a year, a rate six or seven times L'Amour's most productive pace.

In the past ten years, "adult" Westerns, series stories with liberal amounts of sex and violence, have been a mainstay of the Western field. There have been over one hundred and fifty titles published in the "Slocum" series by Jake Logan. "Longarm" by Tabor Evans has also hit the one hundred and fifty title mark. Not far behind these two is "The Gunsmith" by J.R. Roberts and "The Trailsman" by Jon Sharpe, both nearing a hundred and twenty titles printed. No one, however, has suggested that any of these authors has sales figures approaching L'Amour's.

Louis L'Amour became the best-selling Western author of all time, and one of the best-selling modern authors of modern literature, through a combination of three factors: skill, self-promotion, and publisher support. None of them alone accounted for his incredible popularity. They each played an important part in propelling him to the top of the Western hierarchy—a position that seems secure for many years to come.

Though two of his novels were voted among the twenty-five best Westerns ever written, L'Amour has been castigated over the years by critics for his writing skills. Reviewers complain about the sameness of his plots, the simplicity of his characters, and the lack of realism in his stories. All of these criticisms are true within limits. L'Amour was not the most careful of writers. He learned his business in the pulp magazines and many of his stories read like updated pulp adventures. L'Amour quite frankly admitted in interviews that he only wrote one draft of his novels and never used an outline. Oftentimes, his books could have used a bit of polishing.

Still, despite his faults, L'Amour wrote with an energy and excitement that grabbed his readers from page one and refused to let them go until the last words of the book. He was a master of his craft—telling tales people wanted to read. In an article published in *Writer's Digest* in 1980, Irwyn Applebaum, L'Amour's editor for many years at Bantam Books, put it best: "You may find writers who produce a better book in terms of pure literary quality, but I don't think you'll ever find a better storyteller."

Louis L'Amour never lost sight of who he was writing for. His books were aimed at his fans, not his critics. He didn't worry about trying something different or challenging. While the reviewers complained about the lack of variety in his novels, his fans rejoiced in their familiarity. And that was what mattered to L'Amour.

On June 25, 1981, L'Amour was presented the Golden Saddleman Award by the Western Writers of America for his contributions to the Western genre. In his speech accepting the award, L'Amour stated:

> I don't believe that any writer—and this may surprise some of you—should pay any attention to reviews at all. The critics write for the public, so let the public read them. The only people who are important to you and to me are the readers. They're the important people, they are the people we should observe. We have to know what they want and what they are buying. When I'm having an autograph session, I stall long enough to have a word with nearly every person who comes on the line. . . . I learn in every case. Those are the people to learn from.

Writing novels that people wanted to read was not enough to make L'Amour successful. Along with the stories, he needed promotion. The possessor of a keen intellect, L'Amour realized early in his career that publicity played a major role in any literary career. From the time he first started writing until his dying day, L'Amour was an energetic and enthusiastic promoter of his work. And, without question, his efforts paid tremendous dividends.

L'Amour's major break came with the movie *Hondo*. The film promoted the novel, and with it his career. As the novelist put it in his WWA speech, "I managed, by talking to this person and talking to that, to see that whenever *Hondo* was mentioned, Louis L'Amour was mentioned with it. I got an awful lot of mileage out of *Hondo* and an awful lot of help."

L'Amour was the subject of countless short articles and interviews throughout his career. He toured extensively promoting his books, and wherever he went, articles about him appeared in the local papers.

Reading a bunch of these pieces one after another, you are struck by certain common factors they share. L'Amour always managed to mention how authentic his novels were. He usually dropped in a reference to his great-grandfather, scalped by the Sioux, thus tying himself in with the Old West. And never missing were his plans for future novels as well as a plug for his most recent work.

Rarely was L'Amour subjected to detailed, probing questions. Part of the reason, of course, was that usually L'Amour was interviewed by writers who knew nothing about his work. They were sent to get a story. L'Amour was a colorful individual who gave them what they needed without much effort on their part.

Equally important was L'Amour's style and appearance. Born in 1908, L'Amour was forty-five when *Hondo* appeared. A big, impressive looking man with weather-beaten features, he took to wearing Western clothes at all of his public appearances. In *Writer's Digest*, Arturo Gonzalez, Jr., described L'Amour as:

> . . . the epitome of the Western heroes he chronicles in print. His sombrero is edged in a jeweled Indian band; his shoelace necktie is gathered at his throat by an Indian-crafted slide. His tight-fitting Western-style pants are worn over pointed-toe, high-heel cowboy boots. If he were packing a pair of six-guns instead of a battered Olivetti, it wouldn't seem a bit out of place.

L'Amour was a showman, and it paid off time and again in interviews and articles for more than twenty years. Educated in the school of hard knocks, he never counted on anyone else's help in making it to the top. In his WWA speech, he declared:

Before Bantam ever did a thing to promote my books, my name had appeared in every major column in the United States—Louella Parsons, Earl Wilson, Hedda Hopper, Hy Gardner, all the way down the line. I made them all by one means or another. I did all this promotion on my own. . . . It wasn't easy, it was a lot of hard, painstaking work, but it helped so by the time any work was done by Bantam . . . I had already laid a good foundation.

Thus, L'Amour combined his own exceptional writing skill with well-planned promotion to achieve financial success. However, these two traits were not enough to make him the best-selling Western author of all time. It was an inspired publishing decision that provided the necessary third ingredient for his triumph.

In the 1950s, Westerns accounted for between fifteen and twenty percent of all paperback sales. It was a boom market, ripe for expansion. An executive at Bantam Books came up with a plan to increase their share of the marketplace. And, as a result, made Louis L'Amour incredibly rich.

Bantam Books decided to keep all of L'Amour's books in print. This course of action had never been taken for any Western writer up to that time. Normally, whenever a Western title sold out, it was gone and no longer available to the author's fans. Only if there was a great demand did books go into second or third printings. With other Western authors in paperback, this occurrence rarely took place. Publishers treated most of their Western novels as minor books, not worth much notice. Companies rarely kept Westerns as part of their backlist, books that were always available in stock for reorders.

Louis L'Amour made Bantam's backlist extremely profitable. He wrote three Western novels a year for them in the early 1960s. These books proved quite successful. Moderate-size printings sold out quickly, often in a month or two. Quick to respond to market demands, Bantam reprinted the novels as soon as needed. Each L'Amour novel did better than the last. And every time a new L'Amour book appeared, the demand for his backlist grew. People liked what they read and wanted more. Bookstores reordered older titles and kept them on the shelves. Not only was Bantam able to sell the new Louis L'Amour novels, it was also able to sell the older books at the same time.

Thus, it was extremely important that Bantam supported L'Amour by keeping his titles in print. Whenever a novel sold out, it was reprinted, again and again, as necessity and sales dictated. Fans of L'Amour's novels were able to buy all of his novels, something they could not do with other famous Western authors such as Max Brand and Zane Grey.

Even large bookstores have room for only a certain number of genre paperbacks. This space dilemma is even more acute for other stores that handle some books, such as department stores and drugstores. Fiction is categorized by topic—all mysteries are put in one section, science fiction in another, Westerns in yet another. Thus, there is limited room for Western titles.

Many Western writers wrote numerous books. Zane Grey, Max Brand, Luke Short, and Will Henry always sold well in paperback. However, while there were usually a few books by these authors available from their publishers, most of their titles were out of print. If a book sold out, it was considered a success and rarely reprinted. No one considered keeping all of the titles by a Western author in print. No one other than Bantam with Louis L'Amour.

Bookstore managers want to sell books. Route men who fill the shelves for smaller stores serviced by a book distributor have the same desire. The better the sales, the more money the bookstore or distributor makes. There was no question that familiar names sold better than new and unknown authors. L'Amour was a known quantity, with a proven sales record. With limited space available for Westerns in a bookstore, if the choice came between displaying a L'Amour title or another author, L'Amour usually won. And, with all of his titles in print, it was easy to arrange a whole small section of his titles.

Books are sold to bookstores by sales representatives working for the publishers. They are the people who must go out and convince buyers and managers to handle the new releases each month. Faced with hundreds of different titles a year, sales reps welcomed books that sold themselves—books by an author with a proven sales record, like Louis L'Amour.

"Louis is a book salesman's dream," said Louis Satz of Bantam Books, in the December 1980 issue of *Writer's Digest.* "He's met and worked with all 140 of our full-time sales people and he cultivates the wholesalers who are the people who decide which books get rack space."

L'Amour was famous for the attention he paid to the people who sold his books. He treated them with the same respect and interest he gave his fans. Oftentimes, he took important wholesalers and chain store buyers out for dinner. Unconfirmed stories had him buying donuts and coffee for route men, which he delivered to wholesalers' warehouses in the morning, and kegs of beer for the men at night. His novel *The Iron Marshal* was dedicated to the sales people of Bantam Books, and he actually listed all of their names on the first page.

The book field has changed immeasurably since L'Amour started writing in the 1950s. It is common practice now for publishers to keep all of the work by their top authors in constant backlist. Thus, readers are assured of finding any Stephen King or Danielle Steel or Tom Clancy novel at a bookstore and not being told it is currently out of print.

Louis L'Amour is the only Western author accorded this treatment. And with well over a hundred titles in print, it is not surprising that each year his sales figures increase by the millions.

Skill, promotion, and publisher support: the three ingredients that propelled L'Amour to the forefront of Western authors. One of the most astute authors who ever lived, L'Amour summed up the secret of his success in his speech to the Western Writers of America:

> Mere sales are not important to a writer. This sounds like blasphemy, but it's true. It's *repeat* sales that count. All of you should think of that person you are writing for, that reader out there who's going to read you. And you want to write a story that will make him want to come back and buy your next book.

That's the philosophy that made Louis L'Amour the best-selling Western author of all time.

# The Novels of Louis L'Amour—The Fifties: An Annotated Checklist

LOUIS L'AMOUR'S first novel was published in 1950. During the next ten years, twenty more of his novels were published, many of them rewritten versions of earlier pulp stories. It was a decade of change for L'Amour as his focus shifted from short stories to novels. The following annotated chronology lists all of L'Amour's novels during the 1950s, giving original date of publication as well as when the book was first published by Bantam Books.

**1.** *Westward the Tide*—originally published in hardcover by World's Work Publishing, England, in 1950, as part of their Western Fiction Series. It was reprinted unchanged by Bantam Books in February 1977, with no mention of the earlier edition.

In 1877, Matt Bardoul, a typical L'Amour hero, joins a wagon train heading for the Big Horns. Once underway, he learns that Clive Massey and his gang have plans of their own for the settlers. Bardoul foils the villain and wins the heart of Jacquine Coyle.

This is a long, ambitious novel with a fairly large cast of characters and a complex plot.

**2.** *Hopalong Cassidy and the Rustlers of West Fork* by "Tex Burns"—originally published in hardcover by Doubleday Books in 1951. The story behind the Hopalong Cassidy novels is covered in depth in several articles in this section.

**3.** *Hopalong Cassidy and the Trail to Seven Pines* by "Tex Burns"—originally published in hardcover by Doubleday Books in 1951. The story behind the Hopalong Cassidy novels is covered in depth in several articles in this section.

**4.** *Hopalong Cassidy and the Riders of High Rock* by "Tex Burns"—originally published in hardcover by Doubleday Books in 1951. The story behind the Hopalong Cassidy novels is covered in depth in several articles in this section.

**5.** *Hopalong Cassidy, Trouble Shooter* by "Tex Burns"—originally published in hardcover by Doubleday Books in 1952. The story behind the Hopalong Cassidy novels is covered in depth in several articles in this section.

**6.** *Hondo*—originally published by Fawcett-Gold Medal Books in November 1953. The Bantam edition was published in April 1983.

*Hondo* is L'Amour's most successful novel, with over three million copies in print. It was voted one of the twenty-five best Western novels of all time by the Western Writers of America. The story is based on "The Gift of Cochise" published in *Colliers* magazine in 1952. Though L'Amour claimed that the novel was entirely his, it seems likely that the book was actually a novelization of the movie. For a more complete discussion of this question, see the article on *Hondo* by Jon Tuska in this section.

Western scout Hondo Lane comes across Angie Lowe and her young son, Johnnie, on a ranch in the desert during the midst of an Indian uprising. After accidentally killing Angie's husband, Hondo is reunited with the woman by the Apaches.

Whether novel or novelization, *Hondo* remains one of L'Amour's finest works. It was filmed as *Hondo.*

**7.** *Showdown at Yellow Butte* by "Jim Mayo"—published by Ace Books, 1953. The Bantam edition was published in May 1983.

Alton Burwick wants the land at Yellow Butte, so he hires Tom Kedrick and a bunch of tough men to drive out the settlers. But Kedrick refuses to fight innocent men and women and turns against his boss.

Based on the pulp novel "Showdown on the Hogback."

**8.** *Utah Blaine* by "Jim Mayo"—published by Ace Books, 1954. Reprinted by Bantam in September 1983.

Utah Blaine saves Joe Neal from a lynching and is made manager of Neal's ranch. After Neal is killed, Blaine defeats the local vigilantes and wins the girl. Filmed as *Utah Blaine.*

**9.** *Crossfire Trail*—published by Ace Books, 1954. Reprinted by Bantam in August 1983.

Rafe Caradec promises a dying shipmate that he will help the man's wife and daughter save their ranch. He travels to Long Valley, Wyo., to keep his word.

A rewritten version of the pulp story "The Trail to Crazy Man."

**10.** *Kilkenny*—published by Ace Books, 1954. The Bantam edition first appeared in June 1983.

Fast gun Lance Kilkenny wants only to hang up his guns, but he finds himself drawn into a range war with Old Man Tetlow. Chronologically, while this story was the third and final Kilkenny novel, it was the first to be published in paperback. The romantic lead as well as several supporting characters are from the earlier stories, and there are a number of references to the first two adventures.

The other two novels in the series were published in the pulp magazines as "The Rider of Lost Creek" and "A Man Called Trent." They were rewritten and published in paperback more than twenty years after the publication of *Kilkenny* as *The Rider of Lost Creek* and *The Mountain Valley War.* For maximum enjoyment, the series should be read from *Rider* to *Valley* to *Kilkenny.* The short story "A Gun for Kilkenny" also belongs to this same series.

*Kilkenny* was filmed as *Blackjack Ketchum, Desperado.*

**11.** *Guns of the Timberlands*—published in hardcover by Jason Press in June 1955. Reprinted by Bantam Books in November 1955.

Clay Bell and Jud Devitt battle over timber in a clash between two strong, ruthless men.

Slightly expanded from the 1950 pulp novel of the same name. This novel was filmed as *Guns of the Timberlands.*

**12.** *Heller With a Gun*—published by Fawcett–Gold Medal Books in April 1955. Reprinted by Bantam in March 1984.

Gunfighter King Mabry tries to aid a traveling theatrical troupe that has hired a deadly killer as its guide. Filmed as *Heller in Pink Tights.*

**13.** *To Tame a Land*—published by Fawcett–Gold Medal Books in September 1955. Reprinted by Bantam in January 1984.

The story of Rye Tyler, a gunfighter, told in first person, from his youth until his early twenties. In many ways, the episodic story foreshadows many similar events in *The Daybreakers.* One of L'Amour's best books, often underrated by his fans and critics.

**14.** *The Burning Hills*—published in hardcover by Jason Press in May 1956. Reprinted by Bantam Books in August 1956.

Trace Jordan tracks down and kills the murderer of his partner. The dead man's relatives relentlessly pursue Trace in return. Using his knowledge of the hills, he manages to kill most of his enemies until he can finally persuade them of his innocence.

Originally serialized in the *Saturday Evening Post,* this was filmed as *The Burning Hills.*

**15.** *Silver Canyon*—published in hardcover by Avalon Books, October 1956. Reprinted by Bantam Books in November 1957.

Another early novel told in first person. Matt Brennan, a notorious gunfighter, is given partnership in a ranch by a dying man. He has to clear his name and catch a murderer before he can settle down to a peaceful life with Moira Maclaren.

An expanded version of the pulp story "Riders of the Dawn." Brennan, originally named Sabre, also appeared in two other L'Amour short stories in the pulps—"Ride, You Tonto Raiders!" and "The Marshal of Painted Rock."

**16.** *Sitka*—published in hardcover by Hawthorn Books, April 1957. Published in paperback by Bantam Books in January 1957.

L'Amour's most ambitious early novel. Adventurer Jean LaBarge trades with the Russians in Alaska. Fascinated by the country, Jean works with a beautiful Russian countess to make the territory part of America. Not a Western but a historical novel, L'Amour dedicated this book to his wife, Kathy.

**17.** *Last Stand at Papago Wells*—published by Fawcett–Gold Medal Books in July 1957. Reprinted by Bantam Books in July 1986.

Logan Caters and a group of travelers in the desert stand off a siege by Apaches led by the dreaded Churupati. Conflicts among the besieged prove to be nearly as deadly as the attacking Indians. The story is considered in depth in Ed Gorman's article "L'Amour and Gold Medal." This novel was filmed as *Apache Territory.*

**18.** *The Tall Stranger*—published by Fawcett–Gold Medal Books in September 1957. Reprinted by Bantam Books in August 1986.

A rewritten version of the pulp story "Showdown Trail." Rock Bannon, a typical tough L'Amour hero, saves a wagon-train full of settlers from Indians only to have them turn against him when they hook up with the smooth-talking Morton Harper. Bannon instead teams up with rancher Hardy Bishop, whose land is what Harper is really after. The film *The Tall Stranger* was based on the pulp story.

**19.** *Radigan*—published by Bantam Books in October 1958.

The first L'Amour novel done as an original novel for Bantam Books. Angelina Foley rides up from Texas and tries to run her herd on Radigan's ranch. But Radigan has legal claim to the land and refuses to be run off, even when the Foley riders resort to violence.

**20.** *The First Fast Draw*—published by Bantam Books in February 1959.

L'Amour's attempt to write a historical Western novel focusing on real-life gunfighter Cullen Baker. After the Civil War, Baker returns home to Texas and finds himself involved in numerous old feuds as well as new fights. He invents the first fast draw, defeats his enemies, and leaves for the far west. More than most of L'Amour's novels, this book was criticized for its inaccurate portrayal of the facts involving Baker's life. A minor work.

**21.** *Taggart*—published by Bantam Books in April 1959.

The story "Trap of Gold" was modified and incorporated as part of this novel. Taggart is being chased through Apache territory by Pete Shoyer, a notorious bounty hunter who usually brings in his prey dead. Taggart has killed two men in a fair fight but has been branded an outlaw. The Indians trap both men, along with a gold miner, his wife, and his sister. Taggart manages to save the gold, defeats Shoyer in a gunfight, and marries the girl. The story was filmed as *Taggart*.

# Louis L'Amour's Hopalong Cassidy

*by Bernard A. Drew*

Up until early 1990, all four of the "Tex Burns" Hopalong Cassidy novels were available in limited-edition hardcovers from Amerion Press. Located in Mattituck, N.Y., Amerion publishes small printings of hardcover books aimed primarily for libraries. Interested L'Amour readers should check their local library system for these novels.

In 1990, Bantam Books announced plans to reissue in both hardcover and paperback the four "Tex Burns" Hopalong Cassidy novels as part of its Louis L'Amour line. The first of these, *The Rustlers of West Fork*, was published in June 1991.

"THERE WERE many of them," recalled Louis L'Amour of the pulp magazines of the 1930s and '40s, "dozens of Western and mystery magazines, others publishing science fiction, sports stories, romance, war, and air stories. Two of the best were *Adventure* and *Blue Book*. *Black Mask*, one of the mystery magazines, was a breeding ground for such writers as Dashiell Hammett, Raymond Chandler, and Cornell Woolrich, who also wrote as William Irish and was distinctly one of the best."

He elaborated on the subject in *Education of a Wandering Man:* "This was the magazine market I faced as a beginning writer. There were many other magazines that bought articles or occasional fiction, and many of the writers for quality publications were academics teaching at various colleges or employed elsewhere."

Among sagebrush heroes frequently appearing in the early magazines and pulps, enjoying particularly lengthy stays in *Short Stories* and *Argosy,* was Clarence E. Mulford's Hopalong Cassidy. Illinois-born Mulford

(1883–1956) began writing his series of tales about Cassidy, Red Connors, Johnny Nelson, and others of the Bar 20 Ranch in 1905; the short stories and novels would eventually fill eighteen books.

L'Amour was familiar with Mulford's writing. In his memoir describing his self-education through intense and varied reading, L'Amour said that he encountered Mulford's work while caretaking a remote copper mine. "There were other books left by miners or owned by the proprietor. Among these were several volumes by Clarence E. Muhlford [sic], who wrote the Hopalong Cassidy series; a couple of novels by Zane Grey: B.M. Bower's *Chip, of the Flying U;* and novels by James Oliver Curwood and Harold Bell Wright. . . . The loneliness of the mine never affected me, for I had many companions: Hopalong Cassidy, Hamlet, Sancho Panza, and Ulysses were with me."

Little did L'Amour anticipate he would one day write Cassidy stories, after Mulford tired of doing them.

Mulford's Cassidy and other Western novels became sufficiently popular that the writer was able to quit his Civil Service job in Brooklyn, N.Y., in 1926 and relocate with his family to rural Maine. He sold motion picture rights to his characters in 1935, and William Boyd was engaged to appear as the hero in what became a sixty-six-picture string of popular low-budget movies. Boyd's black-garbed, upright Cassidy bore little resemblance to Mulford's cussing, tobacco-spitting original—forever to Mulford's annoyance.

Boyd took Cassidy to programming-starved television in 1949 and was immediately and enormously popular. There were hundreds of Hopalong Cassidy tie-ins brought out—from bicycles and coloring books to badges and lunch pails. The publisher of the series, Doubleday, reissued most of the Mulford books, abridging some, passing over others that perhaps were of a too-dated prose style to appeal to a young readership. The market was still unsatisfied. Mulford had retired from writing in the early 1940s, so four new books were commissioned from Louis L'Amour. A veteran pulp writer, he was anxious to break into the hardcover market. Standard Publications, one of the major pulp publishers in the dying days of cheap magazines, ran two of the novels in *Hopalong Cassidy's Western Magazine* in 1950–51.

The magazine's first issue carried the full-length novel *Rustlers of West Fork* by "Tex Burns." L'Amour's name was never mentioned and Mulford's name only showed up on a back-cover advertisement for Popular Library's paperback edition of *Hopalong Cassidy Takes Cards.*

"Readers familiar with the Bar 20 books, as well as Hoppy's many new fans," explained a publisher's message inside the pulp, "will be glad to know that here in *Hopalong Cassidy's Western Magazine* we are able to bring you, for the first time, brand-new book-length novels which have never before seen print. Each issue will contain a full-length yarn of the adventures of Hoppy, plus other stories and features."

The Hopalong assignment "was really hack writing for L'Amour," according to biographer Robert Phillips in *Louis L'Amour: His Life and Times*. "He not only had to be true to the original characters as developed by Hopalong creator, Clarence E. Mulford, but he also somehow had to make the characters adhere to the characterization of the actors who portrayed them in the popular movies which starred William 'Hopalong' Boyd. This experience had the virtue of giving L'Amour practice in plotting."

According to L'Amour's son, Beau, in an afterword to Bantam's recent hardcover re-publication of the first novel, the stories were initially written more in the Mulford style but the character descriptions were changed to reflect the Boyd persona prior to book publication. This lack of control accounted for L'Amour later disavowing the works. "And for years he worried that these books which he tried so hard to ignore would be reprinted and brought back into circulation," his son said.

The Cassidy in these books is "A tall, well-built man in black sat astride a magnificent white horse . . ." we read. "The man's hair showed silver under the brim of his black hat and his blue eyes were friendly."

L'Amour didn't do a whole lot to imitate Mulford in the books. There are occasional hints of Mulford language. For instance, in *Hopalong Cassidy Trouble Shooter* and *Trail to Seven Pines*, the verb "slope" (meaning "to depart"), frequently used by Mulford but not all that common otherwise, shows up. Mulford character names such as Buck Perks (Peters), Pete Medeford (Wilson?), Tex, and Frenchy are skewed, perhaps intentionally. There are passing references to Lanky and Slim, from the Mulford books as well.

L'Amour and Mulford were more dissimilar than alike. Mulford was an easterner; L'Amour was a Western rover. Mulford was of slight physique; L'Amour was large and robust. Mulford researched the West in books while L'Amour wrote of firsthand experience. Mulford enjoyed almost immediate success with book publication. L'Amour labored for years writing for the low-paying pulp market before breaking into the book field.

L'Amour certainly absorbed the Mulford panorama. With the possible exception of British writer J.T. Edson's Floating Outfit tales, L'Amour's Sackett saga, numbering seventeen books from 1960 to 1985, was the only other prolonged Western series with such historical sweep and scope. L'Amour, like Mulford before him, favored the "realistic" portrayal of the West. "To write a story of the West, one must have more accurate knowledge than for any other writing I can think of, aside from some kinds of science fiction," L'Amour wrote in *Education of a Wandering Man.* "One does not, as some imagine, simply 'dash off a Western.'" And L'Amour, like Mulford, would be criticized for creating male-dominated fictional worlds.

Still, as Beau L'Amour observed, "Although the sound and flow of their writing was different, both wrote with boiling energy."

In the first of the Tex Burns novels, *Rustlers of West Fork* (Doubleday, 1951), Hopalong helps his friends at the Circle J against a range hog.

The hero, having closed a cattle deal for Buck, wants to visit old friend, Dick Jordan, owner of the Circle J. He is warned ahead of time, however, about Avery Sparr, Jordan's new partner and suspected horse thief. When he brazenly rides to the ranch, Cassidy finds Jordan and his pretty eighteen-year-old daughter, Pamela, pretty much held captive. Hoppy, under cover of darkness, squirrels the ranch owner and his daughter into the hill, maneuvers so that a band of roving Apaches confront the pursuing Sparr and his thugs, survives a bitter snowstorm, and finally brings his charges to safety.

Meanwhile, Hoppy's Double Y pards Johnny Nelson and Mesquite Jenkins arrive on the scene. They soon dispose of an encampment of crooks enlisted by Sparr's double-crossing right-hand man, Arnold Soper. The story is one long string of confrontations as Hoppy, or Johnny and Mesquite, boldly face and outshot their opponents. At tale's end, Hoppy returns the Jordans to their ranch, and he rides off to a new adventure.

In the second novel, *Trail to Seven Pines* (Doubleday, 1951), Cassidy arrives at "the toughest town west of anywhere" to help young Bob Ronson, his sister Lenny, and Irene of the Rocking R, in a brewing range war. In a secondary plot line, a gang of crooks takes advantage of the lawlessness to hold up stagecoaches and generally terrorize the citizenry. Hopalong rides into the core of the trouble, hiring on as Ronson's *segundo.* Lenny is immediately at odds with Hoppy, and it takes a while for her to appreciate that her boyfriend, Clarry Jacks, is up to no good.

Hopalong brings his legend with him: "Ben Lock turned and faced the man named as the famous gunfighter on the cattle trails. The man who was like Hickok, a living legend. He looked across the crowded tables, across the noisy room, to see cold, observant blue eyes, firm chin, and a bronzed, handsome face looking from under the wide brim of a black sombrero. Two tied-down guns with white handles, two guns whose use had made their wearer one of the most feared and respected men of his time." Interestingly, Mulford made no secret of having based his version of Cassidy on Wild Bill Hickok: L'Amour's Cassidy, based on the movies, was much more sanitized.

*The Riders of High Rock*, in the next outing (Doubleday, 1951), have stolen more than a thousand head of cattle from Gibson's 3TL and neighboring small ranches. When Red Connors takes to their trail, he is shot and left for dead. Naturally, Hopalong intervenes. The likely rustler mastermind is Jack Bolt of the 8 Boxed H, who is romancing Gibson's daughter, Sue. Hoppy scouts the countryside and finally locates a hidden route the rustlers are using to herd cattle to an illicit market. With the help of a recovered Red and Joe Gamble, and eventually with an eager Mesquite Jenkins, Hoppy dispatches the hoodlums.

In a nod to the evolving West, Hopalong discusses earlier trail driving days with Gibson:

> "You wouldn't like it now." Hopalong dropped into a chair. "Fact is, she's almost gone. Too many fences now. That country is changing. An hombre was plowing up a field sixty miles north of Doan's Crossin' last time I come through. First time I ever saw that country was over the sights of a Sharps with Injuns coming a-whooping. She sure has changed."

The final novel in the series was originally titled *Riders of the Broken Range*. It was announced for the third issue of the Hopalong Cassidy magazine, but the publication folded after two numbers. It finally was published by Doubleday in 1952, renamed *Hopalong Cassidy, Trouble Shooter*.

Hoppy answers a call for help from an old Bar 20 friend, Pete Medford. When Cassidy arrives at Picket Fork, Pete is dead and his niece Cindy Blair and her ranch foreman Rig Taylor can find no trace of the ranch that she has inherited. Hoppy assumes the name Cameron and hires out to Box T owner Justin Tredway, rounding up strays lost in the rattler-infested brush country near Chimney Butte. In a plot as winding and twisted as a cow country trail, Hopalong solves a years-old gold robbery, meets up with members of an isolated religious community, swings dangerously from a rope over a deep gorge, and faces deadly gunmen. All in a day's work.

And then it was over. The books evidently did not sell well enough for Doubleday to continue the series. The pulp magazine died after only two issues. The hardcover series made it through two more volumes before grinding to a halt.

L'Amour's Hopalong Cassidy novels, while suffering from certain similarities of plot situation, and obviously locked into a static characterization, still managed to display the author's affinity for rangeland detail and solid action. They demonstrated that the man behind the Tex Burns house name was definitely a writer to watch.

# Louis L'Amour on
# His Hopalong Cassidy Novels

*by Jon Tuska*

from *A Variable Harvest,* 1990

WHEN I was preparing Louis L'Amour's entry for the *Encyclopedia of Frontier and Western Fiction* (1983), L'Amour objected to the "Tex Burns" Hopalong Cassidy novels being included among his works.

"The situation was this," he wrote to me. "During a period after the collapse of the magazine field when all the pulps and many other publications went under, I was asked to write four Hopalong Cassidy novels. This was during the sudden boom that followed his popularity on TV. I assured the publisher that the books would not sell. The fans of Hopalong were kids and they could get all they wanted in comic books about Hopalong. Moreover, I viewed the Boyd Hopalong with some distaste. However, they preferred to believe the books would sell and I was paid a flat fee to write them. . . . Being broke I was in no position to argue. I wrote the books and they supported me during a very bad year."

Once I responded that nothing in what he had said indicated that he had not written the books and that they were, therefore, among his works, L'Amour became even more adamant.

"To attribute those books to me, in any sense, would not be a credit to your accuracy. The best thing I can advise, in all sincerity and good will, is to forget my connection with them. I deserve no more credit than would a president's speech writer . . . and I have never yet seen one of them given credit. I am trying to help you keep your book honest. If you intend to list those works as mine I shall insist you also list every essay my children have written with which I helped them as well as every other document I can scrape up in which I had a hand. It would make just as much sense."

# Hondo Lane and Louis L'Amour

*by Scott A. Cupp*

ON NOVEMBER 25, 1953, the course of Louis L'Amour's writing career took a big turn. On that date, his sixth published novel, *Hondo,* hit both the bookstores and the movie screens. Both versions were huge successes for the middle-aged writer. Hondo Lane as portrayed by John Wayne dominated the screen and enthralled the audiences. It was a 3-D film, which heightened the curiosity value of the movie, being the only major Western to be filmed in that manner.

Although *Hondo* was Louis L'Amour's sixth novel, it was the first to appear in the United States under his own name. He had previously published four Hopalong Cassidy novels under the house name "Tex Burns" for Doubleday. His first published novel, *Westward the Tide,* had appeared in England in 1950 but had yet to have a popular edition.

Since the movie and book appeared at the same time, many readers thought the book was a novelization of the screenplay. They soon came to realize otherwise. Western readers had found themselves an original writer unlike any they had seen since the appearance of Luke Short, Max Brand, and Zane Grey. During the next five years, eleven novels appeared under L'Amour's name and two others appeared under his pen name, "Jim Mayo." L'Amour's paperback assault had begun.

Louis L'Amour's novels were popular for a variety of reasons—they were well written, had been researched well, they presented an accurate portrait of the West, and they presented characters that the readers could identify with and long to be.

The novels were filled with an authentic vision of the West as L'Amour had seen it when he traveled throughout the mid-1920s while he worked as a cattle skinner, miner, hobo, prizefighter, and roustabout. During this period, L'Amour met a large number of people who had lived through the end of the Indian wars and the passing of the lawless world and the arrival of eastern civilization. The West demanded a hardy, dedicated soul who was willing to face certain death and inevitable failure every day.

In *Hondo,* L'Amour created those basic Western characters who continued throughout his novels, particularly in the Sackett books. The straight-shooting, fair-playing, self-reliant hero and the strong-minded, hard-working, loyal, and dedicated woman who stood by her man and never regretted the life she might have had. L'Amour had examined aspects of these characters in his stories for the pulp magazines and began to bring them to full fruition in Hondo Lane and Angie Lowe.

Hondo remains one of the more enduring of L'Amour's characters. As a scout for the army, he must be resourceful, able to survive off of the land, read the signs of the Indian, and handle himself in a tight situation. As a gunfighter, he had to be quick, accurate, and able to judge a scene quickly. He had to be slow to anger and quick to settle. As a resident in the Indian community, he was able to appreciate the clash of cultures and forced to chose the one he most enjoyed. As a man, he had to be able to protect those unable to help themselves, such as Angie Lowe and her son, Johnnie, and to remove the cancers he found, such as Ed Lowe, Phalinger, and Silva.

We first encounter Hondo on the trail, making himself a cigarette, trying to avoid an ambush set for him by the Apaches. In that first page, we find a wily, self-reliant man who knows the Indians as well as he knows himself. The picture painted of him shows a man whose clothing has been weathered from hard work. He is described as wide-shouldered with no softness about him.

Yet, while possessing all of these earthy qualities, Hondo is also possessed of a poetic spirit. When asked about Destarte, his Indian wife, he explains what her name means:

> It means like Crack of Dawn, the first bronze light that makes the buttes stand out against the gray desert. It means the first sound you hear of a brook curling over some rocks—some trout jumping and a beaver crooning. . . .

Yet he never says that he loved her. Instead he replies that at the time he needed her.

Hondo is a man who values truth and honor above all things. When confronted by the Apache Vittorio with the tintype of Angie Lowe, he responds that he is her husband, for such is how he feels. Ed Lowe had relinquished that right when he abandoned Angie and Johnnie to go wandering and gambling. Hondo, by virtue of his concern and feelings of love for the hardy woman attempting to survive against the relentless odds, promotes himself into that station and no one questions it. Since she has no husband and requires one, and because she has expressed some basic desires to him, it is only natural to him—and to her—that they belong together.

Angie Lowe is as much a representation of the ideal frontier woman as Hondo is the perfect frontier man. Her creed, passed down from her father, was simple:

> To each of us is given a life. To live with honor and to pass on having left our mark, it is essential that we do our part, that we leave our children strong. Nothing exists long when its time is past. Wealth is important only to the small of mind. The important thing is to do the best one can with what one has.

She stays with her ranch when she knows the Indians are on the raid because it is her home and nothing in her character will allow her to admit defeat, run away, and leave everything behind. At the story's end, when Angie, Johnnie, and Hondo are leaving to go to California, she leaves readily because she is with her man, going to make a new life. She is not running from a bad past. She is actively pursuing a strong new future.

In this, his first major novel, Louis L'Amour was able to posit and solidify his ideal man. His work for the pulps had led him to develop Hondo Lane. His story "The Gift of Cochise," published in *Colliers*, provided the impetus to bring *Hondo* to the book-buying public's reach. The success that the book brought him was the final step that he needed to move from pulp writer to national treasure. He knew he was good. Now the whole world knew it.

# Hondo—Novel or Novelization?

*by Jon Tuska*

from *A Variable Harvest*, 1990

LOUIS L'AMOUR'S big break, the one that put him firmly on the road to success, came in 1952. With the short story "The Gift of Cochise," published on July 5, 1952, in *Collie.:s*, L'Amour's career changed dramatically.

In this story, Angie Lowe lives in Apache country with her seven-year-old son Jimmy and her five-year-old daughter Jane. Her husband, Ed Lowe, has gone to El Paso for supplies and he dallies there, drinking and gambling. He is not a bad man, simply an irresponsible one. Cochise comes to visit Angie in Ed's absence and is impressed by her spirit and the spirit of her son, Jimmy. He will allow Angie to wait, unmolested, for the return of her man. In a barroom brawl in El Paso, Ed Lowe steps into a gunfight between hero Ches Lane and the three Tolliver brothers, getting killed in the fracas. Ches learns that Ed has a wife and two children and heads out to pay his respects and see if he can be of some help. On the way there, he is surrounded by Apaches and defeats one of the warriors in a knife fight. This wins him the admiration of Cochise. When Lane finds Angie, the Apaches regard him as her man, a feeling she comes to share. The story ends with the line, "A man could get to like it here."

"The Gift of Cochise" was purchased by Robert Fellows and John Wayne, who wanted to produce it for the screen. James Edward Grant, Wayne's favorite screenwriter, did the screenplay, with Warner Bros. financing and releasing the film. Grant changed the original plot considerably, beginning with the character of the hero, now called Hondo Lane. In the film Hondo was given a dog named Sam as a companion. John Ford acted as an unofficial adviser on the picture, wanting to do what he could to make Wayne's venture into film production a success.

L'Amour had as yet been unable to interest any American paperback publisher in his fiction. He got the Wayne-Fellows group to agree to let him novelize James Edward Grant's screenplay and publish it under his own name, as if it were *his* story, and he even got Wayne to allow himself to be quoted as saying that *Hondo* was the finest Western he had ever read.

When I asked John Wayne about this endorsement, he did not recall

**211**

ever having met Louis L'Amour. His endorsement of the novelization of Grant's screenplay, published as by Louis L'Amour, was supplied at the publisher's request. He did not read the novel. Joel McCrea gave a similar endorsement to Fawcett Books when Les Savage, Jr.'s, *The Wild Horse* was filmed as *Black Horse Canyon* and the paperback original was reissued using this title.

Also, when I contacted James Edward Grant he was quite proud of his screenplay for the film and made it quite clear that it was based on the L'Amour short story and not a book. In the credits for the film, the source material was listed as "The Gift of Cochise."

L'Amour's novelization of *Hondo* follows Grant's screenplay very closely, using much of Grant's dialogue. Angie Lowe was retained as the heroine, but Jane is removed as a character: Angie has only her young son, Johnnie. Her husband is a wicked man and he has deserted her. Hondo, together with his dog, Sam, arrives at the Lowe ranch and stays around to help out. Later, in a fight in the desert, Hondo kills Lowe when Lowe would steal his horse.

L'Amour did add one scene to the novel not in the screenplay, a sexual episode between Hondo and Angie before Hondo tells her that he has killed her husband. Another L'Amour contribution to the novelization was to incorporate his view of marriage when he reflected about Angie and Hondo that "This was as it should be . . . a man and a woman working toward something, for something. Not apart, but as a team."

Fawcett released the paperback original on the same day as the film appeared and henceforth L'Amour always claimed that *Hondo*—when not even the title had been his—was his first novel rather than *Westward the Tide.*

In interviews conducted many years later, L'Amour also projected the notion he was somehow involved with the production of the film and selection of the cast. However, I had someone at the University of Southern California Still Archive photocopy every still from the key book to *Hondo* that was taken behind the set and L'Amour did not appear in any of them.

Movie cowboy Tim McCoy, who knew Buffalo Bill, recalled him as once saying that so much had been written about him and his various exploits that he no longer knew himself what was true and what may have been an exaggeration. In some respects, Louis L'Amour merchandised himself in much the same manner. Creating as much a legend about himself as writing Western fiction, he was willing to take credit for *Hondo*, but not for his "Tex Burns" Hopalong Cassidy novels.

# L'Amour and Gold Medal

*by Ed Gorman*

IN THE good old days, back when you could buy paperbacks for twenty-five cents, my favorite line of books was the Gold Medal suspense novels.

By this time I was in ninth grade and science fiction, my previous passion, had even then begun to seem slightly irrelevant to a teenager just then discovering his loneliness and his loins. Science-fiction writers spoke to my head: Gold Medal writers spoke to my soul.

You know the writers I mean: John D. MacDonald, Charles Williams, Stephen Marlowe, Day Keene, Richard Prather, Vin Packer, Wade Miller, John McPartland, Richard Jessup, and several others.

When you read the Gold Medal books, you found that there were essentially three types of protagonist in this particular universe—the competent, reasonably well-educated middle-class man who found himself in unlikely trouble, as in the early John D. MacDonald novels: the sad, desperate working-class men in most of the books by Charles Williams and Day Keene; and the professional adventurers/detectives prominent in many of the novels of Stephen Marlowe and Wade Miller.

In the early fifties, Louis L'Amour began trying to sell to better markets. Gold Medal was rightly considered the best of the paperback original houses. It had not only been first, it had set the standard for the rest of the industry.

When you read the novels L'Amour did as by "Jim Mayo" for Ace Books, you find pulp fiction in its most primitive if still quite readable form. Action is everything. There is little attempt at either background story or characterization. This isn't criticism. This is simply an observation about the market demands at that time. The editors at Ace would probably have blue-penciled any serious attempts at characterization. They wanted gunsmoke, and little else.

My impression is that L'Amour changed his approach when writing for Gold Medal. My evidence of this is a novel titled *Last Stand at Papago Wells*, a Gold Medal original first published in 1957.

L'Amour seems to have read, if not studied, the Gold Medals of other

**213**

writers, because on the first page you find him trying to do something more sophisticated (for him) with background and characterization.

Yes, we have the mandatory Western novel physical description:

> Logan Cates had the look of the desert about him, a brown, sea-soned man with straight black hair above a triangular face that was all bone and tight-drawn, sun-browned hide. His eyes, narrow from squinting into sun and wind, were a cold green that made a man stop and think before he looked into them a second time.

Usually, L'Amour wouldn't give us much more than this, not in his pure pulp days.

But here, just a few paragraphs later, we find:

> Logan Cates was a man without illusions, without wealth, place, or destination. In the eighteen years since his parents died of cholera when he was fourteen he had driven a freight wagon, punched cows, hunted buffalo, twice gone over the trail from Texas to Kansas with cattle, scouted for the Army and had ridden shotgun on many stages. Twice, also, he had been marshal of boomtowns for brief periods. He had lived without plan, following his horse's ears and coping with each days problems as they arose.

This is a more skillful paragraph than it may superficially appear: it gives us a sense of a man (heroic in the hard-bitten tradition), fixes us in a historical period (just at the end of the frontier), and lends the narrative some authentic Western flavor with the details of a workingman's days.

Logan Cates seems to combine some of the qualities of John D. MacDonald's professionals with some of Charles Williams's sweaty existential decay.

The story itself functions very much like a Gold Medal suspense novel: a variety of people, good and bad, meet by chance at Papago Wells to hold off Indians. Gold Medal editors apparently loved this sort of Grand Hotel action formula: Lionel White did it as a caper novel, Theodore Pratt did it as a forerunner of today's "glitz" novel, and Gil Brewer (in a near perfect novel called *Some Must Die*) did it as a contemporary adventure novel.

What we learn from this "stand at Papago Wells" is that the enemy is both without and within—Logan Cates sees a lot of dark humanity among those gathered for mutual protection at the wells.

L'Amour learned his pulp lessons well. The novel builds to several very well-executed cliff-hangers and is filled with a lot of Western color.

His depiction of Indian savagery would probably seem in questionable taste in these more liberal times, but his version of Indian raids is both authentic and frightening.

In all, the novel has the feel of a Gold Medal "Giant," a thirty-five-cent book rather than a quarter one. There are eight or nine principle characters, several subplots, and some nicely stage-managed action scenes. To date, this had to have been L'Amour's most ambitious book.

This is not to say that L'Amour was Gold Medal's best Western writer. Some readers preferred the quirky poetry of Clifton Adams (whose *The Desperado* is probably the best Western Gold Medal ever published) or the wry, melancholy tales of Richard Jessup under both his own name and his Richard Telfair handle. The great Gold Medal historical novel belongs to the now-forgotten William Forrest and his beautiful *White Apache*.

But *Last Stand* is a very good L'Amour, filled with all the color and clamor his fans came to expect from him. His experience at Gold Medal helped him grow into the giant storyteller he later became, teaching him how to paint with more colors, and how to use those colors more subtly.

# The Twenty-five Best
# Western Novels of All Time

IN 1977, the Western Writers of America conducted a poll among its current members as to their choices of the twenty-five best Western novels ever written. Two Louis L'Amour novels were among the twenty-five chosen.

1. *The Virginian* by Owen Wister
2. *The Ox Bow Incident* by Walter Van Tilburg Clark
3. *Shane* by Jack Shaefer
4. *The Big Sky* by A.B. Guthrie, Jr.
5. *The Searchers* by Alan LeMay
6. *Riders of the Purple Sage* by Zane Grey
7. *Paso Por Aqui* by Eugene Manlove Rhodes
8. *Bugles in the Afternoon* by Ernest Haycox
9. *The Long Rifle* by Stewart Edward White
10. *Vengeance Valley* by Luke Short
11. *The Hell Bent Kid* by Charles O. Locke
12. *Cheyenne Autumn* by Mari Sandoz
13. *Destry Rides Again* by Max Brand
14. *Hondo* by Louis L'Amour
15. *The Sea of Grass* by Conrad Richter
16. *Ride the Man Down* by Luke Short
17. *The Day the Cowboys Quit* by Elmer Kelton
18. *Stay Away Joe* by Dan Cushman
19. *The Time It Never Rained* by Elmer Kelton
20. *True Grit* by Charles Portis
21. *Monte Walsh* by Jack Schaefer
22. *Flint* by Louis L'Amour
23. *From Where the Sun Now Stands* by Will Henry
24. *Hombre* by Elmore Leonard
25. *Wonderful Country* by Tom Lea

# The Novels of Louis L'Amour—
# The Sixties:
# An Annotated Checklist

DURING THE 1960s, Louis L'Amour's name appeared on twenty-nine books, almost three a year. It was a decade in which the Sacketts first appeared and L'Amour did some of his finest writing. The numbering of this checklist continues from the chronology of his fifties work.

**22.** *The Daybreakers*—published by Bantam Books in February 1960.

The first Sackett novel, and in the opinion of many, the best. Told in first person by Tyrel Sackett, the fastest gun alive. After killing a man in a feud, Tyrel and his brother Orrin flee Tennessee and head west. After a number of adventures, they settle in New Mexico.

There are numerous similarities between the structure and style of this novel and *To Tame a Land*. Along with the first-person narration and the deadly nature of the hero, the chief villain in both stories is a close friend of the protagonist who has gone bad. And in each novel, the climactic gunfight hinges on the mention of a book shared by both men.

While L'Amour may have been planning more Sackett novels, it seems unlikely judging by the tone of the end of this story that he planned using Tyrel or Orrin in another adventure. This was one of L'Amour's best novels. Along with *Sackett*, this novel was filmed as the TV miniseries "The Sacketts."

**23.** *Flint*—published by Bantam Books in November 1960.

James Kettleman, a successful East Coast financier, returns to the West to die. No one knows that he was the famous "Kid at the Crossing," who had killed five men in a furious gunfight many years earlier. Kettleman, who thinks he is dying of cancer, finds himself caught up in the middle of a range war. Before long, he is battling an old enemy, helping a beautiful girl in distress, and discovering the truth about himself and his desires.

This novel was voted by the Western Writers of America as one of the twenty-five best Westerns of all time in 1977. It is one of L'Amour's finest works.

**24.** *Sackett*—published by Bantam Books in May 1961.

The second Sackett novel. Tyrel and Orrin's older brother, Tell, stumbles across Angie Kerry in the mountains, alone after the death of her grandfather. Along with his friend Cap Rountree, Tell defeats the Bigelow clan.

Along with *The Daybreakers,* this novel served as the basis for the TV miniseries "The Sacketts."

**25.** *Shalako*—published by Bantam Books in February 1962.

A typical L'Amour hero, Shalako Carlin tries to help a hunting party of Europeans in New Mexico, who are being pursued by a party of renegade Apaches. One of L'Amour's best novels, this was filmed as *Shalako* in 1968.

**26.** *Killoe*—published by Bantam Books in May 1962.

Young Dan Killoe, wise beyond his years, helps his father and neighbors move a huge herd of cattle west, looking for open range. Accompanying them is Dan's half brother, Tap Henry. They are beset by renegades and Indians and Tap's apparent treachery, but Dan proves up to all challenges. Another entertaining read.

This book was dedicated by L'Amour to Bill Tilghman, "Who Showed Me How It Was Done With a Six-Gun."

**27.** *High Lonesome*—published by Bantam Books in September 1962.

Considine, Dutch, Hardy, and the Kiowa rob a bank and head for the border. However, on the way they encounter an old man and his daughter, being pursued by the Apaches. Instead of riding away, Considine and his men fight off the Indians, making their stand on the peak High Lonesome. This novel was a much expanded version of the short story "In Victorio's Country."

**28.** *Lando*—published by Bantam Books in December 1962.

Orlando Sackett and his friend the Tinker search for buried gold in Mexico, as well as trying to discover the whereabouts of Orlando's father, Falcon. But Lando is caught by the Mexican authorities and imprisoned for six years, until he finally escapes and goes after the man who betrayed him.

Lando is an unconventional hero, a boxer who rides a racing mule, and not the usual L'Amour fast gun. The Tinker makes an unusual sidekick. The two characters help make this an enjoyable change of pace for L'Amour.

**29.** *Fallon*—published by Bantam Books in February 1963.

Macon Fallon, a con man and expert at cards, turns a ghost town into a thriving community. In doing so, he slowly becomes respectable—marrying and fighting off a band of outlaws. A minor novel.

**30.** *How the West Was Won*—published by Bantam Books in March 1963.
Novelization of the movie of the same name, based on the screenplay by James B. Webb.

**31.** *Catlow*—published by Bantam Books in June 1963.
Abijah Catlow is a legendary outlaw of the Old West. His childhood friend Ben Cowan is a marshal who has to bring him in.

**32.** *Dark Canyon*—published by Bantam Books in November 1963.
Gaylord Riley, the youngest member of the Jim Colburn gang, goes straight and buys a ranch using money given him by the outlaw leader. He promises his friends that there will always be a place for them there. Riley doesn't realize he has bought himself an outfit set right in the middle of a battle between the two richest men in the territory. But neither do his enemies realize that Riley has such dangerous friends. Tell Sackett appears as a minor character in this novel.
This novel is a slight expansion of the pulp story "Lost Mountain."

**33.** *Mojave Crossing*—published by Bantam Books in January 1964.
The fourth Sackett novel. Tell Sackett fights to protect his gold from an outlaw gang of 1870s California. Nolan Sackett makes a brief appearance in this story.

**34.** *Hanging Woman Creek*—published by Bantam Books in April 1964.
Pronto Pike, a man who tries to steer clear from a fight, finds himself forced to take sides in a battle between a powerful rancher and a small operator, Philo Farley, and his sister Ann. Pronto's best friend and partner, Eddie Holt, is black, one of the few African-American characters in L'Amour's novels.

**35.** *Kiowa Trail*—published by Bantam Books in October 1964.
Kate Lundy, owner of the Tumbling B ranch, drives her cattle north with the help of her foreman, Conn Drury, her kid brother Tom, and the rest of her tough outfit. When Tom is shot in the back in a nameless town, Kate vows to get her revenge on the townspeople. She does so in a unique manner by cutting off further herds coming up the Kiowa trail, destroying the townspeople's major source of revenue.

**36.** *The High Graders*—published by Bantam Books in January 1965.

Mike Shevlin comes back to the town of Rafter Crossing to find the killer of an old friend, Eli Patterson. Hired by Laine Tennison to find out who was stealing the high-grade ore from her mine, Mike also discovers a plot to turn the local cattlemen against the miners.

**37.** *The Sackett Brand*—published by Bantam Books in June 1965.

Tell Sackett is ambushed and left for dead. When he recovers, he finds his wife has been attacked and murdered. It turns out that the killer is the boss of a tough outfit who sends his men after Tell. But the gunfighters of the Lazy A never counted on the entire Sackett clan learning of Tell's problems and coming to his aid. Told primarily in first person, the book gets extremely choppy about halfway through when L'Amour suddenly switches to third person to introduce other Sacketts riding to the rescue.

**38.** *The Key Lock Man*—published by Bantam Books in December 1965.

Matt Keelock is pursued by a posse of six men who are out to lynch him. But he is not ready to surrender without a fight. A variation on the same theme as *The Lonesome Hills*, with an added subplot about a lost gold train.

**39.** *The Broken Gun*—published by Bantam Books in January 1966.

L'Amour's one modern Western novel. Dan Sheridan comes to Arizona to solve an eighty-year-old mystery and finds himself fighting modern-day outlaws. This was filmed as *Cancel My Reservation*.

**40.** *Kid Rodelo*—published by Bantam Books in March 1966.

Kid Rodelo is released from prison. With the help of Nora Paxton and three escaped prisoners, he goes after the gold from an old robbery. Yaqui Indians provide only some of the perils. This book was filmed as *Kid Rodelo*.

**41.** *Mustang Man*—published by Bantam Books in May 1966.

Nolan Sackett, the outlaw Sackett, helps Sylvie, a girl in distress, only to be ambushed by her. As soon as he escapes from her clutches, he runs into Penelope—and gold—and a lot more trouble.

**42.** *Kilrone*—published by Bantam Books in October 1966.

Barney Kilrone rides into a fort in Nevada to report the massacre of a troop of soldiers. The commander of the fort turns out to be Frank Paddock, an old friend who has turned to drink. When Paddock leaves to fight the rampaging Indians, he turns over the defense of the fort to Kilrone. Needless to say, the Indians attack. And an old enemy of Kilrone, Iron Dave Sproul, tries to steal the army payroll. A fast-paced adventure.

**43.** *The Sky-Liners*—published by Bantam Books in April 1967.

Flagan and Galloway Sackett, two brothers, promise to escort Judith Costello and her herd of horses out West. Black Fetchen, an enemy of the Sacketts and an outlaw, wants the horses and assembles a tough gang to steal the herd. But Flagan and Galloway are typical Sacketts and are no strangers to trouble. This is one of L'Amour's longest novels in the 1960s, and is one of the best.

**44.** *Matagorda*—published by Bantam Books in November 1967.

Tap Duvarney travels to Matagorda, Tex., looking to help his friend Tom Kittery in the cattle business. However, he instead finds himself in a town split by a feud between Kittery and the Munsons of the Circle M Ranch. The Munsons have Jackson Huddy, a deadly quick gunfighter, on their side. But Tap Duvarney has friends as well.

**45.** *Down the Long Hills*—published by Bantam Books in January 1968.

The only survivors of a wagon train massacre are seven-year-old Hardy Collins and three-year-old Betty Sue Powell. On their own, they make their way west toward Fort Bridger, keeping hidden from Indians, outlaws, and even a bear. They are eventually found by Hardy's father. One of L'Amour's best books, this novel was a definite change of pace for the author. It won the Western Writers of America Spur Award for best novel in 1969. It was filmed as *Down the Long Hills*.

**46.** *Chancy*—published by Bantam Books in April 1968.

Otis Chancy, a young man from Tennessee, puts his money into a herd of cattle. Out West, he fights Indians, outlaws, and a crooked sheriff as he tries to make his fortune. After many adventures, he settles down as boss of his own outfit in Wyoming, only to find he still has to fight some old enemies.

**47.** *Brionne*—published by Bantam Books in August 1968.

Major James Brionne was responsible for Dave Allard being tried and hung for murder. Four years later, Allard's brothers kill Brionne's wife and burn down his home. The Major and his young son head West, but the Allards follow. When they attack again, Brionne knows that this time it is kill or be killed.

**48.** *The Empty Land*—published by Bantam Books in January 1969.

Matt Coburn was a town-tamer. He comes to the gold rush town of Confusion to bring law and order when outlaws, gunfighters, and gamblers threaten to bust the place wide open. Matt does what he must and then moves on to other challenges.

**49.** *The Lonely Men*—published by Bantam Books in May 1969.

A Sackett novel, tying together elements of several earlier books. Laura Pritts, the estranged wife of Orrin Sackett, lies to his brother Tell, saying that her son has been kidnapped by Apaches. Tell, not knowing that Laura merely wants revenge against the Sackett family, heads off to Mexico with a small band of tough companions. They end up rescuing two captives and thwart Laura's plans.

**50.** *Conagher*—published by Bantam Books in September 1969.

Evie Teale and her husband, Jacob, settle out West with their two children, Laban and Ruthie. When Jacob dies unexpectedly, Evie struggles to make ends meet. Turning her house into a stagecoach stopover, she manages to prosper. Lonely, though, she writes poetic notes that she scatters on drifting tumbleweeds. They are found by Conn Conagher, a typical L'Amour cowboy. Conagher settles the score with a band of outlaws, the Ladder Five, and then comes calling on Evie.

# An Open Letter to the Old Bookaroos

*by Louis L'Amour*

*The Roundup,* September/October 1963

Gentlemen:

First, allow me to congratulate you on the selection of Fred Grove's *Comanche Captives* and Hal G. Evarts' *Massacre Creek.* I have read both novels and enjoyed them very much, and believe both are among the best tradition of the frontier novel.

However, I must take exception to a phrase in your comments on my novel, *Shalako.* You say: "Despite a highly improbable cast . . ." and then you list the German baron, the French count, the senator's daughter, etc. who made up that cast, the hunting party which figured largely in my novel. For some reason you call these people highly improbable. Unfortunately, I can only put this down to a complete forgetfulness of what was happening in the American West.

After living in the West much of my life, and years of research in the field, *I can think of no Western cast I would consider improbable.* One of the great charms of the West, and one of the things that cause me to continue to write about it, as well as one of the reasons people like to read about it, was that the West was a place where the improbable happened every day.

However, as to my cast: let me remind the judges that in the summer of 1855, some thirty years before my story, Sir George Gore, of Sligo, Ireland, came hunting buffalo. He had 43 men in his party, 112 horses, 12 yokes of cattle, 14 dogs, 6 wagons, and 21 carts, many of the carts loaded with the finest luxury foods money could buy.

Sir George went hunting in the heart of Sioux country, and if he did not have the trouble my party of hunters had it was perhaps due to a guide named Jim Bridger.

Arriving a few years before, but living on the edge of the Dakota Badlands at the same time as my story, was the Frenchman who founded the town of Medora, named for his wife. This was Antoine-Marie-Vincent-Manca de Valombrosa, otherwise known as the Marquis de Mores.

The handsome marquis, an improbable character indeed, built a chateau where he entertained forty or fifty of Europe's greatest nobility. They hunted buffalo, antelope, and grizzlies. Many of them were accompanied by their wives, and the wife of the Marquis, the Baroness Medora von Hoffman, was the daughter of a New York banker.

Quite incidentally, the baroness came west with the fervent ambition to kill a grizzly with a pistol. A noted horsewoman and an excellent shot, she lived for many years after, so I do not believe she tried it. Not to say that it couldn't be done.

Living in the same area at the same time, was another extremely improbable character named Teddy Roosevelt.

However, the marquis to make certain of his improbability, engaged in a minor range war, including a gun battle in which he and a companion killed one man and wounded another. So here we have an improbable French nobleman engaging in an improbable gun battle, and in a very improbable way, winning the fight.

Ten years earlier than my story, the Grand Duke Alexis came hunting. Gen. Sheridan supervised the party for him, with Buffalo Bill as guide. Accompanying the party were Consul Bodisco, Chancellor Machen, Admiral Possiet, Gen. George A. Custer, Lt. Stordegraff, Count Olsonfieff and a number of others, including that same Col. George A. Forsyth who figured in my story.

Among others, touring or hunting before and after the period of my novel, were the Viscountess of Avonmore, the Earl of Dunraven, Lady Guest, Lady Duffus Hardy, Lady Rose Pender (she rode from Cheyenne to Rapid City and then to Miles City in a buggy in 1883, the year following my story), the Baron of Swansea, and the party of the Duke of Sutherland. There were others too numerous to mention. In my files I have a list of forty-nine such groups and there were many more.

Visiting the Marquis de Mores at about this time was the very improbable character named Galiot Francois Edmond, Baron de Mandat-Grancey, who not only toured the West but wrote an excellent book about it called *Cowboys and Colonels*.

Another equally improbable visitor was Oscar Wilde, who stood at the bar in velvet knee breeches belting the juice with the miners of Leadville and nearby points. Later, he even shared a bottled lunch with a group of miners at the bottom of a mine shaft.

The Apache raid and the resulting army maneuvers as related in my story are factual. The names of the officers, the Indians and all the places are factual. Even the Apache called the Quick-Killer was a real warrior, and known to be as I have written of him. The locale of the story is correct down to the finest point, and I invite any reader to look over the ground in that southwestern corner of New Mexico below Lordsburg.

What the judges objected to in my story was not the writing, which could be much, much better, but the history. True, I used a fictional device in placing one of the many such parties of hunters in the midst of an actual Indian outbreak, but this is accepted practice.

The judges added this unkindest cut of all: "L'Amour all but convinced us that it could have happened."

Gentlemen, I stand by my story. You go back and read it again. I did convince you.

Sincerely,
LOUIS L'AMOUR

# The Novels of Louis L'Amour—
# The Seventies:
# An Annotated Checklist

DURING THE 1970s, Louis L'Amour's name appeared on twenty-six novels. During this decade, L'Amour began writing longer novels and went back in history to chronicle the early adventures of the Sackett family in America. The numbering of this checklist continues from the chronology of his sixties books.

**51.** *The Man Called Noon*—published by Bantam Books in February 1970.

There was gold buried somewhere on Fan Davidge's ranch. A crooked judge named Niland, Peg Cullane, a cold-blooded beauty, and German Bayles, a deadly gunfighter, all wanted it. But standing against them was an amnesia victim who calls himself Jonas and was as tough as they come.

This novel was filmed as *A Man Called Noon*.

**52.** *Galloway*—published by Bantam Books in July 1970.

A Sackett novel. Flagan Sackett escapes from a band of Apaches and heads for sanctuary in the mountains. Alone and weaponless, he tames a wolf. Meanwhile, his brother Galloway searches for him and becomes involved in a range war. Another one of L'Amour's annoying novels told in alternate first- and third-person viewpoints.

**53.** *Reilly's Luck*—published by Bantam Books in October 1970.

When a young boy, Val Darrant, is abandoned by his mother, he is taken in by a gambler, Will Reilly. Together the two travel across America and Europe. When Reilly horsewhips the brutal Prince Paval, he makes a deadly enemy.

L'Amour often went to great lengths detailing the European backgrounds of many Westerners. In this novel, he reversed himself and placed a Western gambler in Europe. One of his longer and more ambitions books of the period.

**54.** *North to the Rails*—published by Bantam Books in February 1971.

Tom Chantry comes West to buy cattle and is mistaken by the locals as a Easterner. When French Williams and his outlaws try to steal his herd, they learn differently. Chantry is the son of a frontier lawman and knows how to fight.

**55.** *Under the Sweetwater Rim*—published by Bantam Books in May 1971.

"Ten" Brian is a frontiersman with experience in the French foreign legion. When renegades and Indians raid the wagon train he is guarding, Ten manages to escape with the major's daughter and the army payroll. The renegades continue to follow the wagon until Ten finally kills their leader.

**56.** *Tucker*—published by Bantam Books in October 1971.

Shell Tucker's father is ambushed by three gunmen who steal his gold and leave him to die. Determined to regain the money, Shell hunts down the outlaws.

**57.** *Callaghen*—published by Bantam Books in February 1972.

Morty Callaghen is a twenty-year army veteran waiting for his discharge from the service. In the meantime he battles Indians and outlaws in the desert and finds an underground river of gold.

**58.** *Ride the Dark Trail*—published by Bantam Books in June 1972.

A Sackett novel. Em Talon is fighting to hold her ranch from Jake Flanner and his men when Nolan Sackett comes by. Em is a Sackett who married a Talon so Nolan, the outlaw Sackett, stays to help. When events reach a climax, Em's two sons, Milo and Barnabas, come riding home and help even the odds.

**59.** *Treasure Mountain*—published by Bantam Books in October 1972.

A Sackett novel. Trying to learn the fate of their long-missing father, Tell and Orrin Sackett go to New Orleans. There, they find clues to a twenty-year-old mystery centered around a lost cache of gold. Along with the Tinker, they find the treasure and their father's murderer.

**60.** *The Ferguson Rifle*—published by Bantam Books in March 1973.

Another treasure novel. Ronan Chantry leaves Boston after his wife and son are killed in a fire. An educated man, he is also a tough, capable fighter. In the Rocky Mountains, he meets Lucinda Falvey, who is searching for a lost treasure of gold. He helps the girl in her quest, fighting her outlaw uncle, Rafen Falvey, and his gang, who also seek the treasure.

**61.** *The Man From Skibbereen*—published by Bantam Books in July 1973.

Crispin Mayo is an Irishman traveling west to work on the railroad. He witnesses the kidnapping of Major McClean by a band of renegades. With the major's daughter, Barda, he heads after the bandits.

**62.** *The Quick and the Dead*—published by Bantam Books in November 1973.

Con Vallian, a typical L'Amour hero, comes across Duncan and Susanna McKaskel and their son, Tom, who are traveling west. The McKaskels plan to settle on the prairie, but are threatened by Doc Shabbitt and his gang. Vallian stays around to help the family and battle the outlaws.

**63.** *The Californios*—published in hardcover by Saturday Review Press, April 1974. Reprinted by Bantam Books in October 1974.

L'Amour's mystical novel of California right before the gold rush. Sean Mulkerin saves his family's ranch from creditors using gold provided by the Old One, an Indian with magical powers. This novel foreshadows the theme of *The Haunted Mesa*. See R. Jeff Bank's article, "The Mix Master," for a more detailed study of this story.

**64.** *Sackett's Land*—published in hardcover by Saturday Review Press, May 1974. Reprinted by Bantam Books in May 1975.

A Sackett novel. Though packaged to resemble a Western, this story is actually a historical novel, telling of Barnabas Sackett's adventures in England and America at the turn of the seventeenth century. Chronologically, the first of the Sackett novels.

**65.** *Rivers West*—published in hardcover by Saturday Review Press, March 1975. Reprinted by Bantam in August 1984.

A Talon novel. Jean Talon, a young shipbuilder from Quebec, comes across a plot to take over the Louisiana territory by Baron Torville. Again, more of a historical novel than a Western.

**66.** *The Man from the Broken Hills*—published by Bantam Books in October 1975.

A Talon novel. Milo Talon, Em's son, joins up with the Stirrup-Iron outfit during roundup time. He learns that the ranch along with several others is losing cattle to an unknown rustler. After several adventures, he retrieves the missing herd and puts the rustlers out of business.

**67.** *Over on the Dry Side*—published in hardcover by Saturday Review Press, October 1975. Reprinted by Bantam Books in May 1976.

Young Doby Kenohan and his father are moving West when they come across the Chantry ranch, abandoned with a dead man in the house. They are there for a few weeks when Chantry's brother Owen comes riding in. Before long, all three of them are fighting to keep the ranch against the vicious Mowat gang who are searching for a lost treasure.

**68.** *The Rider of Lost Creek*—published by Bantam Books, August 1976.

The first Kilkenny novel. Lance Kilkenny helps his friend Mort Davis, whose outfit is caught in the middle of a range war. He tangles with the Brockmann brothers and falls in love with Nita Riordan. Based on the 1947 pulp novel of the same name. One of L'Amour's best action novels.

**69.** *To the Far Blue Mountains*—published in hardcover by E.P. Dutton in October 1976. Reprinted by Bantam Books in June 1977.

A Sackett novel. Chronologically the second Sackett novel, this closely follows the events of *Sackett's Land.* Barnabas Sackett departs England for the last time and returns to America, where he and his wife Abigail struggle to raise a family in the wilderness of the Carolinas. Like the first book in the series, this is not a Western but a historical novel with a frontier setting.

**70.** *Where the Long Grass Blows*—published by Bantam Books in November 1976.

Ben Canavan rides into Soledad with hopes of establishing a ranch. He finds himself in the midst of a land war between two powerful ranchers, neither of them particularly honest. Siding with Dixie Venable, owner of a small ranch, Canavan brings about the downfall of both the land barons. This novel is a rewritten version of the pulp story "The Rider of the Ruby Hills."

**71.** *Borden Chantry*—published by Bantam Books in October 1977.

A Chantry novel. Borden Chantry, a Western marshal, has to solve the murder of Joe Sackett, but finds himself after a killer who is wiping out all the witnesses to his crime. A combination Western and mystery novel, this book is discussed in depth in R. Jeff Banks's article, "The Mix Master."

**72.** *Fair Blows the Wind*—published in hardcover by E.P. Dutton in April 1978. Reprinted by Bantam Books in October 1978.

A Chantry novel. Chronologically, the first in the Chantry series. Tatton Chantry is left to die on the coast of North Carolina. Traveling south, he stumbles upon a party of shipwrecked Spaniards and joins forces with them. He fights pirates, treasure hunters, and Indians before returning home to Ireland. Another historical novel in the style of *Sackett's Land.*

**73.** *The Mountain Valley War*—published in paperback by Bantam Books in May 1978.

Chronologically, the second Kilkenny novel. King Bill Hale tries to take over the high country but soon discovers he is fighting a tough mountain family as well as Kilkenny, one of the fastest guns alive. An expanded version of the pulp story "A Man Called Trent."

**74.** *Bendigo Shafter*—published in hardcover by Dutton in January 1979. Reprinted by Bantam Books in September 1979.

L'Amour's most ambitious Western novel of the seventies. Young Bendigo Shafter and his family, along with several other families, start a town in Wyoming. They survive Indian trouble, outlaw attacks, and the harsh weather and slowly build their community. Later, Bendigo travels East and meets a number of famous people in New York. The novel ends with a number of mysterious events left unresolved. A sequel is called for but was never written. One of L'Amour's best books.

**75.** *The Proving Trail*—published by Bantam Books in January 1979.

Kearney McRaven rides down from the high country to find that his dad has been killed by mysterious gunmen in long, black coats. Soon, Kearney finds these same men are after him as well.

**76.** *The Iron Marshall*—published by Bantam Books in June 1979.

Tom Shanaghy, a rough, tough New Yorker, jumps a train heading west to escape a gang out for his blood. He ends up in a small Kansas town where a combination of circumstances makes him the marshal. Soon, Tom finds himself investigating a plot to steal $250,000 in gold. In a change of pace, Shanaghy is not much of a gunfighter but a rough-and-tumble fist fighter.

L'Amour dedicated this book to all the Bantam Books and Select Magazines sales representatives and sales managers.

# Louis L'Amour

by *Barbara A. Bannon*
*Publishers Weekly,* October 8, 1973

LOUIS L'AMOUR is quite probably the most prolific, best selling, and most highly rated writer of Westerns in this country today. He currently has forty-eight titles in print as paperback originals with Bantam, many of which have been sold to the movies. It is not unusual for a L'Amour book to go into as many as ten, thirteen, sixteen printings. The total number of copies of his books in print is now 32,225,000, and his audience comes from all over the world.

What makes a L'Amour Western so popular, in addition to his solid story-telling ability, is the carefully researched and authentic historical background. "History is my bag, I like it," he told *PW* in a recent interview in his West Hollywood home, and, indeed, every available area of wall space in the L'Amour household is given over to floor-to-ceiling bookcases crammed with books—books not only on American history but on many aspects of world literature and culture, including the Far East, about which L'Amour is as knowledgeable as he is about the American West.

Because he is well aware of the hack writing associated in many people's minds with the category "Western," Louis L'Amour winces slightly when you use that word to describe what he is doing.

"I do not distinguish Westerns at all from other kinds of novels," he says. "If you are going to characterize my stories I would prefer to have them called stories of the frontier. What is attractive to people reading this kind of book is the idea of the freedom of the Western man, getting on a horse and moving on somewhere else. We all have dreams of wanting to be this kind of a free agent. To me there is no period in the world's history that is so fascinating as the era in which the American West was opening up. You cannot invent people like the real-life Molly Brown or silver mining baron Spencer Penrose, who built his house in Virginia City, Nevada, with solid silver doorknobs throughout. They were all bigger than life and they did fantastic things."

Another reason why Mr. L'Amour does not care for the categorization inherent in the word "Western" is the fact that it seems to isolate its characters too much. "These were not just people who lived and died in the West," he says. "They were constantly coming from and going out to all parts of the world all the time. They came from everywhere. Oliver Wollop came out to Wyoming from England and later went back there to serve in the House of Lords. Chris Madsen, a famous frontier marshal, was a Dane. Five of the men who died with Custer had been in the Vatican Guard. Once I met up with a big fellow, bearded and dirty, who told me authentically about how he had rowed in the Henley Regatta, the Oxford-Cambridge boat race. These old characters were tough. If you don't shoot them they live forever."

As a serious professional writer, L'Amour believes that "no matter what you write you must respect your audience. I write for very bright people, as I can tell from the kind of fan letters I get. I know a great deal about nature, tracking, wild animals, horseback riding. All of this works its way into my books. I used to drop in tidbits of history for myself. Then I found I was getting more and more of a response to them from my readers. A writer owes a debt of authenticity to his readers."

L'Amour's readers write to him constantly about the minutiae of the West and he tries to answer every letter he gets. One unexpected bonus has been the fact that a number of them have unearthed old, privately printed journals or diaries, which they gladly send on to him, and which are of considerable interest in filling in background details. The day *PW* visited him, a coffee table in the living room boasted such intriguing old journals as *My Experiences and Investment in the Badlands of Dakota and Some of the Men I Met There,* and *Soldiering in Dakota Among the Indians in 1863–4–5.*

L'Amour can trace his own family history in this country back to 1638 and follows the family's steady progression westward, "always on the frontier." He was born in North Dakota. His great-grandfather was scalped by the Sioux and he grew up on stories of the Old West. His wife's family, too, can trace its ancestry in America back a long time. "Her family and my family had to have known each other at various times along the way," he told *PW.* "There were times when we both had ancestors in the same town with a population of just two or three thousand people."

That idea of families moving westward at about the same time and meeting up with each other at different periods of history has given Louis L'Amour his most ambitious writing project yet, one that he expects "will last for the rest of my life." He is writing a series of novels dealing with three immigrant families coming to this country from Europe: the Sacketts, who are Welsh and English, the Talons, who come from France, and the Chantrys from Ireland. "As they move westward in different generations they brush elbows with each other and intermarry over a period of forty years. In the end all their fates will be woven in together and in the course of writing these books I plan to tell the whole story of the West. I have my characters well established now and people are really curious about them. From time to time I refer back to earlier characters in the series and even their ancestors in Europe. Here, too, I do very careful research. When I write about inns and road conditions in sixteenth-century Ireland or England, I am using the names of real inns and making sure my people are traveling over real roads.

"I'm a very up person," L'Amour says of himself frankly. "Any writer writes to be read. I think in the next ten years I will sell forty to sixty million copies of my books, and I want to reach as wide an audience as possible. Most writers pamper themselves. I do not believe in this 'I am not in the mood to write' business. I think you have to just sit down at the typewriter and stick with it. (L'Amour's contract with Bantam calls for three books a year. If he only had the time, he'd love to do ten a year.) I would lay a lot of money that I am read by whole families more than any other writer in the world. I think just as many women as men read my books, and I get a lot of letters from women asking, "Where are the men like the ones in your books these days?"

The range of L'Amour's readership can be demonstrated by two items he showed *PW.* One was a picture of a sixth or seventh grade class in a Canadian school, each child holding a copy of a different L'Amour novel which was assigned classroom reading in history. The other was a letter from the head of the Department of Earth Sciences at Stanford inquiring about additional information on an aspect of science mentioned in a L'Amour novel. He estimates that at the present time there are five or six people doing doctoral dissertations on his work.

Sandwiched in between his writing for a few years now has been a pet L'Amour project that he hopes will be completed in the next year. He is part of a multimillion dollar investment in acquiring land in Colorado eleven miles west of Durango, where there is still an old narrow-gauge railway. The aim will be to set up an authentic Western town (circa 1865–1886) after the fashion of Colonial Williamsburg or Old Sturbridge, and to have it both a tourist attraction and possibly a site for filming movies. The Durango project, which will be called Shalako, has been mentioned in news stories and L'Amour says he is "already getting applications from all over the world from people who want to work there."

Neither Indians nor white men in the L'Amour novels are all good or all bad. "The Indian was a primitive, a savage: bravery was the basis of his thinking," he says. "They had no conception about mercy according to our standards. It was an accepted part of their life to torture. Many of the white men of the time had no better standards than the Indian. Most of the pioneers who came West had nothing against the Indian, but when you were kind to an Indian he misunderstood and interpreted it as being afraid of him. The Western migration came so fast, because of the gold rush, that the Indian never had a chance to adjust to the cultural shock of the white man.

"You cannot write about the West without living in it," L'Amour is convinced. He, his wife and son and daughter regularly spend as much time as possible in the countryside around Caliente Creek and a month in Colorado each year, hiking in the mountains, following old trails. "As a writer and as a human being I agree wholeheartedly with what Robinson Jeffers once wrote," he told *PW:* "'When the cities lie at the monster's feet, there are left the mountains.'"

# The Mix Master—
# L'Amour's Crossover Novels

*by R. Jeff Banks*

THE GENRES of popular fiction provide structure for writer, reader, and editor. Their exact definition varies from time to time, but never so much that we have trouble recognizing the generic identity of a particular work. Each usually has its best or best-loved (and they are not always the same) writer clearly identified. Sometimes those writers whose careers define their genres are as inventive as Ellery Queen *within* their chosen field of popular fiction. Sometimes their inventiveness leads them beyond such narrow confines.

Louis L'Amour belonged to the latter type. His works were usually Westerns, but especially in his last two decades those Westerns were enriched and enlivened with characters, scenes, incidents, and other characteristics more typical of fiction *outside* the Western genre. This did not make him unique, but it did make his work much more interesting and enduring than if he had confined himself to the same familiar Western elements in each novel.

When genre mixing is carried to extremes, hybrid or "hyphenated" genres result. There are probably as many of these as possible combinations of the recognized genres will allow, but the most successful has been the Western-mystery.

After achieving success with Westerns during his pulp writing days, L'Amour expended considerable effort on the pulp mystery. One of his pulp series detailed the adventures of hard-boiled private detective Kip Morgan. The Los Angeles setting was in the West, but these stories were not "modern Westerns," for those require a rural or at least small-town locale. Morgan was certainly not a Western hero, though all heroes do have common characteristics. Like his creator, he had been a professional boxer, and the background was quite convincing. In this, L'Amour anticipated by almost forty years the creation of more than one novel series about the adventures of former-boxer private eyes.

The Morgan stories, some of them reprinted in *The Hills of Homicide*

(1983), one of L'Amour's earlier pulp reprint collections, were not sports-mysteries either. They were just very good detective stories *made better* by borrowing some elements (including their hero) from sports fiction. They illustrate as well as any of his novels how much he could add to work in any genre through borrowing from another.

L'Amour's longest-running pulp series, with eighteen stories reprinted in *Bowdrie* (1983) and *Bowdrie's Law* (1984), was about Texas Ranger Chick Bowdrie. Real-life Western lawmen might occasionally be called upon to function as detectives, but in fictional life during the pulp era (c. 1920–1950) that occurred less frequently. It was rare for Bowdrie, who like most of the fictional sheriffs, marshals, and rangers, ordinarily engaged in a chase, a shoot-out, or both. But he did a spot of detective work more frequently than the rest of his fraternity of rangers, making his reprinted adventures more readable today (and probably when they first appeared) than those of lawmen who never did. Certainly there was usually only one suspect who made any sense in those few Bowdrie stories where the villain was not clearly identified from the first.

The Bowdrie story with the most mystery elements was "Case Closed—No Prisoners," which concerned the robbery of a small-town bank and murder of the banker. His dying words included the name of one of the robbers, something noticed only by the readers. Bowdrie solved the mystery using other clues, mostly the later acts of guilty men trying to cover up what they had done, just as many straight fictional mysteries are solved. He also paraphrased a Sherlock Holmes truism about the more complicated mysteries being the easiest to solve. On finishing the story, the reader felt the same smug self-satisfaction as the Ellery Queen reader who caught the significance of a "dying message" at the earliest possible moment.

Yet, like all of L'Amour's pulp work, this story stops short of a true hybrid. It is not a Western-mystery.

A couple of his nonseries Western shorts with almost as much material borrowed from the mystery genre are "Four Card Draw" and "Lit a Shuck for Texas." Both are reprinted in *Riding for the Brand* (1986). The former story has a more conventional "dying message" than "Case Closed—No Prisoners."

L'Amour's only true Western-mystery was the novel *The Broken Gun* (1966), one of his most underrated books. The hero is a contemporary writer, specializing in Western history, thus making the book a modern Western, as most Western-mysteries are. The mystery is the disappearance of Texan trail drivers and their herd, seventy years earlier, in New Mexico. The author-hero is drawn into it by his discovery of yet another "dying message." His investigation prompts attempts by the descendants of the original villains to kill him. He survives and brings these modern criminals to justice for having continued their traditional family route to riches, calling upon typical Western skills from his own upbringing, plus advanced military training and experience, and mountain climbing techniques to do so. He is aided by one of the most unusual Indian sidekicks in any Western, and a young woman who is considerably more than the traditional hand-wringing damsel in distress. This is a fine mystery and a fine Western all rolled into one.

Sports fiction was another pulp field natural for L'Amour to work in. Readers of his novels are aware that a boxing background for the hero played an important role in the climactic fight scene in both *The Man from Skibbereen* (1973) and *The Iron Marshall*—(1979). *Lando* has those same qualities and more! Orlando Sackett also owns a racing mule whose success provides another important climax. But even that novel stops short of being a sports-Western.

However, *Lando's* boxing climax is an interestingly rewritten version of the one in the short story "Barney Takes a Hand," reprinted in *Riding for the Brand.* Barney is both a former boxer and an ex-convict. He agrees to save a young widow's ranch after discovering her original defender about to die. He can only do it by returning to the ring. There he wins a purse that prevents foreclosure, and the widow's heart. The sports-Western is a very small hybrid genre; this is L'Amour's only story in it, and it is quite possibly the only one by any writer.

When L'Amour wrote in other genres, the stuff of the Western was likely to appear in those stories and novels. The early historical novel *Sitka* (1957) has a primarily Western setting, yet only the needs of paperback marketing gave it the "Western" label. Many of the best scenes occur at sea. Yes, there is an almost conventional "walkdown" between the hero and a (rather minor, hired killer) villain, but the fight occurs in the exotic capital of imperial Russia.

Such later historical novels as *Sackett's Land* (1974) and *The Walking Drum* (1984) feature borrowings, sometimes liberal ones, from other genres, including, but not restricted to, the Western. Those two books have the pacing of adventure novels—a form which L'Amour finally turned to in *The Last of the Breed* (1986), which is also similarly enhanced with Western story materials. Rafael Sabatini's work of a half a century earlier and the more recent Flashman series are the only well-known historical novels with comparable sustained levels of action as these two adventures.

Both books are also spiced with a hint of the supernatural taken from the fantasy genre. In *The Walking Drum,* there is a single paragraph on premonition. In the Sackett novel, Barnabas Sackett has vague bad feelings, sometimes connected with following bad events. These may be examples of his second sight, so prominent in the sequel, *To the Far Blue Mountains* (1976), a Western with many supernatural elements. Several times the narrator is simply expressing emotion with poetic emphasis that has a supernatural ring to it. We cannot count his feeling upon reaching the American shore that this land is the place of destiny for himself and his descendants as prescience, no matter how much the rest of the Sackett series makes the feeling a true one, since most immigrants to any place have likely felt the same thing.

*To the Far Blue Mountains* establishes Barnabas's second sight as hereditary, the staple science-fictional explanation for "wild talents." Furthermore, it and that of his wife's maid are relentlessly accurate. The Bermuda Triangle and a Phantom Island that may be interdimensional or intertemporal "true visions" both appear near the end of the novel. There is even a suggestion of racial memory.

Barnabas's son, in *Jubal Sackett* (1985), has recurrent nightmares of a woolly mammoth and hears frequent reports of isolated survivors of the beast in post-Columbian America. His encounter with one provides the book's major climax. His inherited second sight is mentioned or shown in action at least four times exclusive of the elephant. His Indian sidekick guides him to a "ghost cave" where mummified corpses are still able to communicate after a fashion. Thematically related to that, and, from the angle of genre mixing, this book's most interesting feature, is the report of spirit mediums in New England. This account comes two centuries before the Fox sisters began the historical fad, and it is both a dark fantasy and science fiction element, the latter because of its anachronistic forward shift.

So two of the three chronological foundation volumes of the Sackett series are brightened by the furnishings of science fiction. Two of his nonseries books that featured even more are his only other genre hybrids, science fiction–Westerns.

The better of the pair is *The Californios* (1974). Set mostly along Southern California shores, it is far removed from the cattle drives, cavalry outposts, mines, and Plains Indians of conventional Westerns. Its time setting is also atypical, before the gold rush: a recurrent irony is characters scoffing at the notion of gold discoveries in California. The hero is a sea captain, and seafaring men, even displaced to land, are rarely prominent in Westerns except those by L'Amour.

Conventional Western elements are many, including the hero's goal of saving the ranch, a prominent gang of bad men, and the importance of gold. A cache of just enough gold to save the family ranch had appeared just in time a generation before the beginning of the book; this is recalled three times, beginning in chapter one. The mystery of the route to the gold is foreshadowing for the opening of a passage to a parallel world near the book's end.

A "White Indian," a frequent fantastic character of pulp Westerns, is an important and consistently mysterious character in the novel. This "Old One," who is well over one hundred years old, is a mystical adept, able to "know" by unconventional means and reputed to "call up spirits." The outlaw gang meets a series of disasters that seem part induced hallucination (another science fiction element), part the work of those spirits.

The hero's Irish ancestry brings two brief suggestions his family may be fey. The old/lonesome gods of *The Lonesome Gods* (1983) are first mentioned, three times, in *The Californios*. Gold from "the other side" is provided at book's end to save the ranch again. Finally, one villain who has disappeared to "the other side" reappears, having aged fifty years in a few weeks. This proves the earlier contention, "Time is different there."

L'Amour's worst book was a sort of sequel, *The Haunted Mesa* (1987). The situation (the existence of parallel worlds and of passageways linking them with our own) but not the characters continues from *The Californios*. The book shares characteristics with his other "hyphenated" novel, *The Broken Gun*, also. The time is contemporary, the hero an author.

This hero's specialty is debunking the supernatural. It is for that reason a friend thought of him upon discovering an interdimensional door at his remote homesite. The friend's plea for help is substantiated by his diary or "daybook," and its delivery by a beautiful girl from "the other side." The diary documents the door in too much convincing detail, and extensive quoting from it is one of the novel's major flaws. Except in very bad science fiction, large documentary blocks stopped being an acceptable story-telling device more than a century ago. In science fiction, the practice hardly survived the pulps.

This diary fills most of chapters three through six, with bits spilling over into one chapter on either side. L'Amour sought to sugarcoat the documentary pill with six switches between the diary and straight narration (infused with too little action). At first clever, his transitions soon become repetitious and predictable, leaving even the most sympathetic reader wishing he would get on with the story.

The hero is a problem (or two) himself. No less reluctant than you or I would be to pass through to a threatening "other side" where a militaristic dictatorship controls a typically 1930s-ish mix of antique and futuristic weapons, he is also reluctant to credit the existence of such a place. Both concerns are brought up over and over in an intermittent interior monologue that wears out both sides of both questions. Like the attempt with the diary to make the situation credible, this one attempting to do the same for the hero's misgivings is grossly overdone.

He finally does enter the alternate world on page 253 of the hardcover edition of the novel. After that, the story is a very well written "adventure" science fiction novelette or short novella. Unfortunately, that is not enough to redeem what has taken place before. With better editing and cut to paperback original length, *The Haunted Mesa* might have been a good read, though below average for L'Amour. As published it is a padded failure.

Even a rare L'Amour failure has many redeeming qualities. The modern Western lawman who is the hero's chief liaison with "authority" on "this side" is cut from the author's familiar hero cloth and pattern. Several "inexplicable disappearances" from our world are explained as cleverly and *interestingly* as few writers other than L'Amour could manage. There are interesting encounters with, and an explanation of, Bigfoot creatures.

Another version of Bigfoot is featured in *The Lonesome Gods.* The title gods in this essentially conventional Western are mostly symbolic, except for Tahquitz, who has a real presence and profound effect upon events. Until a rather prosaic but still emotionally charged explanation, Tahquitz spreads a supernatural flavor over the book. The reader is expertly manipulated to believe that this is a possible source for the "Bigfoot myth." Here, as in many other books, L'Amour mixed genres for a positive effect. He did this in small measure through much of his work, with the frequency and effectiveness increasing as he matured as an author.

Many very successful writers find genre writing a frustrating straitjacket. L'Amour was nearly unique in his ability to borrow this and that from any genre with a usually sure hand, and the result was a feast of delightful reading. The cost, for the most part nothing more serious than the mislabeling of some of his non-Western books as Westerns, was amazingly slight. That his reach occasionally exceeded his grasp, most notably in *The Haunted Mesa,* does not lessen the wonderment of such a reach.

Who would not gladly trade off reading one such novel for the chance to read a *Jubal Sackett* or a *Walking Drum*? And who would imagine a Western writer of such conventional (though outstanding) books as *Hondo* (1953) and the various adventures of Tell Sackett and his brothers and cousins producing three such entirely different works?

Who?

Anyone lucky enough to have discovered Louis L'Amour.

# The Novels of Louis L'Amour— The Eighties: An Annotated Checklist

DURING THE 1980s, Louis L'Amour's name appeared on fourteen novels. L'Amour was now established as a best-selling author and he had his greatest success during the final years of his life. The numbering of this checklist continues from the chronology of his seventies novels.

**77.** *The Warrior's Path*—published by Bantam Books in July 1980.

A Sackett novel. When Carrie Penny and Diana Macklin are kidnapped in seventeenth-century America, Kin and Yance Sackett go hunting for them on the famous Indian trail, the Warriors Path. The two Sacketts soon discover that the girls have been taken not by Indians but by renegade white men hoping to sell the girls into slavery. Another frontier novel, a historical adventure, not a Western.

**78.** *Lonely on the Mountain*—published by Bantam Books in November 1980.

Logan Sackett needs help driving a herd of cattle from Canada through the Dakotas. Tyrel, Tell, and Orrin Sackett, along with Cap Rountree, ride north to help him. They encounter the usual problems with Indians and outlaws, but the Sacketts manage to defeat all comers. A minor work.

**79.** *The Comstock Lode*—published in hardcover and trade paperbound format by Bantam Books in March 1981. Reprinted by Bantam Books in March 1982.

A long novel, released with much fanfare, the first in Bantam's trade paperbound line. Young Val Trevallion watches the murder of his parents and swears he will have his revenge against the killers. When he grows up, Val goes into mining and becomes quite successful. Events conspire to bring him up against the murderers of his relatives, who are now out to kill him as well.

**80.** *Milo Talon*—published by Bantam Books in August 1981.

A Talon novel. Milo Talon is hired by Jefferson Henry to find his missing granddaughter. However, Milo senses that there is a great deal left unsaid by Henry and investigates the case further. He discovers a web of treachery and deceit involving a lost will and a huge inheritance. One of L'Amour's more complicated plots with a broader cast of characters than usual. Told in first person through most of the book, it annoyingly breaks to third person late in the story to introduce a pair of unusual cutthroats.

**81.** *The Cherokee Trail*—published in hardcover and paperback by Bantam Books in August 1982.

Mary Brendon takes over a rundown stagecoach station on the Cherokee Trail after her husband is killed on the way there. Widowed, and without any other place to go, she has no choice but to make the station a success. With her young daughter and several friends, she succeeds, as well as ruining the schemes of Jason Flandrau, the man who killed her husband.

**82.** *The Shadow Riders*—published by Bantam Books in October 1982.

Two brothers, Dal and Mac Traven, fight on opposite sides during the Civil War. When the war ends, they ride home together, hoping to rebuild their ranch. They find that the place has been attacked by a band of Southern raiders hoping to continue the war. The Traven brothers, with some unexpected allies, hunt down the raiders who have kidnapped their sister and Dal's girlfriend. A book very much in the Sackett tradition, but without the Sacketts. This was filmed as *The Shadow Riders*.

**83.** *The Lonesome Gods*—published by Bantam Books in hardcover in April 1983. Reprinted by Bantam Books in January 1984.

Another very long, ambitious novel by L'Amour. A story of the California frontier before the Civil War. Johannes Verne, an orphan, is left to die in the desert by his cruel grandfather. He is rescued and raised by mysterious Indians. He grows into a strong young man who learns the truth about his life.

**84.** *Ride the River*—published in hardcover by Bantam Books in June 1983. Reprinted in paperback by Bantam Books in July 1983.

A Sackett novel. Another historical Sackett novel, set in the 1840s on the East Coast. When Echo Sackett, a young girl, learns that she has inherited some money, she leaves the hill country and travels to Philadelphia to claim it. However, once she has the money she finds herself the object of attention of a ruthless band of outlaws. She fights the crooks with the aid of several cousins and Dorain Chantry. An entertaining and somewhat different Sackett adventure.

**85.** *Son of a Wanted Man*—published by Bantam Books in May 1984.

Mike Bastian, the son of Ben Curry, was raised by his outlaw father to take command of his gang when his father was ready to retire. But Mike, in love with a beautiful young woman and faced with jealous members of his father's gang, isn't sure he wants to be an outlaw. This novel is a rewritten version of the pulp story "The Trail to Peach Meadow." The basic story remains unchanged, with the main difference being the addition of several scenes featuring Tyrel Sackett and Borden Chantry. On the whole, perhaps L'Amour's worst novel in paperback and one that should never have been published.

**86.** *The Walking Drum*—published by Bantam Books in hardcover in June 1984. Reprinted in paperback by Bantam Books in May 1985.

L'Amour's twelfth-century historical novel, the first of a projected trilogy. Mathurin Kerbouchard has numerous adventures in Europe and the Middle East. He avenges the murder of his mother and rescues his father held captive by the Old Man of the Mountain. This novel is discussed in depth in both an interview with L'Amour and an article by Judith Tarr further on in this section.

According to L'Amour this novel was actually written in 1970 but Bantam refused to publish it because readers only wanted Westerns from him.

**87.** *Jubal Sackett*—published in hardcover by Bantam Books in June 1985. Reprinted in paperback by Bantam Books in June 1986.

A Sackett novel. The last Sackett novel to be published, this is another historical novel about the early days of that family. Jubal Sackett is the son of Barnabas and Abigail Sackett, brother of Yance and Kin-Ring of *The Warrior's Path*. Born with a desire to explore, Jubal travels from the Carolinas all the way west to the Rocky Mountains in the early seventeenth century. At the end of his adventures, he encounters a beast out of legend. This novel is covered in greater detail in R. Jeff Banks's article, "The Mix Master."

**88.** *Passin' Through*—published by Bantam Books in October 1985.

Passin' Through, a man without a name, escapes a hanging for a killing committed in self-defense. Leaving the immediate area, he stumbles across a ranch run by a mysterious actress. Before long, Passin' finds himself investigating an attempted land grab involving a beautiful girl and a deadly outlaw.

**89.** *Last of the Breed*—published in hardcover by Bantam Books in July 1986. Reprinted in paperback by Bantam Books in July 1987.

A modern-day adventure. Joe Makatozi, the pilot of an experimental U.S. aircraft, is forced down in Russia and imprisoned in a labor camp in Siberia. He escapes and heads for the Bering Straits. Descended from American Indians, Joe uses all of his native skills to stay alive. Meanwhile, the Russians have sent Alekhin, a famous Yakut hunter and tracker, after Joe.

**90.** *The Haunted Mesa*—published in hardcover by Bantam Books in May 1987. Reprinted in paperback by Bantam Books in May 1988.

L'Amour's last novel, a science fiction and modern Western combination. Mike Ragland, an investigator into the supernatural, answers a plea for help from his friend Erik Hokart. On a lonely mesa in Utah, he discovers a doorway into another dimension. This novel is covered in greater detail in R. Jeff Banks's article, "The Mix Master." Reading very much like a 1930s science fiction pulp story, *The Haunted Mesa* became a number one hardcover best-seller, a tribute to L'Amour's popularity more than his skill as a fantasy writer.

# "Bantam Announces Plans for the Louis L'Amour Overland Express"

*Publishers Weekly,* May 9, 1980

HITTING the trail won't be a lonesome experience for Western author Louis L'Amour as he saddles up early next month to begin a three-week publicity tour of Midwestern and Southwestern cities. Bantam's popular author is celebrating a number of achievements: he joins the rank of the few privileged living American writers with one hundred million copies of his/her books in print; he may be the first living author to have all of his/her books in print at once (that means seventy-five for L'Amour); and he is marking twenty-five years with Bantam.

To start L'Amour and his books on the road to his second hundred million sales, Bantam has planned a junket that resembles promotional travels of country-Western stars more closely than of conventional book authors. L'Amour will ride out to greet the fans in a 1972 Luxury Custom Silver Eagle bus replete with master bedroom, sitting room, refrigerator, sofas, TV, stereo, and Beta Max rented from Stagecoach VIP, a Nashville-based firm that supplies such vehicles to country and rock music bands for concert tours.

L'Amour's bus will have a stagecoach design and banners on its sides proclaiming it "The Louis L'Amour Overland Express." Scheduled for visits after a stop at the ABA in Chicago on June 8 and 9, are the Quad Cities (Moline, East Moline, and Rock Island in Illinois, and Davenport, Iowa), as well as Des Moines, Omaha, Kansas City, Mo., Nashville, Little Rock, Tulsa, and Oklahoma City. According to Stuart Applebaum, Bantam's director of publicity and public relations, "These are cities where L'Amour has not had that much exposure as yet."

Plans are for L'Amour to be interviewed by local broadcast and media press in each of the cities and to have as many of these interviews as possible take place in The Overland Express.

In addition, the bus will make the rounds of wholesale agencies and bookstores (independents as well as chains) and variety accounts.

Two new titles will also contribute to L'Amour's progress toward a

246

second hundred million in sales. July will see publication of the fifteenth Sackett novel, *The Warrior's Path,* and an official commemoration title, *Yondering.* The latter, a collection of short fictional tales inspired by the author's extensive travels, will also be published in a collector's first edition of five thousand special hardbound copies ($9.95), available only through direct-response ads at the back of the two new books. Applebaum notes that L'Amour is not only Bantam's most popular author in bookstores—"with all his books going over one million copies in print within eighteen months of publication and enjoying less than a 10 percent return"—but is also the company's "most successful draw in direct-response ads."

# Louis L'Amour on *The Walking Drum*— An Interview

*(The following is part of a long interview with Louis L'Amour conducted by Lawrence Davidson, Richard Lupoff, and Richard Wolinsky for KIOU radio in San Francisco in 1986. In this portion of the interview L'Amour discussed his novel* The Walking Drum.*)*

**LAWRENCE DAVIDSON:** I would like to ask a couple of questions about the actual process of writing. Harold Keith [in his article about L'Amour in *The Roundup* magazine] suggested that you could sit down at a typewriter and blast away with no outline, no preparation—research but no preparation in the sense of preparing a specific story.

**LOUIS L'AMOUR:** That's exactly true.

**LD:** You don't have character lists or plans?

**LL:** No.

**LD:** That's just amazing. Just amazing.

**LL:** I saturate myself with the period of the time. I just saturate myself in it and then when I sit down at the typewriter, I put a couple of characters in a historical situation and let it happen to them. Sometimes, I'll spend a little time on the character. For example, in *Ride the River*, I wanted to do a story about a girl. All right, what's the problem? I had to figure out whatever the problem had to be. What she had to accomplish. In this case, she heard of a small inheritance she had down in Philadelphia and she had to go down and get it. The story takes place getting down there, getting the money, and returning safely with it.

In another case, I was doing *The Ferguson Rifle*. I wanted to present a story of the West seen through different eyes. So my protagonist in that case was a university professor. Kind of a rebel. Well, not really a rebel but a guy that's not strictly in line with the rest of the world. He lectured at the Sorbonne and he'd been at Heidelberg and places like that. He's living back in the eastern states. His wife is killed in a fire. Fires were very frequent in those days. Frame houses and everything. He wants to get

**248**

away from everything he knows. Just wants to leave everything that reminds him of her behind him, you know. Since he's been so upset with the whole thing. So he goes West and becomes a mountain man briefly. I did this because I wanted to put a man with his intellectual capacity and with his knowledge of things out there. I wanted to have him observe what was happening in the West and not just have the run-of-the-mill Western type character.

**LD:** Now, is this the way you did *The Walking Drum?* I find this such a huge story with such a large cast, a variety of characters and settings and things going on. How do you keep that all straight?

**LL:** No problem. That was a picaresque novel. A picaro in the old version of the term was a wandering rogue, a wandering rascal. Well, he's not really a rascal, he's on the verge a little bit. He's as they used to say, anything to get the food. He'll work with what he has to. The European type of hero was the swashbuckler, as he is. The Asiatic type of hero was the conniver or the shrewd man. He's partly that too. I did this right off the cuff. I saturated myself in the period, of course. I had been doing that for more years than I care to mention. I traveled and wandered around the nation. Anyway, I just took this character and put him in the situation of what was happening and let it happen again.

**LD:** It never lets up. I haven't finished reading the book yet. Don't tell me how it comes out.

**LL:** I won't. I'm following it up with two others. One where he goes on to India and one where he goes to China.

**RICHARD LUPOFF:** Why the sudden switch from Westerns? Is there any reason other than a break?

**LL:** I haven't switched. I'm still going to write a lot of them. In fact, I have another one coming out soon. I'll have a big one out early next year. This is just a challenge and change of pace. Something I wanted to do. We live by challenges, we grow by challenges. If you always stay in the same level, you're never going to get anywhere you know. I feel that as a writer, I'm at about my halfway point. I'm continually improving. And now I can improve faster because I know more what I have to do.

**LD:** I find your protagonist in *The Walking Drum* most intriguing because his prime motivation is not wealth, power, women, the usual. He is a seeker for knowledge. Wherever he goes, he studies. He looks for the town scholar, the town library, which I love. You have some amazing information in there about medieval libraries I didn't realize existed.

**LL:** Well, I have a lot of information. There are some other fascinating things I didn't get into the book. I will probably touch on them in the second book if I didn't yet. But in the Arab world at that time, they had no copyright laws, and also, they had no printing presses at first. They copied books. A writer of a book had to have a fantastic memory because he would sit down with men, I've forgotten the exact word for them, but they were a special class of person who were copiers, who copied books. They were like a witness in a courtroom. They didn't have to take an oath on the Koran, but it was practically so. They were regarded as sworn copiers. They would sit down and this man would dictate the book to them and they would copy it down word for word. In the Islamic world at this time, they did not trust the written word. They had everything by oral means before. That book had to be letter perfect and if there were any copies, they could not deviate in the slightest degree or it had no value. Some of these men, this is hard to believe, but there is a lot of evidence to prove it, some of these men had literally hundreds of books in their minds. They could recite on a moment's notice.

**LD:** Memorized books.

**LL:** Yes.

**LD:** In the fashion Ray Bradbury used in *Fahrenheit 451.* He restores that in the future.

**LL:** It was a Danish scholar who wrote a book that's been translated recently. I've forgotten the translator and I've even forgotten the scholar's name. It was a very famous Danish scholar who wrote a book called *The Arab Book.* He goes into the subject at quite some length about how it was done.

**RL:** Were there actually tunnels all under Europe as you've described?

**LL:** Now there you touch on a very interesting question. I'm going to France soon. I'm hoping there are some repercussions on that story. Because I have every reason to believe that tunnel existed and probably still exists. When I was over there, times were very hard in France. The war was still going on. Food was very hard to find. There was a Frenchman who'd been very cooperative and helpful, so from time to time I used to give him a bucket of pineapple or something you know. Some surplus we had in the mess and he was very behooved to me. One day he told me a story that led to this. I was always interested in tunnels and secret passages and that sort of thing. Always had been. Right close to us there was a castle where the secret passage was known and tourists could go through it even. We were talking about the passage and he said, "You know, I've never told this to anybody, but when I was a very small boy I heard my father and my grandfather talking about it. It seems that my great-grandfather was awakened one night in the middle of the night by the village priest and told to get his shovel and to come and be very quiet. To bring the lantern but not to light it. When he got to the chapel, which was built in 550 A.D., there were already four or five men there with shovels and lanterns waiting. They lit their lanterns and took them into the chapel. A great big slab had fallen into the floor of the chapel, into this tunnel. They were going to have to repair that, shore it up underneath before the mass the next morning. So they worked on it and during the course of time, this story emerged that the monks had built this tunnel years ago so they could travel without being afraid of the robber barons. Incidentally, the monks did their own raiding at times, too. They were a war-like bunch in this town.

**LD:** Thank you very much. I wish we had more time.

# Striding to Byzantium:
# Louis L'Amour's *The Walking Drum*

*by Judith Tarr*

"ONE OF THE best means of introduction to any history," writes Louis L'Amour in his Author's Note to *The Walking Drum* (New York, 1984, p. 462—references throughout will be to this Bantam paperback edition), "is the historical novel." This note, like the novel that precedes it, shows evidence of broad and painstaking research as well as a genuine fascination with the Middle Ages. L'Amour himself, of course, is best known as a writer of Westerns; the American West, in the nineteenth century, is "his" period, and the major body of his work, in both quantity and quality, resides there. *The Walking Drum,* first of a projected trilogy (L'Amour died before further volumes could be published), represents a change of place, period, and genre—from Western to medieval historical.

The picaresque tale of the warrior-scholar Kerbouchard operates on several levels. First and most obviously, it is a story, an entertainment. The young Kerbouchard sees his home destroyed and his mother murdered; escapes only to fall into slavery; escapes again into Moorish Spain; returns educated and wealthy to avenge his mother's death, and sets forth on a quest to find his lost father; finds Kerbouchard the elder at last, enslaved in the fortress of Alamut; frees him, says farewell, and sets off into the distant East to find his destined bride. The pace is swift, the plotting repetitive (each of Kerbouchard's adventures is connected with a woman and spiced with the malice of an enemy), the prose workmanlike and suitably transparent to the progression of the story, except when L'Amour interrupts the action to insert a passage of exposition, or Kerbouchard pauses for a peroration upon the meaning of his existence. For Kerbouchard is a scholar, and as a scholar, he stops on occasion to analyze, to comment, or to proclaim a manifesto, such as that on love (pp. 180f.). These interruptions, however, are easily and quickly passed over in reading purely for story. Kerbouchard's tale is amply entertaining, full of danger and adventure, exotic sounds and sights, beautiful women, malevolent enemies, and a hero cast in the heroic mold, but with a touch of the contemplative.

From the point of view of the medieval scholar, the book is less successful. L'Amour's research is broad, to be sure. It is not, unfortunately, deep, nor is it excessively reliable. One error is particularly important to the book. Alamut is properly placed, and while its fabled garden probably did not exist, L'Amour portrays it as well-hidden and all but inaccessible—a fair enough use of novelist's license. The Old Man of the Mountain, however, was neither the Master of the Assassins nor the lord of Alamut. Sinan Rashid al-Din was a subordinate and somewhat of a maverick in the Ismaili sect of the Assassins, and he ruled in Masyaf in Syria, some hundreds of miles from Alamut.

Other errors are less obvious. Some, like the mention of "the writings of Constantine Porphyrogentus [*sic*] who traveled [to Kiev] in the ninth century" (p. 300), seem to result from a confusion of references: Constantine Porphyrogenitus (i.e., "Born in the Purple Chamber") was Emperor of Byzantium in the tenth (not ninth) century, and certainly did not travel to Kiev, although a princess of that city is said to have traveled to Byzantium for Christian baptism. Others seem to be based on popular assumptions, such as L'Amour's arming of Moors with scimitars. In fact the scimitar did not come into use in the Muslim world until after the Mongol invasions some fifty years later than the date of L'Amour's novel. The warriors of Islam, like the Franks, wielded a straight sword. In a Western, L'Amour would have committed a similar error in arming his cowboys with tommy guns.

That L'Amour was not fully comfortable with the period or the genre, however perceptible his love of both, shows not only in the failure of details but in the way these details are incorporated into the narrative. The story pauses every few pages, sometimes every few paragraphs, for the insertion of an expository lump: a bit of history or biography, a disquisition on the (highly simplistic and sometimes misinterpreted) contrast between the barbarian West and the civilized lands of Islam, a list of books and authors that Kerbouchard has read in his quest for knowledge as well as revenge—an advertisement, in short, of research done and facts recorded. Sometimes the information is useful, even entertaining. Sometimes, as when the text veers from the caravan in Spain to a description of the fairs in France (pp. 200f.), the result is confusion; are we in France, are we still in Spain, what is the relevance of this information to this particular point? Occasionally the information is startling to a scholar of the period: for example, L'Amour's apparent belief that women in Moorish Spain, and by implication in Islam in general, lived under no restrictions

(p. 153), and that French women by contrast were no more than chattels. L'Amour seems to have been unaware of the principle and purpose of the harem, or of the Muslim view of Frankish women as distressingly free and alarmingly immodest.

Kerbouchard himself reveals a range of knowledge that would not have been possible in the year A.D. 1176. He speaks of the pharaohs of Egypt (p. 196) and of a papyrus of the Egyptian priest Imhotep (p. 185) at a time when the lore of Egypt was all but lost and the hieroglyphic writing completely forgotten. The Pyramids in fact were thought to have been the work of jinn or giants, not of the pharaohs. He refers to "some laws of physics" (p. 150) or to "experimental science" (p. 256) before either concept was known or named. Frequently he cites specific dates, anno Domini, for the historical event or personage to whom he is referring. In fact the medieval sense of time was less precise than our own, and exact dates much less likely to be known even by a scholar. That Kerbouchard is not a man of his time but a mouthpiece for the author comes clearest in such history-book declarations as, "It was a time when all knowledge lay open to him who would seek it" (p. 85), or "Perhaps no period in history had so many writers enamored of historical writing" (p. 375), or "Mine was the day of the adventurer" (p. 372)—followed in the last example by a mention of the Norman Conquest as "only a few years before," as if L'Amour had forgotten the actual, considerable interval between 1066 and 1176.

Kerbouchard stands out of time, an alien not only as a Breton pagan in Christian Europe and Muslim Asia (itself somewhat improbable), but as the possessor of distinctly modern views and information in a distinctly nonmodern setting. L'Amour does not portray the world and its people as they truly were, in a universe constricted by the loss of classical learning and the absence of any solid conception of the scientific method. Rather, he places contemporary characters in a carefully constructed stage setting, supplies them with a modern researcher's arsenal of information, and tells his story with frequent pauses to relay that information.

This is neither good historical fiction nor good scholarship: nor, as riddled with lumps of exposition as it is, is it remarkably good writing. And yet, the medievalist can read on yet another level and find *The Walking Drum* profoundly medieval in its sensibility. Read as a medieval romance, as a hero tale, as a *chanson de geste*, L'Amour's novel works amazingly well. Kerbouchard is the hero, the knight-errant, wandering the world in search of revenge, rescuing fair ladies, defeating wicked foes, and achieving hairbreadth escapes from seemingly impossible predicaments. He is a master swordsman, a master horseman, a master scholar, a master physician, a master of everything he does or claims to do; an inheritor of the secret knowledge of the ancient Druids, a friend and associate of scholars and princes, and of course a magnet for the ladies. His characterization is thin, given over to heroic wish fulfillment and claims to skin-deep scholarship; characterization in the manner of the romances, in which the merely human is laid aside for the depiction of the ideal. He is, in short, a very perfect gentle—if not medieval—knight.

The contrast between extreme precision in dates and places and such apparent chronological errors as the presence of Visigoths in Spain in the late 1100s, the reference to Gauls rather than Franks (as if Rome had never fallen), the misplacement of Constantine Porphyrogenitus by a century, creates a very medieval sense of time out of time, of all times as one and all periods as essentially the present. The progression of the plot, linear (if occasionally convoluted) in space and time but cyclic in its repetition of events, is much like the medieval pattern of narrative. Kerbouchard's first adventure with the wicked Tournemine comes round to its conclusion at the end of Part I, with Tournemine's death and Kerbouchard's revenge for the death of his mother. On a smaller scale, the adventure of Aziza and her promised husband not only returns later to haunt Kerbouchard but is reflected almost immediately in the adventure of Sharasa and her own jealous would-be lover, then later, again, in the adventure of Sundari which is still in progress at the novel's end. Like the medieval romance, of which Malory's *Morte D'Arthur* is perhaps the greatest and most comprehensive example, *The Walking Drum* sends its perfect knight upon his errantries, provides him with beautiful ladies and worthy adversaries, and continues even beyond the actual end of the book. The conclusion leaves the reader with the impression of a quest continued, a story carried on through yet another cycle of romance and adventure.

Kerbouchard's quest is not for the Grail but for knowledge, and in that he is primarily a man of our own century: but there are those who believe that the Grail itself was not a cup or a bowl, but an idea, and that idea was the comprehension of divinity. Kerbouchard has a more earthly ambition, in keeping with the tradition of the modern novel: to see and to know and to learn all that this world holds. Yet his credo, in the end, is the knight's credo. As he himself puts it (p. 415): "I have only a sword, but a strong man need wish for no more than this: a sword in the hand, a horse between his knees, and the woman he loves at the battle's end." A declaration very much in the vein of Roland or El Cid Campeador, or Sir Lancelot himself.

# The *Contemporary Authors* Interview

*(This interview with Louis L'Amour was conducted for* Contemporary Authors, *a hardcover library reference series containing biographical and bibliographical sketches of American writers, by Mary Scott Dye, over the telephone on November 2, 1987, approximately seven months before L'Amour's death from lung cancer on June 19, 1988. One of the last interviews granted by L'Amour, it covered a wide range of topics concerning both L'Amour's life and his work.)*

**CONTEMPORARY AUTHORS:** In 1983 you received both the Congressional Gold Medal for literary lifetime achievement and the Medal of Freedom, the nation's highest civilian award. You must have had a great feeling about that kind of recognition.

**LOUIS L'AMOUR:** It was marvelous, absolutely marvelous. The Congressional Gold Medal had been only given to one other writer in American history—Robert Frost—and no novelist had ever received it. It's a difficult award to get. I was also very pleased to receive the Medal of Freedom. I thought it was interesting that over half of the other recipients of the Medal of Freedom who were on the platform with me had read my books.

**CA:** Do you find it unfair that your writing is sometimes categorically overlooked by "serious" reviewers?

**LL:** It doesn't bother me in the least. It's their ignorance, not mine. I pay no attention to critics. The only people I pay attention to are the readers, the audience. In the first place most critics don't know what they're talking about. They don't even know how stories are written or how they're composed. And then most of their comments are made for themselves and a small coterie about them. A writer should go ahead and write his books and say what he has to say; if he paid attention to the critics, he'd soon be writing for them instead of for the audience.

**CA:** From the time you left home at fifteen, you were self-educated, primarily through extensive reading and through the practical experience you gained while traveling as a young man. Was this more beneficial than completing a formal education?

**LL:** It was for me and for what I was doing. I wouldn't recommend it for everybody. I doubt very much that many people have the discipline that it takes to educate themselves. There are too many distractions when you're not settled down to a formal education, where you go to a class-room every day. You have to choose your own times to study and to read. It requires a great deal of attention to what you're doing. Many times people wanted me to do something else—go to football games or baseball games or a movie—but I had to stay home and study.

**CA:** Who were some of your mentors?

**LL:** I had no mentors. Everything I've learned I've learned by myself. I studied many great writers, of course, such as Maxim Gorky, Guy de Maupassant, O. Henry, and Robert Louis Stevenson. Hopefully I've learned from them and the way they operated. I tried to.

**CA:** A book of poetry entitled *Smoke from This Altar* was your first published work. Was there a progression from poetry to short stories to novels?

**LL:** I wouldn't say a progression. I like writing poetry very much, but a person can starve to death writing poetry, and I had to make a living. I had nobody to take care of me. Poetry doesn't have a very big market in the world. However, I still like to write poetry and would like to write some more. But I wanted to tell stories so I moved into fiction. Some of the characters in my novels originated in short stories. I published several hundred short stories before I ever wrote a novel.

**CA:** According to previous interviews and articles, you didn't set out to be a writer of Westerns.

**LL:** When I began writing I wrote about the Far East; I wrote a number of adventure stories about Indonesia and China. I also wrote some sport stories, some detective stories, and some Western stories. It so happens that the Westerns caught on and there was a big demand for them. I grew up in the West, of course, and loved it, but I never really intended to write Westerns at all.

**CA:** Beginning in the 1950s with *Hondo,* you found your success in the field of paperback originals, a format that drew readers and authors from the newly defunct pulp magazines.

**LL:** That's not true. The same format is used for any novel. It has noth-ing to do with the pulp magazines. I got my short story apprenticeship writing for the pulp magazines, but the story you tell for any novel is the same whether you tell it for the pulps or anything else. There's no distinc-tion, though people make that mistake often. For me, there are only thirty-six plots—that's all there are, and that's all there ever will be. And 90 percent of *all* fiction is based on twelve or eighteen plots, whether it's written by William Shakespeare or anybody else. They are very simple, basic plots, of course, but nevertheless they're all the same. For example, my story *The Last of the Breed* has the same plot that Victor Hugo used for *Les Miserables.* It's about a pursuer and a pursued.

**CA:** The main theme of many of your novels seems to be that the strong in body and character will survive and the weak will not. Do you think this is an accurate formula for 1987?

**LL:** It's an accurate formula for any period of history since the beginning of time. The strong will survive and the weak will not. Now more weak are surviving because the strong are protecting them and making laws to help them. In many ways that is the kind, gentle, decent thing to do. But it is not really the best thing for our people, our race, our species on earth, because people are staying alive who really shouldn't be, and wouldn't be if it was left up to nature. But that, of course, isn't a nice way to look at it. We all try to protect the weak and help them. Today there are lawyers who go out and fight your battles. In my books people took care of themselves because they had to.

**CA:** Why do you prefer the term "frontier" to "Western" when describing your books?

**LL:** I use the term frontier because many of my stories do not apply to the West at all. For example, there's *Sackett's Land* and *The Far Blue Mountain* and *Fair Blows the Wind.* They all start in England in Shakespeare's time and come over to this country. If they're going to be called anything they should be called "Easterns." My stories are of the frontier wherever it happens to be. Right now we're facing a frontier in space, which is the greatest frontier of all and the endless frontier. There are frontiers in medicine, there are frontiers in chemistry, there are frontiers everywhere. Wherever there's a frontier, there's a possibility for one of my stories. I deal with man on the edge.

**CA:** You used the pseudonyms Tex Burns and Jim Mayo early in your writing career. Why?

**LL:** I had no connection with the name Tex Burns; it belonged to a publishing firm. Jim Mayo I did use. My publisher at the time said nobody would ever buy a Western story written by a guy named L'Amour, and I'd have to use a different name. I had written some short stories about the Far East and a character named Pongo Jim Mayo. Jim Mayo was the only name I could think of on the spur of the moment, so I used it. As soon as I began to acquire some kind of a following, I switched back to my own name. And I made them like it.

*CA:*  Your devotion to detail and authenticity are legendary trademarks. How much time do you spend researching the average book?

**LL:**  I do research as a continuing process. I never stop. Much of my research for the material about the American frontier was done while I was knocking around as a kid, working around the country. Also I've studied a great deal, and continue to do so. I study plants and animals. I have a ranch in Colorado of something over a thousand acres, and I use it as a working laboratory. Due to the formation of the land there, it has several microclimates where different kinds of plants grow, so I get a chance to study them at every stage. When I tell about a plant in my story, even if I only mention it in passing, I describe it as it grows on my land. I try to be extremely authentic, not only about such things as plants but historically also. When I write about a journey across the country in the 1600s, I've checked every possible source to see what that terrain was like at that crossing. I make a diagram and write down my point of origin and my point of destination. In between I read memoirs; I check old travel books and old army record books describing the army marching over the area. If they passed through a swamp, I put it on the map; if they stopped at an inn and they called the bartender by name I put it on the map. Maybe only one-tenth of this is used in the story, but that trip is so authentic that a man of the 1600s could follow it and be perfectly at home. It's something I enjoy doing.

*CA:*  Did you have to do an inordinate amount of preparation for *The Walking Drum*?

**LL:**  Originally my intention was to write that sort of story. As I said earlier, I didn't intend to write about the West. I had traveled in the Far East a good deal and had read a lot about it. So writing *The Walking Drum* was comparatively easy because I was ready for it. I'm researching the sequel now. I've checked the medical practices of the time, the ways inns were kept, everything. There will be two more books in the series. In the next one I'm taking Kerbouchard through Central Asia, then into India; and the third book will take him on to China—all in the twelfth century.

*CA:*  You've been writing books at the rate of approximately three per year for the last thirty-four years. With well over one hundred books published, will you allow yourself to slow down?

**LL:**  Of course not. A book will be published later this year or early next year called *The Sackett Companion*. It will offer brief résumés of the

Sackett books and will also contain some additional historical material. I've done an enormous amount of research for that. My readers have been asking for a genealogy of the Sackett family beginning with the revolutionary war, so I've been putting that together. I'd worked with genealogy before; my family started in the 1600s and I'd researched that. Whether I complete it or not, I have started the biggest literary project that anybody ever attempted. Balzac's *Human Comedy* is the closest thing to it. I have started out to try and tell the story of the opening of the United States and Canada as seen through the eyes of three families: the Sacketts, the Chantrys, and the Talons. When it's finished, this project will comprise at least fifty books. About half of them are done now. And in putting together this genealogy, I have stumbled on dozens of stories I want to write. I had thirty-four stories planned originally; now I'd be afraid to tell you how many.

*CA:* Is your first draft of a book usually the finished form?

**LL:** Yes, it is. I do a lot of thinking beforehand about what country a book will cover and about the background and that sort of thing, so when I start to write it goes pretty fast. I never know how it will turn out. Sometimes stories have been years developing. For example, I first got the idea for *The Last of the Breed* when I was nineteen years old. The same is true of *The Haunted Mesa,* my latest story. My ideas come from various things. In the case of *The Haunted Mesa* I heard an old cowboy tell some really strange stories about an area that I was going through, and that started me researching it. But it wasn't until just a couple of years ago that I wrote the book.

*CA:* In *The Haunted Mesa* you combined two very different genres, the Western and the supernatural. . . .

**LL:** The word *genre* is used all the time now, I know, but I don't like it. Writing is writing and a story is a story regardless of what it is. I see no difference in a story of the West and a story of New York City today; they're all stories of people. If you were talking strictly about genre, the best of Edgar Allan Poe and the best of Dostoyevski would have to go in the detective story genre, because *Crime and Punishment* is certainly a crime story. Genre is a bad way of classifying.

*CA:* You must not have time for much else other than writing.

**LL:** I write, read, spend time with my family, and do very little else. I don't have much time for myself. I recently went to Paris, where I appeared at an exhibit of Western paintings at the Grand Palais. I went at the request of the National Cowboy Hall of Fame. That's the first time the

Parisians had really seen an exhibit of Western paintings. They were quite impressed.

*CA:* Is there one book of yours that is most popular with your readers?

**LL:** No, all my books are equally popular. I don't have a book that's sold fewer than a million copies, and most of them have sold well over that. You have to be very accurate in writing, because when you sell to that many people, somebody out there knows everything you're writing about, and there are specialists in every area. A long time ago, when I was a small boy, I grew up hearing Indian stories. My great-grandfather was scalped by Indians, my grandfather fought Indians. I knew the stories very well and I knew a great deal about Indians. I came out of the movies one night with my father and I heard a man say to his wife, "That's how it was." And it wasn't at all—the movie was entirely false. I thought that nobody had the right to mislead people that way. From that time on I knew that when I wrote I was going to be authentic. The American frontier has never been properly written about. There's too much stress on the cowboys-and-Indians type of thing, the buckskins, the Daniel Boone types, when so much else was happening. Some of the weirdest stories of the world happened out there—including thousands of ghost stories. The Indian was never properly presented. He was both better and worse than the way he's been depicted. He wasn't a nice, kindly individual, he was a savage. Yet he had a spiritual life that was unique and exciting.

*CA:* Has your readership changed over the years?

**LL:** No, but it has grown. About half my readers are women. A lot of people don't realize that. At least sixty percent of my letters are from women.

*CA:* That certainly should discredit the criticism that your novels are sexist, which one sometimes hears.

**LL:** How could they be sexist? Whoever said that has never read my books. My women are strong, interesting people. For example, read *The Cherokee Trail*, which is about a woman on a stage station, or *Ride the River*. There's no sexism in my stories at all. I like women. I admire them as people. I just got through writing a letter to a young lady, a teacher who wrote to me about something in one of my books, and I was commenting that I can't understand why the feminists don't object to the fact that in every horror movie or crime movie you see, some woman's screaming her bloody head off. That isn't true; women don't do that. I've been around them under stressful circumstances and they don't scream. They're just as solid as any man would be. There's an old saying in the West: The cowards didn't start and the weak didn't make it. That was true for the women as it was for the men. Many times a woman lost her husband in the move West, and she took on the work herself and filed the land claim herself. No, I'm not the least bit sexist—very much to the contrary. I'm a great admirer of women. I've made love to lots of them and enjoyed it very much. I think they're exciting, wonderful, interesting people.

*CA:* In an introduction to the thirtieth-anniversary hardcover edition of *Hondo,* you suggest that the American West is for our society the equivalent of the Homeric Bronze Age. Do you find any problems in putting the two together? Do they mesh easily?

**LL:** Oh, of course, they mesh perfectly. Not only Homer's period, but also the Elizabethan period in England. You could take Jim Bowie or Wild Bill Hickok or Buffalo Bill or any famous character you know about in the West and put him in the streets of Troy, and he'd be perfectly at home. You could take Achilles or Ajax and put them on the deck of one of Sir Francis Drake's ships and they'd be perfectly at home. The men of those periods thought very much alike. They were dynamic periods, periods when much was being done, when a lot of fighting was going on, and men were moving out in the world and doing things, so the characters are very similar.

*CA:* I've read that you have a massive personal library, over ten thousand books.

**LL:** Yes and they're very carefully selected. These aren't just books. I have about twenty Chinese classic novels, about as many from India, and some Arab stories. That's about the only fiction I have, except for a few of the classics which I continue to return to. Most of my stuff is history, or books related to history.

*CA:* Your books obviously have a large impact on the writing that you do.

**LL:** Very definitely. I've always been an enormous reader. I started reading nonfiction when I was twelve and I've been reading it ever since. I'm very much involved in everything that's going on today. I'm interested in politics and foreign affairs and the space movement. I've made several speeches to the National Commission on Space and I expect to be doing more in that direction. I'm interested in the possible voyage to Mars and the settlement up there. My reading goes off in all directions. Only about 20 percent of my library is concerned with the West. The rest of it is concerned with history and other places and other times. I have seven shelves on Tibet and China alone. I have a great deal on medical history, and on the development of the railroad and the speedboat and that sort of thing.

*CA:* In an article published in a 1983 issue of *Publishers Weekly,* Richard Wheeler, another respected author of Westerns, was quoted as saying that Westerns were part of a dying breed. How do you manage to stay so popular and keep your material fresh?

**LL:** There's no problem with it at all. There's a lot of Western material out there that's very fresh. And the Western novel is not dying, it's doing very well. It's selling every place but in the movies. Moviemakers use demographics that are collected only in New York and Los Angeles, and they think that speaks for the whole country. Consequently they don't know what they're talking about. There seems to be some misconceptions about me and my type of writing which have been perpetuated by several articles that weren't written too well. To fully understand me, I think a person should come here and spend a few hours just walking through my library, looking at the books, getting an idea of the range of my thinking and the things which I'm involved in. Too often people start out with a clichéd idea of a Western writer. That automatically eliminates an awful lot of things that interest me. There's no difference in the Western novel and any other novel, as I said earlier. A Western starts with a beginning and it goes to an end. It's a story about people, and that's the important thing to always remember. Every story is about people—people against the canvas of their times.

# Louis L'Amour's Nonfiction Books

LOUIS L'AMOUR wrote three nonfiction books, all of which appeared in the 1980s. Each one of them shares a special place in the L'Amour canon. They are on three entirely different topics, but each book, in its own way, sheds a great deal of light on Louis L'Amour, the man and the writer.

The first of this trio is *Louis L'Amour's Frontier,* published as an oversize hardcover by Bantam Books in 1984. This stunning book features twenty-five essays written by L'Amour about the frontier, not only out West, but throughout the entire country. Accompanying the text are 140 full-color photographs that illustrate the land L'Amour describes. The photos are the work of acclaimed landscape photographer David Muench, and many are full-page or double-page spreads.

In *Frontier,* L'Amour has a chance to set down on paper his feelings for the land and the people who settled America without resorting to fiction. It is as close to an actual history book as he ever wrote. The book is filled with all the color of his novels without depending on created characters to forward the story. It is a book that no L'Amour fan should be without.

*The Sackett Companion* was published in 1988, several months after L'Amour's death. Subtitled *A Personal Guide to the Sackett Novels,* it is a book aimed not at the casual reader but at the hard-core L'Amour fan and collector. Unfortunately, the book is a disappointment for anyone reading it.

Most of the volume is taken up with long studies of each Sackett novel. Characters and places are described, and some background, but not much, is given. There is nothing new in any of these studies for people who have already read the books in question. And for those who have not, the details mean little.

There is a Sackett family tree and a genealogy, but it is incomplete and information is left out to be filled in by future Sackett novels. L'Amour makes passing reference to other books to be written, but gives precious few details about them.

The other feature of the book is a long glossary for the Sackett novels. This lists each character and person mentioned in all the books and tells which book he or she appeared in. Along with that information, all of the rifles and pistols mentioned in the books are indexed, as are the books, and various other items. These lists are basically nothing more than long strings of words. What does it matter if the Picts are mentioned in three different Sackett novels? Or that The Congress Hall Saloon is named in *The Lonely Men*? Or that *Pilgrim's Progress* is mentioned in *Galloway*?

Only those desiring a complete collection of L'Amour's works need to buy *The Sackett Companion*. It is filled with minutiae, but offers very little new and interesting for the longtime L'Amour reader.

The third and final nonfiction book written by L'Amour, appearing a little more than a year after his death, is *Education of a Wandering Man*. Wisely listed as "a memoir" by Louis L'Amour, the book is a rambling sort of autobiography of the author's early life. Much of the book is spent describing L'Amour's reading and how it shaped his future life and philosophy. As L'Amour himself put it at the end of the book, "What has been offered here is one man's quest for knowledge."

The volume is of some interest to the L'Amour fan as it does give details of L'Amour's life not published elsewhere. However, L'Amour rambles off on sidetracks too often. Too much of the book tells what books L'Amour read when, but does not go into his thoughts or opinions of the volumes. The book primarily covers L'Amour's early life and little is said about his war experiences or his life as a writer afterward. There is even a long list of what books L'Amour read in the 1930s.

*Education of a Wandering Man* is important to the L'Amour fan who is interested in L'Amour's early life and his opinions about books. To the millions of fans of his Western novels, it is a distinctly minor work.

Of L'Amour's three nonfiction volumes, only *Frontier* is a must buy for the collector. The other two are minor works of limited interest. Along with the recently reissued *Smoke from This Altar* (Bantam Books, 1990), they are aimed at those people who want everything ever written by L'Amour.

# Part 4:
# Audio and Video

There can be good Western movies but they have to
be *good* stories. There is no bandwagon. There
is no thing you can get on and ride to glory, you know.
Each one has to make it on its own.

Louis L'Amour, interviewed by Lawrence Davidson,
Richard Lupoff, and Richard Wolinsky, KIOU Radio, 1986

# Introduction

MOVIES PLAYED an important role in Louis L'Amour's career. *Hondo* provided the boost necessary to break him out of the pulps into the paperback field. More than a dozen films based on his novels appeared in the 1950s and 1960s. Though none of the movies were major blockbusters, they helped keep L'Amour's name in the public eye.

The astonishing growth in the spoken-word audiotape field owes a great deal to L'Amour's work. His short stories worked wonderfully well when adapted to tape, dramatized much like old radio shows. Tape adaptations of L'Amour's work constantly filled the best-seller lists of spoken audio tapes. His success boosted the entire industry.

This section of *The Louis L'Amour Companion* covers these two areas of Louis L'Amour's work. We lead off with a letter from L'Amour written in the 1940s discussing one of the more controversial Westerns ever made. As always, the piece demonstrates both L'Amour's wide range of knowledge of the times and his passion for authenticity.

Following the letter is a detailed article by Jim Hitt on adaptations of L'Amour's work from book into film. Next, L'Amour discusses his films in a wide-ranging interview with Lawrence Davidson, Richard Lupoff, and Richard Wolinsky. The last two pieces in the section are a comprehensive checklist of L'Amour's film and TV adaptations and a checklist of L'Amour audiotape adaptations.

# The Outlaw Rides Again

*by Louis L'Amour*

a letter to *Rob Wagner's Script,* August 17, 1946

IF HOWARD HUGHES intends to continue producing pictures like *The Outlaw,* his studio had better do something about research.

At any moment now I am expecting to walk into a theater to see Ulysses S. Grant attacking the Maginot Line, or Lydia Pinkham doing the Salome dance with the head of Senator Bilbo.

To anyone with the slightest knowledge of Western history, this most recent display of Western lore is painful, to say the least.

If I were a relative of either Pat Garrett or Doc Halliday I'd sure sue somebody.

Of course, the following points may seem unimportant:

> Pat Garrett did not kill Doc Halliday.
> Doc Halliday does not lie in Billy the Kid's grave.
> There is no evidence that Halliday ever knew either Billy the Kid or Pat Garrett.
> Pat Garrett was not the weak, frightened character he appeared in the movie.
> Nobody ever shot any holes in the Kid's ears and, as that proved a man a coward, the Kid would have shot his own mother rather than have it happen.

If Howard Hughes wants to do a Western, why not do one entirely fictional instead of taking the facts of known lives and distorting them out of all reason?

All credit to the cast. They did a good job with their material. From my seat, Jane Russell's mammary display was adequate. Jack Buetel looked youthful enough for Billy the Kid. Walter Huston, as always, turned in a fine performance, as did Thomas Mitchell.

If Hughes wanted to do the story of Billy the Kid, why did he not use the real story, which is packed with dramatic dynamite? If he needed a deadly gunman as the friendly antagonist of Billy, why not the man who was actually that?

I refer to Jesse Evans. Evans and the Kid stole horses together, fought Indians together, and gambled together. Evans was, by reputation, fully as dangerous with a gun as Billy. Then, in the Lincoln County war, they took opposite sides. Three times during the months that followed they met under tensely dramatic circumstances where the slightest wrong word would have ended in a shoot-out.

Why junk a valuable, interesting, exciting story to distort the facts? Doc Halliday, known as "the most cold-blooded killer in Tombstone," was the son of a fine old Southern family. He came from Georgia, and, for a brief time, was a dentist in Dallas. He met Wyatt Earp, thereafter his greatest friend, in West Texas. They were in Dodge together, later they rode together to Tombstone, and when they left Tombstone, they left together.

During his life he offered odds of eight to five that he would die with his boots on in a gun fight. He would have lost.

A lifelong sufferer from tuberculosis, he died in Cottonwood Springs, Colorado, and it struck him as so amusing that he should die in bed, his last words were, "This is funny!"

He was a pale man with ash blond hair. Intelligent, witty, and with a hot temper, under fire he was as cold as ice. He always stood (as many gunmen did) with his side toward an enemy when he fired. As he was unusually thin due to his illness, he made a small target. While he was an excellent shot with a pistol, he usually used a sawed-off double-barreled shotgun. In other words, when he shot, he shot for keeps!

Pat Garrett, instead of being the weak, sloppy character offered by the movie, was a successful rancher and famous peace officer. He was six feet four inches tall, very fast with a gun, and he killed Billy in Fort Sumner; shot him in Pete Maxwell's bedroom there. Several years ago I was shown Billy's grave by an old Indian woman. At that time the grave was abandoned, known to few, and unmarked.

In the past few years I've written a number of Western stories, and in the past five months, have sold six Western shorts and two full length novels of the West, aside from a few other things, and have been a student of Western history since I was a youngster. The trouble with pictures of this kind is that thousands upon thousands of people know no better.

It is never a good thing to underestimate one's audience, and Hughes is guilty of that. The facts of this story are known to most of the population of New Mexico, Arizona and Texas. Accounts of the doings of the Kid and of Doc Halliday have been written in many Western magazines, and biographies of the Kid are on the market at present.

Aside from the fact that it reflects on the historical integrity of all films and is therefore distinctly harmful, it is absolutely useless and serves no artistic purpose.

A great deal has been written about the lengths to which a producer will go to make a picture authentic; certainly, this was a bad slip-up. The ear-shooting episode was impossible from the standpoint of Billy's character. The scene where he makes his bed in the moonlight was absurd. Too many men wanted to kill Billy for him ever to do that. The final wrong touch was Billy's taking the girl up behind him when Halliday's horse was available. No man in his right mind ever started off on a long ride in Apache country with a horse carrying double.

But of all this composite of mistakes, the worst was dragging Doc Halliday into the story at all. He had no place there, wasn't needed, and as I've said, didn't die that way.

Dramatic necessity may sometimes demand the distortion of minor details. There was no such necessity here. The picture could have been done much better and remained historically accurate and authentic as to character.

# From Fiction into Film

*by Jim Hitt*

from *American West from Fiction (1823–1976)*

*into Film (1909–1976),* 1990

LOUIS L'AMOUR was a prolific writer, and it is only natural that many of his formulary Western novels and short stories have been adapted for the films. The most important has remained his first, *Hondo.*

The Apache was treated with respect in L'Amour's *Hondo* (1953). The author himself in a 1982 introduction to a reprint of the novel wrote of the Apache:

> He was no poor, pathetic red man being put upon by whites, but a fierce warrior, a veteran of many battles, asking favors of no man. He did not fear the pony soldiers, but welcomed them, for they brought into his harsh land the horses, the food, the clothing, and the weapons he could take from them. Often he admired the men he killed, often he was contemptuous of their ignorance and lack of skills.

The Apache chief Vittoro keeps appearing and reappearing throughout the novel, and his presence, or lack thereof, often dominates and determines the actions of Hondo Lane and those around him. Vittoro is L'Amour's ideal Apache, an honorable man and a fierce warrior, a rebel of sorts, a defender of his homeland intent upon pushing the white man out. The treaty has been broken by the white man, and as Hondo points out, "There's no word in the Apache language for 'lie,' and they've been lied to."

Hondo Lane is part Indian himself and has lived among the Mescalero Apaches for five years, even taking an Apache wife, Destarte. When he is asked what her name means, Hondo gives an eloquent, poetic speech.

> It means like Crack of Dawn, the first bronze light that makes the buttes stand out against the gray desert. It means the first sound you hear of a brook curling over some rocks—some trout jumping and a

**273**

beaver crooning. It means the sound a stallion makes when he whistles at some mares just as the first puff of wind kicks up at daybreak. It means like you get up in the first light and you and her go out of the wickiup, where it smells smoky and private and just the two of you there, and you stand outside and smell the first bit of wind coming down from the high divide and promising the first snowfall.

Yet the Apaches are warriors, and their society can be cruel. When he is captured by Vittoro and his braves, Hondo is threatened with an excruciatingly slow death, and for a start, hot coals are poured over his hand. Only an old tintype that Vittoro recognizes saves Hondo's life.

The film *Hondo* (Warner Bros., 1953) retains most of the novel's plot and dialogue. The story opens in 1874 with Hondo (John Wayne) riding dispatch for the cavalry when he comes across Angie Lowe (Geraldine Page) and her son Johnny, abandoned on their small ranch. Equal time is then divided between the growing romance of Hondo and Angie and the constant incursions of the Apaches. Some incursions are benevolent, some not. More importantly, however, the novel's attitude toward the Indians is not only left intact but expounded upon. The entire sequence explaining Destarte's name is lifted straight from the book, and Hondo's admiration of the Apache extends far beyond his dead wife. After Vittoro's death and the defeat of the Apaches, Hondo says, "It means the end of a way of life. Too bad. It was a good life." His eulogy is the last words spoken in the film.

Two major scenes from the novel have been omitted. The first is the massacre of Company C by Vittoro and his warriors, which is the only section of the novel that shifts the action away from Hondo, and while it may illustrate the tactical skill of the Apache, it weakens the story. The film's exposition speeds things up by having Hondo mention finding the dead troopers and presenting the ragged guidon flag as evidence. A more important scene omitted is when Hondo and Johnny are threatened by four mountain Apaches not associated with Vittoro. Hondo is forced to kill one, and immediately thereafter Vittoro rides up. The mutual respect between these two men is never more evident than in this scene, and as Hondo and Johnny ride back to the ranch, the depth of their relationship is exposed when the young boy jumps into Hondo's arms and cries.

Although *The Burning Hills* (1956) by L'Amour uses Indians to resolve part of its plot, it is really a formula Western. When Trace Jordan's partner is killed, he goes looking for the men who did it and winds up killing Bob Sutton. Immediately, he is on the run from Sutton's relatives. Along the way, he meets Maria Cristina, who joins him. By clever tricks and ruses, Jordan avoids his pursuers, managing to kill many of them, and leads them into an ambush by Apaches. Eventually, Jordan captures the wounded Ben Hinderman, the leader of the pursuers, who realizes that Jordan has been in the right all along, and he calls off the vendetta, allowing Maria and Jordan to escape. It is all pretty standard stuff with much action and very little characterization. As with so many of L'Amour's women, Maria never comes alive, and her accent reads as phony as it sounds on the screen. The only interesting thing about her is that she is no starry-eyed heroine, but a woman who has lost one husband and who has been pawed by so many gringos that she is sick of the sight of men. However, L'Amour's strong point has always been his ability to tell a fast-paced, lean story without too much extraneous interferences like character and meaning. *The Burning Hills* fits the mold.

The movie *The Burning Hills* (Warner Bros., 1956) was scripted by Irving Wallace before he became a popular novelist, and it sticks fairly closely to the novel. At first, it is Trace Jordan (Tab Hunter) who seeks revenge on the men who killed his brother, but soon he becomes the hunted. After Trace shoots the head of the Sutton clan (Ray Teal), his son Wes (Skip Homeier) leads his men in pursuit of Jordan. Wounded, Trace is befriended by Maria (Natalie Wood), who nurses him back to health and then is forced to flee with him into the hills. Slowly Trace decimates the men after him, wounding and killing them one by one and finally leading the last dozen or so into an ambush by Comanches. Wes and one of his henchmen escape along with their guide. In the final confrontation on the cliffs high above the rushing river, Trace stands his ground and wins his victory. The guide, half Indian himself, says that he promised to lead Wes to Trace but that he had no part in the fighting and he rides off leaving the young lovers in a clinch.

*The Burning Hills* is an important Western in that it signaled a move toward youth in Westerns during the 1950s. In addition, Skip Homeier is a fine villain, chillingly cold, who backshoots his foreman without a second thought. The script helped to flesh out a thin plot, except that Maria became a virginal Mexican girl completely worthy of the blond hero's love. But the real problems lie with Tab Hunter, who gives his customary wood performance as the hero, and Natalie Wood, whose accent is so unbelievable as to defy description. Even though the film tried to copy the theme and style of *Hondo*, it lacked all the qualities that made the earlier film a superior work. When *Hondo* showed sympathy and understanding of the Indians, this film, like the novel, relegated them to the role of *deus ex machina,* a force which, at the moment of decision, becomes the hero and Maria's salvation. Like the novel, the film moves quickly and tells its story with economy, but also like the novel it is standard fare, despite its influence on other Westerns.

Louis L'Amour wrote another novel involving Apaches that became a film, *Last Stand at Papago Wells* (1957), also one of the author's weaker efforts. There is not one sympathetic character among the Indians. They are simply savages who attack a disparate group of travelers at Papago Wells, New Mexico. The defenders are led by Logan Cates, a Hondo-like character who once scouted for the army, and only his knowledge and courage keep the group together. Much of the tension comes from the relationships within the group rather than from the Apaches without. The film became *Apache Territory* (Columbia, 1958), an undistinguished oater. The plot, including the love interests and the film's attitude toward the Indians, remains basically the same as the novel. It is an obvious attempt by the studio to cash in on the success of *Hondo,* but too much of the basic premise of both the novel and film depends upon coincidence. There are also too many plots and subplots cluttering things up, and the basic simplicity of *Hondo* is missing.

Most other adaptations of L'Amour novels have not fared well. A minor short story, "Rider of the Ruby Hills," was turned into *Treasure of the Ruby Hills* (United Artists, 1955), wherein a rancher (Zachary Scott) gets mixed up in a range war with hidden treasure on the side. It is a routine effort at best. *Kilkenny* (1954) became *Blackjack Ketchum, Desperado* (Columbia, 1956), a standard tale of a gunman (Howard Duff) who tries to live down his reputation but is forced to strap on his six-shooters one last time when an evil cattle baron (Victor Jory) attempts to take over a peaceful valley. Though it has overtones of *Shane,* the film went in another direction by having the hero pursue romance rather vigorously. *Utah Blaine* (Columbia, 1957), based on the novel (1954) written under the pseudonym Jim Mayo, looks better than it plays due to imaginative camera angles, but the plot is all too predictable. Utah Blaine (Rory Calhoun) is given half a ranch when he saves a man from hanging, then finds the ranch is under siege by a local cattle baron. By story's end, he has taken the measure of the villain. *Guns of the Timberland* (Warner Bros., 1960) is offbeat in that it concerns partners in a logging business who conflict with local ranchers. Overall, it is a dreary affair, and even the novel (1955) was not up to L'Amour's usual standards.

With the possible exception of *Hondo,* Louis L'Amour has written competent and exciting Westerns but no great ones. *Heller with a Gun* (1955) is a good example. It is the story of King Marby, a typical L'Amour hero, who gets involved with a traveling theatrical troupe. Filmed as *Heller in Pink Tights* (Paramount, 1960), the film shifts the emphasis from the gunfighter (Steve Forrest) to the troupe itself, the manager (Anthony Quinn), and the leading lady, Angel (Sophia Loren). Director George Cukor, helming his only Western, produced a wonderful film, deepening the characters and situations and turning the whole thing into a romantic comedy mixed with slices of Americana, but in the process, most of the L'Amour novel disappeared. Even the character of King Marby has been radically changed.

Several important differences exist between book and film. A subplot in the novel involving a ruthless killer who is hired by the troupe to guide them across the prairies is dropped. The film has Marby tag along because he is interested in Angela. In the novel, Angela turns against Marby because she cannot understand the Western code, just as Molly rebels in *The Virginian,* and Marby understands that their values will always be in conflict. He voluntarily rides out of her life, leaving her to Tom Healy, the manager. In the film, Healy proves himself an equal of Marby, not with a gun, but with his spirit and determination, and Angela realizes that it is Healy she loves. There is also the emphasis on secondary characters. L'Amour spent little time developing them, consigning most of his efforts to the story of King Marby. On the other hand, Cukor gives us some wonderful supporting characters. There's Doc Montague (Edmund Lowe), a broken-down, hypochondriacal Shakespearean ham; Loran Hathaway (Eileen Heckart), the second leading lady dressed in a red fright wig constantly chuckling wildly over her daughter; the daughter, Della Southby (Margaret O'Brien), the pretty and guarded ingenue; and finally, De Leon (Raymond Novarro), the villainous employer of Marby. The novel is fluff, entertaining fluff to be sure, but fluff. The film has many wonderful Cukor touches that enrich it far beyond what the novel accomplished.

Two other adaptations of L'Amour novels rate mention. *Kid Rodelo* (Trident Films, 1966) was in reality a Spanish film based on L'Amour's novel (1966). This was typical L'Amour, but American director Richard Carlson, who also appeared in the film with a cast principally of Americans, turned the story of an ex-convict (Don Murray) wreaking vengeance on the men who bilked him and sent him to prison into a blood-splattered spaghetti-like Western amazingly aimed at the juvenile audience. *Catalow* (MGM, 1971), although distributed by MGM, was another European Western with an American director (Sam Wanamaker) and American cast; it misses all the humor in the L'Amour novel (1963) and butchers the book.

# Louis L'Amour's Films—An Interview

*(The following is part of a long interview with Louis L'Amour conducted by Lawrence Davidson, Richard Lupoff, and Richard Wolinsky for KIOU radio in San Francisco in 1986. In this portion of the interview L'Amour comments on some of the films made for the large screen and TV from his novels.)*

> When *The Godfather* came out, within
> a few days after it appeared and proved a hit,
> I had at least a dozen calls, "Do you have a
> story in the West about a Godfather?"
>
> Louis L'Amour

**LAWRENCE DAVIDSON:**   I was wondering, there are about thirty of your books that have been turned into films.

**LOUIS L'AMOUR:**   Well, yes, just about that. Sold about thirty-five to movies, but there are three or four on the shelf.

**LD:**   And how do you feel about the way Hollywood treated your books?

**LL:**   Generally speaking, very badly. *Hondo* was excellent, I thought. *How the West Was Won,* I thought, was very good. The movie—I had nothing to do with the TV series. The picture *Heller in Pink Tights,* with Sophia Loren, just missed. So did *Shalako.* Both of them had the ingredients but they just missed what they should have been.

**LD:**   Well, I enjoyed *The Shadow Riders* very much.

**LL:**   Mmm-hmm. I did too.

**LD:** I wished it had been . . . the one character that got left out of the movie that was in the book—her uncle, a seafaring man. I thought he was a gem, I thought he was wonderful. It was disappointing when he didn't show up in the movie.

**LL:** Well, you see that was nobody's fault. I'll tell you what happened in that situation. This is one of the things that happens in Hollywood. We had done *The Sacketts,* you know, and that was where Tom Selleck was really discovered. He had been playing bits and pieces around but nothing important. We gave him his first really important role as Orrin Sackett and that's what got him the series and what started him. He'll say so himself. I was the one who put up the big fight to get him, because they had somebody else in mind who had made more pictures than Tom had. Tom was tall and lean and rangy and we needed somebody like that in a lot of my stories.

Anyway, to get back to the serious things about it. We had done that and Tom was gonna have a hiatus. He was gonna have a break. Vern Noble was a good friend of his. He came to me and said, "Look, I've got a chance to get Tom if it's your story and can we have a story by such and such a time." Well, I had no story that would fit him. They also wanted to use Sam Elliott. So I very hurriedly sketched out the characters, outlined the general trend of the story, and gave it to them. They wrote the screenplay from that. Then I added more to the story and they checked with me every once in a while. Jim Burns and I talked back and forth. Then my story went on and became a completely different story.

The scene where the girl has the fight with the guy in the woods for example, if you remember, where he is drowning and says "I can't swim" and she says "You should have learned" or something like that—I forget what it was now—and leaves him there. That was strictly mine, and it wasn't in the movie at all. But those things happen occasionally.

**LD:** *Hondo* was originally filmed in 3-D and was never released as such. Did you ever see the 3-D version?

**LL:** Yes, it was released in 3-D.

**LD:** Oh?

**LL:** But only very briefly. It was shot in both versions.

**LD:** There are a few scenes in there that are obvious, like an arrow coming at the camera. It's a wonderful movie. It just seems really odd that it doesn't get more play than it seems to get.

**LL:** Well, it should. Alan Ladd was a great friend of mine. And *Shane* was a good picture. But, actually, if you look at the ingredients, *Shane* wasn't near as good a picture as *Hondo*. I liked *Shane*, and Alan was very close to me, but *Shane* hit the screen a little bit earlier. Both of them had the same ingredients. My short story had been published earlier than his story had.* But they both had a boy, a woman and her husband, and their kid. It was a good deal the same setup. Anyway, his got the attention and *Hondo* slipped through the cracks. His story was the oldest story that has ever been written in the West. Every Western writer has written it. The strange gunfighter who comes riding into town and allies himself with the community then goes on. The story of *Hondo* was different. It was a story of a fiercely independent man. So independent his own dog was independent, it wasn't his dog, it was just with him. A woman who wanted to keep her home regardless of everything. And an Indian who was leading his people in a fight he knew they couldn't win in the long run. It was these three people playing out their lives against a background of this Indian outbreak, which is a totally different thing.

**RICHARD LUPOFF:** One thing that we've discussed with other Western writers is what has happened to the Western in terms of films. There have been virtually no films. In terms of books these days, it seems that the only names we see on the shelves are Louis L'Amour and Max Brand. Sadly, only two names. What's going on? What happened?

**LL:** There are other Western writers around. Will Henry, for example, is a very good writer. I don't read Westerns because I'm too busy working on my own. But there are some good Western writers around. And it's not the fault of the Western writers or the fault of anybody. Hollywood is a place of whim. Purely whim. There are a few creative people and many of them are not creative at all. Each one of those guys who is not creative is sitting there waiting for something to happen, so they can jump on it. When *The Godfather* came out, within a few days after it appeared and proved a hit, I had at least a dozen calls, "Do you have a story in the West about a Godfather?" [Hilarious laughter] I mean it, seriously, and then everybody wanted big teeth because of *Jaws*. The thing is, that *Star Wars* was a good story. *The Godfather* was a good story. *Jaws* was a good story. There can be good Western movies but they have to be *good* stories. There is no bandwagon. There is no thing you can get on and ride to glory, you know. Each one has to make it on its own. Every one of these

---

*L'Amour was mistaken about which story came first. The magazine version of *Shane*, titled "The Rider to Nowhere," was published in *Argosy* magazine in 1946. It was published in book form in 1949, three years before "The Gift of Cochise" appeared in print.—REW

guys, if the Western does it now, everybody will be making Westerns and happily.

**RL:**   Do you think that might happen?

**LL:**   Yes. It can happen at any moment. Because right now there's some developing interest in that sort of thing. If they feel maybe that's the way they should go now, it can happen any minute.

# L'Amour on Film: A Checklist of His Movies and Television Adaptations

*by Hal Hall and Robert Weinberg*

1. *East of Sumatra*—Universal, 1953. Color, 82 minutes. Story by Louis L'Amour and Jack Natteford.

Cast: Jeff Chandler, Marilyn Maxwell, Anthony Quinn, Suzanne Ball, Peter Graves.

2. *Hondo*—Wayne-Fellows/Warner Bros., 1953. Color, 84 minutes. Based on the story "The Gift of Cochise" by Louis L'Amour.

Cast: John Wayne, Geraldine Page, Michael Pate, Ward Bond, James Arness, Lee Aaker, Rudolfo Acosta, Leo Gordon, Tom Irish, Paul Fix, Rayford Barnes.

3. *Four Guns to the Border*—Universal, 1954. Color, 84 minutes. Story by Louis L'Amour.

Cast: Rory Calhoun, Colleen Miller, George Nader, Walter Brennan, Nina Foch, John McIntire, Charles Drake, Jay Silverheels, Nestor Paiva, Mary Field, Bob Herron, Bob Hoy, Peg Parton.

4. *Treasure of the Ruby Hills*—Allied Artists, 1955. Black and white, 71 minutes. Based on "The Rider of the Ruby Hills" by "Jim Mayo."

Cast: Zachery Scott, Carole Matthews, Barton MacLane, Dick Foran, Lola Albright, Raymond Hutton.

5. *Stranger on Horseback*—United Artists, 1955. Color, 66 minutes. Based on a story by Louis L'Amour.

Cast: Joel McCrea, Kevin McCarthy, Jaclynne Greene, Miroslava, Nancy Gates, John Carradine, John McIntire, Emile Meyer, Robert Cornthwaite, James Bell, Walter Baldwin.

6. *Blackjack Ketchum, Desperado*—Columbia, 1956. Black and white, 76 minutes. Based on the novel *Kilkenny* by Louis L'Amour.

Cast: Howard Duff, Victor Jory, Maggie Mahoney, Angela Stevens, David Orrick, William Tannen, Ken Christie, Martin Garralaga, Robert

Roark, Don C. Harvey, Pat O'Malley, Jack Littlefield, Sidney Mason, Ralph Sanford, George Edward Mather, Charles Wagneheim, Wes Hudman.

7. *The Burning Hills*—Warner Brothers, 1956. Color, 94 minutes. Based on the novel by Louis L'Amour.
   Cast: Tab Hunter, Natalie Wood, Skip Homeier, Eduard Franz, Earl Holliman, Claude Akins, Ray Teal, Frank Puglia, Hal Baylor, Tyler Mac-Duff, Rayford Barnes, Tony Terry.

8. *Utah Blaine*—Columbia, 1956. Black and white, 75 minutes. Based on the novel by Louis L'Amour.
   Cast: Rory Calhoun, Susan Cummings, Angela Stevens, Max Baer, Paul Langton, George Keymas, Ray Teal, Gene Roth, Norman Fredric, Ken Christy, Steve Darrell, Terry Frost, Dennis Moore, Jack Ingram.

9. *The Tall Stranger*—Allied Artists, 1957. Color, 81 minutes. Based on the story "Showdown Trail" by "Jim Mayo."
   Cast: Joel McCrea, Virginia Mayo, Michael Ansara, Michael Pate, Barry Kelley, Whit Bissell, James Dobson, George Neise, Adam Kennedy, Leo Gordon, Ray Teal, Philip Phillips, Robert Fould, Jennifer Lea, George J. Lewis, Guy Prescott, Ralph Reed.

10. *Apache Territory*—Columbia, 1958. Color, 75 minutes. Based on the novel *Last Stand at Papago Wells* by Louis L'Amour.
    Cast: Rory Calhoun, Barbara Bates, John Dehner, Carolyn Craig, Thomas Pittman, Leo Gordon, Myron Healey, Francis de Sales, Frank de Kova, Reg Parton, Bob Woodward, Fred Krone.

11. *Guns of the Timberland*—Warner Brothers, 1960. Color, 91 minutes. Based on the novel by Louis L'Amour.
    Cast: Alan Ladd, Jeanne Crain, Gilbert Roland, Frankie Avalon, Lyle Bettger, Noah Berry, Jr., Vena Relton, Alana Ladd, Regis Toomey, Johnny Seven, George Selk, Paul E. Bruns, Henry Kulky.

12. *Heller in Pink Tights*—Paramount, 1960. Color, 100 minutes. Based on the novel *Heller with a Gun* by Louis L'Amour.
    Cast: Sophia Loren, Anthony Quinn, Margaret O'Brien, Steve Forrest, Eileen Heckart, Edmund Lowe, Ramon Navarro.

13. *Taggart*—Universal, 1964. Color, 85 minutes. Based on the novel by Louis L'Amour.
    Cast: Tony Young, Dan Duryea, Dick Foran, Elsa Cardenas, John

Hale, Emile Meyer, Peter Duryea, David Carradine, Tom Reese, Ray Teal, Claudia Barrett, Stuart Randall, Harry Carey, Jr., Bill Henry, Sarah Selby, George Murdock, Arthur Space, Bob Steele.

**14.** *Kid Rodelo*—Paramount, 1966. Black and white, 91 minutes. Based on the novel by Louis L'Amour.
    Cast: Don Murray, Janet Leigh, Broderick Crawford, Richard Carlson.

**15.** *Hondo and the Apaches*—MGM, 1967. Color, 85 minutes. Based on the story "The Gift of Cochise." This was the TV pilot for the series *Hondo,* which ran for seventeen one-hour episodes on ABC TV in 1967–68. It was released in theaters in Europe.
    Cast: Ralph Taeger, Michael Rennie, John Smith, Gary Clark, Kathie Browne, Buddy Foster, Victor Lunden, Steve Mario, William Bryant, Gary Merrill, Noah Berry, Jr., Randy Boone, Michael Pate, Jim Davis, John Pickard, Robert Taylor.

**16.** *Shalako*—Cinerama Releasing, 1968. Color, 113 minutes. Based on the novel by Louis L'Amour.
    Cast: Sean Connery, Brigitte Bardot, Stephen Boyd, Jack Hawkins, Peter Van Eyck, Honor Blackman, Woody Strode, Eric Sykes, Alexander Knox, Valerie French, Julian Mateos, Donald Barry, Rodd Redwing, Chief Tug Smith, Hans De Vries, Walter Brown, Charles Stainaker, John Clark, Bob Hall.

**17.** *Catlow*—MGM-EMI, 1971. Color, 103 minutes. Based on the novel by Louis L'Amour.
    Cast: Yul Brynner, Richard Crenna, Leonard Nimoy, Daliah Lavi, Jo Ann Pflug, Jeff Corey.

**18.** *Cancel My Reservations*—Hope Enterprises/MGM-EMI, 1972. Color, 99 minutes. Based on the novel *The Broken Gun* by Louis L'Amour.
    Cast: Bob Hope, Eva Marie Saint, Ralph Bellamy, Forrest Tucker, Anne Archer, Keenan Wynn, Ned Beatty.

**19.** *A Man Called Noon*—National General/Scotia-Barber, 1973. Color, 97 minutes. Based on the novel by Louis L'Amour.
    Cast: Richard Crenna, Stephen Boyd, Rosanna Schiaffino, Farley Grainger.

**20.** *The Sacketts*—Douglas Netter/M.B. Scott Productions, 1979. Color, 191 minutes. Based on the novels *The Daybreakers* and *Sackett* by Louis

L'Amour. Two-part miniseries made for TV. An edited version was later released as a TV movie.

The miniseries was voted the most authentic Western of the 1970s by the Cowboy Hall of Fame.

Cast: Glenn Ford, Ben Johnson, Sam Elliott, Tom Selleck, Gilbert Roland, Ruth Roman, Jack Elam, Mercedes McCambridge, Jeff Osterhage, Slim Pickens.

**21.** *The Shadow Riders*—TVM, 1982. Color, 100 minutes. Based on the novel by Louis L'Amour. Made-for-TV movie.

Cast: Tom Selleck, Sam Elliott, Ben Johnson, Katherine Ross, Geoffrey Lewis, Jeffery Osterhage.

**22.** *The Cherokee Trail*—Walt Disney, 1986. Color, 40 minutes. Based on the novel by Louis L'Amour. Made-for-TV movie.

Cast: Cindy Picket, Mary Larkin, Timothy Scott, David Hayward, Richard Farnsworth, Victor French.

**23.** *The Quick and the Dead*—HBO Pictures, 1987. Color, 90 minutes. Based on the novel by Louis L'Amour. Made-for-TV movie.

Cast: Sam Elliott, Kate Capshaw, Tom Conti.

**24.** *Down the Long Hills*—Disney, 1987. Color, 90 minutes. Based on the novel by Louis L'Amour.

Cast: Bruce Boxleitner, Bo Hopkins, Michael Ween, Don Shanks, Ed Bruce, Buck Taylor, Thomas Wilson Brown, Lisa MacFarlane.

In addition to the films listed above, in 1955 Popular Publications sold film rights to "Ride, You Tonto Raiders!" to Universal Pictures. No existing records indicate if this story was made into a film.

In 1956, Popular Publications sold film rights to "Death Song of the Sombrero" and "The Guns Talk Loud" to Universal Pictures. No existing records indicate if either of these stories were made into films.

# L'Amour Audiotape Adaptations: A Checklist

*by Hal Hall and Robert Weinberg*

THE 1980s saw an explosion in the spoken-word cassette market in bookstores. Spurred by the tremendous interest in self-help books, audio cassettes became a mainstay of the sideline departments of most stores. Adaptations of best-sellers, both nonfiction and fiction, grew so popular that often the tapes were released at the same time as the books. In most cases, the audio versions were condensed "adaptations" of the work. By the late 1980s, *Publishers Weekly* was running audiotape reviews every month along with an audiotape best-seller list.

Louis L'Amour's short fiction helped spark this audio revolution. L'Amour's short stories about Texas Ranger Chick Bowdrie worked wonderfully as audio dramas—complete with actors and sound effects. In actuality, the tapes were more dramatizations of the stories than actual readings. In most cases, L'Amour added a personal introduction to each tape.

Written for the pulp magazines, the Bowdrie stories were fast-paced, action-packed, and told a tale that could be fit easily on a one-hour tape. With slick packaging and promotion from Bantam Books, the tapes consistently made the spoken audio best-seller list. Though the list of yet-untaped Bowdrie adventures is slowly decreasing, there are still well over a hundred other L'Amour pulp adventures suitable for tape adaptation. No doubt they will be appearing with regularity for years to come.

The following list consists primarily of audio adaptations of L'Amour's work, along with a few earlier tapes done featuring L'Amour lectures. This list does not include several recordings done of complete L'Amour novels by the National Library Service for the Blind. The interested reader is referred to Hal Hall's comprehensive bibliography of L'Amour's work for more details on those record sets.

**1.** *The Wild West: What Was It Like?*—New York: Grolier Education Corp, 1976. 1 cassette, 16 minutes. L'Amour discusses Westerns.

**2.** *The American West*—North Hollywood, Ca.: Convention Seminar Cassettes, 1978. 1 cassette. L'Amour discusses teaching Westerns in American literature classes.

**3.** *Strange Pursuit: A Chick Bowdrie Story*—New York: Bantam Audio Publishing, 1986. 1 cassette, 60 minutes. A multivoiced adaptation of the story of the same name.

**4.** *Trail to the West: A Chick Bowdrie Story*—New York: Bantam Audio Publishing, 1986. 1 cassette, 60 minutes. A multivoiced adaptation of the story of the same name.

**5.** *Where Buzzards Fly: A Chick Bowdrie Story*—New York: Bantam Audio Publishing, 1986. 1 cassette, 50 minutes. A multivoiced adaption of the story of the same name.

**6.** *South of Deadwood: A Chick Bowdrie Story*—New York: Bantam Audio Publishing, 1986. 1 cassette, 60 minutes. A multivoiced adaption of the story of the same name.

**7.** *Survival: From My Yondering Days*—New York: Bantam Audio Publishing, 1986. 1 cassette, 60 minutes. Reminiscences by L'Amour along with a reading of L'Amour's short story "Survival" by Richard Crenna.

**8.** *The Black Rock Coffin Makers*—New York: Bantam Audio Publishing, 1987. 1 cassette, 60 minutes. Multivoiced adaptation of the story of the same name.

**9.** *Case Closed—No Prisoners: A Chick Bowdrie Story*—New York: Bantam Audio Publishing, 1987. 1 cassette, 60 minutes. Multivoiced adaptation of the story of the same name.

**10.** *Dead End Drift*—New York: Bantam Audio Publishing, 1987. 1 cassette, 60 minutes. L'Amour discusses his experiences as a miner. Richard Crenna reads the story "Dead End Drift."

**11.** *Old Doc Yak; Thicker Than Blood*—New York: Bantam Audio Publishing, 1987. 1 cassette, 60 minutes. L'Amour discusses his early days as a merchant seaman. Richard Crenna reads "Old Doc Yak" and "Thicker Than Blood."

**12.** *Showdown Trail*—New York: Bantam Audio Publishing, 1987. 2 cassettes, 180 minutes. Multivoiced adaptation of the story of the same name.

**13.** *Stay Out of My Nightmare!*—Miami: Book of the Road, 1987. 2 cassettes, 180 minutes. Readings by Charles Dean and J.C. Sealy of "Stay Out of My Nightmare!," "Street of Lost Corpses," and "Collect from a Corpse."

**14.** *The Hills of Homicide* and *I Hate To Tell His Widow*—Miami: Book of the Road, 1987. 2 cassettes, 180 minutes. Readings by Charles Dean and Michelle Morain of "The Hills of Homicide" and "I Hate to Tell His Widow."

**15.** *Keep Travelin', Rider* and *Ride You Tonto Raiders*—Miami: Book of the Road, 1987. 2 cassettes, 180 minutes. Readings by Jarion Monroe and Michelle Morain of "Keep Travelin', Rider" and "Ride You Tonto Raiders."

**16.** *Law of the Desert Born*—Miami: Book of the Road, 1987. 2 cassettes, 180 minutes. Readings by Charles Dean and Susan Marr of "Mistakes Can Kill You," "Desert Death Song," "Trap of Gold," "The Black Rock Coffin Makers," "Big Medicine," and "Law of the Desert Born."

**17.** *Riding for the Brand*—Miami: Book of the Road, 1987. 2 cassettes, 180 minutes. Readings by Mark Murphey and Jill Fine of "Riding for the Brand," "The Nester and the Piute," "Lit a Shuck for Texas," and "The Turkeyfeather Riders."

**18.** *Dutchman's Flat*—Miami: Book of the Road, 1987. 2 cassettes, 180 minutes. Readings by Mark Murphey and Jill Fine of "His Brother's Debt," "Dutchman's Flat," "Trail to Pie Town," "Four Card Draw," and "McQueen of the Tumbling K."

**19.** *Man Riding West* and *The Trail to Peach Meadow Canyon*—Miami: Book of the Road, 1987. 2 cassettes, 180 minutes. Readings by Jarion Monroe and Jill Fine of "Man Riding West" and "The Trail to Peach Meadow Canyon."

**20.** *Trap of Gold* and *Hattan's Castle*—New York: Bantam Audio Publishing, 1987. 1 cassette, 60 minutes. Multivoiced dramatizations of the two stories.

**21.** *The Trail to Peach Meadow Canyon*—New York: Bantam Audio Publishing, 1987. 2 cassettes, 140 minutes. Multivoiced dramatization of the story of the same name.

**22.** *The Turkeyfeather Riders*—New York: Bantam Audio Publishing, 1988. 1 cassette, 60 minutes. Multivoice adaptation of the story of the same name.

**23.** *Bowdrie Passes Through: A Chick Bowdrie Story*—New York: Bantam Audio Publishing, 1988. 1 cassette, 60 minutes. A multivoiced adaptation of the story of the same name.

**24.** *One For the Mohave Kid*—New York: Bantam Audio Publishing, 1988. 1 cassette, 60 minutes. A multivoiced adaptation of the story of the same name.

**25.** *Four-Card Draw*—New York: Bantam Audio Publishing, 1988. 1 cassette, 60 minutes. Multivoiced adaptation of the story of the same name.

**26.** *Keep Travelin', Rider*—New York: Bantam Audio Publishing, 1988. 1 cassette, 60 minutes. Multivoiced adaptation of the story of the same name.

**27.** *Riding for the Brand*—New York: Bantam Audio Publishing, 1988. 1 cassette, 60 minutes. Multivoiced adaptation of the story of the same name.

**28.** *Unguarded Moment*—New York: Bantam Audio Publishing, 1989. 1 cassette, 60 minutes. Multivoiced adaptation of the story of the same name.

**29.** *Too Tough to Brand*—New York: Bantam Audio Publishing, 1989. 1 cassette, 60 minutes. Multivoiced adaptation of the story of the same name.

**30.** *McNeilly Knows a Ranger: A Chick Bowdrie Story*—New York: Bantam Audio Publishing, 1989. 1 cassette, 60 minutes. Multivoiced adaptation of the story of the same name.

**31.** *Man Riding West*—New York: Bantam Audio Publishing, 1989. 1 cassette, 60 minutes. Multivoiced adaptation of story of the same name.

**32.** *No Man's Man*—New York: Bantam Audio Publishing, 1989. 1 cassette, 60 minutes. Multivoiced adaptation of the story of the same name.

**33.** *Lonigan*—New York: Bantam Audio Publishing, 1990. 1 cassette, 60 minutes. Multivoiced adaptation of the story of the same name.

**34.** *Down Pogonip Trail*—New York: Bantam Audio Publishing, 1990. 1 cassette, 60 minutes. Multivoiced adaptation of the story of the same name.

**35.** *The Strong Shall Live*—New York: Bantam Audio Publishing, 1990. 1

cassette, 60 minutes. Multivoiced adaptation of the story of the same name.

**36.** *A Ranger Rides to Town: A Chick Bowdrie Story*—New York: Bantam Audio Publishing, 1990. 1 cassette, 60 minutes. Multivoiced adaptation of the story of the same name.

**37.** *The Sixth Shotgun*—New York: Bantam Audio Publishing, 1990. 1 cassette, 60 minutes. Multivoiced adaptation of the story of the same name.

**38.** *Merrano of the Dry Country*—New York: Bantam Audio Publishing, 1990. 1 cassette, 60 minutes. Multivoiced adaptation of the story of the same name.

**39.** *Road to Casa Piedras: A Chick Bowdrie Story*—New York: Bantam Audio Publishing, 1990. 1 cassette, 60 minutes. Multivoiced adaptation of the story of the same name.

**40.** *Keep Travelin', Rider*—LFPL Audio, 1990. 2 cassettes, 120 minutes. An abridged reading of the story.

**41.** *Desert Death Song*—LFPL Audio, 1990. 2 cassettes, 120 minutes. An abridged reading of the story.

**42.** *Grub Line Rider*—New York: Bantam Audio Publishing, 1990. 1 cassette, 60 minutes. Multivoiced adaptation of the story of the same name.

**43.** *Bill Carey Rides West*—New York: Bantam Audio Publishing, 1991. 1 cassette, 60 minutes. Multivoiced adaptation of the story of the same name.

**44.** *One for the Pot*—New York: Bantam Audio Publishing, 1991. 1 cassette, 60 minutes. Multivoiced adaptation of the story of the same name.

# Appendices

# Appendix 1:
# Collecting Louis L'Amour: Hardcovers, Paperbacks, Magazines, Esoterica

REPEATING a very old joke, there is good news and bad news for people interested in collecting Louis L'Amour material. The good news is that there is a wide range of interesting books, magazines, and esoterica by and about L'Amour for fans to collect. And, price-wise, the items are not very expensive, especially when compared to collectibles by most other authors of equal popularity.

The bad news is that except for fairly recent publications, the items are difficult to find. There are few book dealers or stores that handle L'Amour material, and the demand for rarities by him is much greater than the supply. A collector has to be willing to spend a good amount of time and effort to assemble an attractive L'Amour collection. But it can be done by anyone, whether or not he or she have ever collected rare books or magazines before.

L'Amour collecting breaks down into four easily defined categories: hardcovers, paperbacks, magazines, and esoterica (which takes in such items as newspaper articles, advertising material for L'Amour books, etc). Each of these branches can be broken down even further.

Hardcover collections can consist of all hardcover editions of L'Amour's work, or only first editions, or foreign hardcover editions of L'Amour books. Paperbacks can also be subcategorized as to first editions, different printings with new covers, movie tie-in editions, and more. The same holds true in both other sections. These various subgroupings point out an important facet of book and magazine collecting. Before starting out, you must know exactly what you are looking for and what exists.

Fortunately, included in this book are checklists of all of L'Amour's published work. Highly recommended is Hal Hall's *The Works of Louis L'Amour: An Annotated Bibliography and Guide,* which is a comprehensive listing of L'Amour's work in both American and in foreign editions. Checking through these two volumes is a necessary first step in assembling a L'Amour collection. Before starting to collect, you have to decide exactly what you want to find.

If you want to collect *all* of L'Amour's work be prepared to spend a good amount of money and time. A number of people (the editor of this book included) have been collecting L'Amour's work for years and have yet to assemble a complete collection of all his appearances in print.

In the sections following, we have tried to give some basic information and ideas for the L'Amour collector. Along with these hints, we have given at the end of this appendix the names and addresses of bookstores and mail-order outlets who oftentimes offer L'Amour material.

## *L'Amour in Hardcover*

Louis L'Amour achieved his greatest fame as a paperback writer. However, a number of his books appeared in hardcover and are well worth owning. Some of the rarest L'Amour collectibles are hardcover editions of his early work.

As with all hardcover books, certain basic rules apply. First editions are much more valuable than later editions. (First editions are usually identified as such on the copyright page of most hardcovers.) A book without a dust jacket is worth approximately half the price of a copy with jacket. Copies in beat-up or worn condition are not worth nearly as much as copies in nice shape. The most desirable condition of any hardcover book is like new condition in the original jacket.

Autographed books are worth approximately double the value of an unsigned book. Later L'Amour hardcovers (such as *The Lonesome Gods* and *Last of the Breed*) turn up much more frequently than early hardcovers. Oddly enough, L'Amour's first hardcover (and one of the most desirable L'Amour collectibles), *Smoke from This Altar,* frequently turns up signed. This is probably due to the fact that the book was partly financed by L'Amour and only distributed in the Oklahoma City area, where he lived. Many of the copies probably were sold to friends or people who attended lectures on writing given by L'Amour at the time.

As L'Amour's first published book, *Smoke from This Altar* is quite collectible. Since it was published in a very small edition (probably under a thousand copies) and only available in the Oklahoma City area, it is now quite rare. Still, copies do show up from time to time on the rare-book market. A few have even been found in the plain paper dust jacket. Prices range widely on this book, with copies priced from two hundred to five hundred dollars, depending primarily on condition and whether or not it is autographed.

L'Amour's second published book was *Westward the Tide,* published in England in 1950 by Worlds Work Publishers. This book is extremely scarce and is probably the hardest L'Amour book to find. Though it was probably done in an edition of a thousand or more copies, most of them went to libraries in England. The book was published in an illustrated dust jacket, but copies in jacket are almost impossible to obtain.

Not as rare, but also quite collectible, are the four Hopalong Cassidy novels published by Doubleday Books as by "Tex Burns" in 1951 and 1952. These volumes are scarce but not impossible to find. They usually sell for between sixty and a hundred dollars each.

Much harder to find are the British hardcover editions of these same novels. These were published in Great Britain by Hodder and Stoughton approximately a year after the Doubleday editions appeared.

Several other L'Amour books were published in hardcover in the 1950s. While not as rare as the above mentioned volumes, they are all still quite collectible.

L'Amour turned to paperbacks in the 1960s and not many of his books appeared in hardcover. However, in the mid-1970s, the Saturday Review Press started publishing his work in hardcover. These books, including *Sackett's Land, Rivers West,* and others, are collectible and reasonably easy to find. They make a nice addition to any L'Amour collector's library.

L'Amour became a hardcover bestselling author in the 1980s. His books from this period are quite common and should not go for a great deal of money. As L'Amour spent a great deal of time promoting his work, autographed copies of these later books are not difficult to find and should not command outrageous prices.

Bantam Books has published a set of all of L'Amour's work in hardcover. These editions are advertised in inserts at the center of most L'Amour paperbacks. While these volumes are reasonably well done, they have little value as collector's items. They are comparable to book club editions published by such presses as the Literary Guild and the Book of the Month Club. The books are aimed at people who want hardcover editions of favorite novels. As they are done in open editions without regard to printings, they have no real value as collectibles. These volumes are also available bound in leather, but unfortunately the cost of the binding material has little to do with the value of a book. These artificial collectibles are the Franklin Mint items of the L'Amour field. Collectors are better off spending their money on truly rare or unusual items.

## *L'Amour in Paperback*

Louis L'Amour became famous as a paperback author and any comprehensive collection of L'Amour material should include a good selection of his paperbacks. Collecting rare paperbacks is not very difficult and good books still are available at decent prices. A useful tool in collecting L'Amour paperbacks is *The Official Price Guide: Paperbacks* by Jon Warren, published by House of Collectibles Press in trade paperbound format. It is available in the collectibles section of most bookstores. Along with listing many of the L'Amour books, it also provides a good summary of how to judge condition of books, determine first editions, and other necessary information for a beginning collector.

As with hardcovers, the most desirable L'Amour paperbacks are the earliest ones. Topping the list is the Gold Medal first edition of *Hondo,* with the famous quote by John Wayne. As L'Amour's first paperback and one of his most famous novels, it is one of the cornerstones of a L'Amour collection. A first printing of this paperback in very good condition usually sells for about seventy-five to a hundred dollars.

L'Amour's four paperback appearances with Ace Books, two under his own name and the other two under the pseudonym Jim Mayo, are also quite collectible. These books normally sell for between forty to seventy-five dollars a copy, depending as always on condition. First editions of L'Amour's early novels for Gold Medal Books are also worthwhile additions to a L'Amour paperback library and sell for prices somewhat lower than those quoted for the Ace paperbacks.

L'Amour's principle publisher in paperback was Bantam Books. At present, all of L'Amour's work is in print in Bantam paperbacks. However, every one of these novels has gone through multiple printings. While a few of the later books, such as *The Haunted Mesa,* have used the same cover on every printing, most of L'Amour's Bantam Books have been published with a number of different cover paintings for the same volume. An interested collector could assemble a huge and varied collection of L'Amour's work concentrating solely on different editions of the Bantam publications featuring different cover art.

As always, the first editions of these paperbacks are the most collectible (and the most expensive) of the various printings. However, later editions often featured cover art by well-known Western painters that makes them quite desirable. Oftentimes, when a movie was made of a particular novel, the next printing of the book featured a photo taken from the film as the cover. Many paperback fans collect these movie tie-in editions.

L'Amour Bantam paperback editions range in price from ten to fifteen dollars for first editions to one or two dollars for recent printings. However, a casual collector with a little luck should be able to find many of these books in local used bookstores. Oftentimes, even early L'Amour paperbacks including the Ace and Gold Medal editions turn up as well. Half the fun of collecting L'Amour in paperback is finding a bargain in the used-book racks.

A very useful article on L'Amour's first-edition paperbacks is "A Guide for Collecting L'Amour Paperbacks" by Dean L. Mawdsley, which appeared in *Paperback Parade* magazine in August 1987. The issue is still available, for five dollars a copy from Gryphon Publications, Box 209, Brooklyn, NY 11228.

Nearly all of L'Amour's work has appeared in foreign paperback editions. A number of these books feature cover art different than the American printings. L'Amour is especially popular in England and Germany. According to publicity from Bantam Books, L'Amour has appeared in twenty-eight languages. Foreign editions of his paperbacks have not attracted much attention but they are an interesting and unusual sidelight to collecting L'Amour's work.

## *L'Amour in Magazines*

While Louis L'Amour made his mark as an author of paperback Western novels, he wrote steadily for the pulp magazines for fifteen years before *Hondo*. And even before he sold any fiction, L'Amour placed numerous articles and poems in small, out-of-the-way publications. Collecting these magazines is difficult but by no means impossible.

Among the most difficult items for any L'Amour collector to obtain are the early semiprofessional magazines to which L'Amour sold his earliest nonfiction. Publications such as *Lands of Romance* and *Tanager* received limited circulation and copies of these magazines rarely show up in book catalogs at any price.

L'Amour's first professionally published story appeared in *True Gang Life* in 1935. While all issues of this magazine are notoriously scarce, this particular number seems to be one of the rarest of the entire run, probably because of the L'Amour story. It has a value of three hundred to four hundred dollars in fine condition.

Pulp magazines from the 1930s through 1950s are not nearly as common as old paperbacks from the same period. A much smaller group of people collects these magazines. However, there are a number of book dealers who handle pulps and they sometimes turn up at flea markets and old bookstores. By and large, Western pulps are not as collected as mystery or science fiction magazines, and they usually can be found for reasonable prices. As always, condition and age are the major factors in determining price. Because of L'Amour's popularity, many knowledgeable dealers charge a premium for pulps with his stories.

Most Western pulp magazines containing L'Amour stories should sell in the ten-to-twenty-dollar price range. The major exceptions to this rule are the two issues of the *Hopalong Cassidy* pulps, which are quite rare. The first issue of this magazine usually sells for one hundred dollars in good condition. The second issue, which is much scarcer, sells for double that price.

Issues of *Thrilling Adventures,* which contained L'Amour's early Ponga Jim Mayo stories (and often letters by L'Amour in the letter pages of the magazine) sell for about double the price of the Westerns. Issues of non-pulp magazines such as *Colliers* and *The Saturday Evening Post* vary in price depending on the seller, but they should not cost any more than the pulps, and in most cases should be priced less.

Each year, collectors from across the United States gather for PULP-con, a convention aimed at pulp magazine fans and collectors. Approximately two hundred people attend the show, including fifty to sixty dealers in pulp magazines. Along with many thousands of pulp magazines for sale, there are also large displays of rare paperbacks that can be purchased. PULPcon is aimed at the hard-core pulp magazine buyer, but it is an excellent place to obtain a good number of L'Amour pulps at one time. For more information about PULPcon, write to: PULPcon Information, Box 1332, Dayton, OH 45401.

## *L'Amour Esoterica*

Another interesting area of L'Amour collecting is a vast undefined territory covered under the catch-all category "Esoterica." This section includes anything and everything not included in the better-defined listings above. Esoterica includes newspaper articles by or about L'Amour, giveaways from publishers associated with L'Amour books, magazine articles on L'Amour, radio interviews with L'Amour, and a hundred other equally interesting but hard to pin down collectibles. It is an area where a dedicated collector can find terrific material for hardly any cost at all other than time.

L'Amour was a tremendous self-promoter. Wherever he went, he made himself available for interviews to the local newspapers, radio, and television. In Hal Hall's bibliography of L'Amour, nearly two hundred interviews and articles about L'Amour are listed in his secondary bibliography. And Hall is first to admit that his checklist barely scratches the surface of what exists.

Articles about L'Amour appeared everywhere from *The New York Times Book Review* to *Time Magazine.* Pete Hamill wrote a column about Louis L'Amour and boxing. Jim Tibbetts, a Kansas City sports columnist, once interviewed L'Amour on old-time baseball. L'Amour himself wrote an article "Of Guns and Gunmen" for *Gun World Magazine* in 1984. The list of L'Amour appearances is long and fascinating—a challenge to any collector.

In the early 1950s, *Argosy* published a slender paperbound collection of some of the best adventure stories published in the magazine over the past few years. The booklet was only available as a free giveaway to new subscribers to the magazine. It was titled *Trap of Gold,* taken from Louis L'Amour's story of that name, the first reprint in the book. This booklet seems to be L'Amour's first appearance in book form in the United States and is incredibly rare. It is an important part of any collection of L'Amour esoterica.

L'Amour material turns up in the oddest places. John Wayne Adventure Comics #25 (March 1954) features a cover photo from the John Wayne movie *Hondo.* Inside is a two-page adaptation of the torture scene from the movie.

Hiram Walker whiskey ran a series of magazine ads in the 1950s profiling men of action. One of these ads featured Louis L'Amour—"His hobby is writing. His business: adventure." When L'Amour was awarded the Congressional Gold Medal in 1983, Bantam Books ran a full-page ad in *The New York Times* congratulating their most famous author. Both of these items belong in any L'Amour collection.

Bantam Books, L'Amour's long time publisher, created numerous special displays for advertising and promoting L'Amour's books. Some of these unique stands are well worth owning. In 1983, Bantam published a special booklet entitled *Louis L'Amour: America's Storyteller* and produced a half-hour video commemorating L'Amour's twenty-five years with the company.

A number of L'Amour films are available on videotape, including *The Sacketts* miniseries. Again, they definitely belong in any Louis L'Amour collection.

The items mentioned in this essay are but a small sampling of the many varied and interesting collectibles available to the L'Amour collector. Unlike Stephen King, whose early first editions are already going for many hundreds (and sometimes thousands) of dollars, L'Amour books are still reasonably priced. With L'Amour's incredible and continued popularity, this situation will probably change in the years to come. Now is the time to start collecting L'Amour material.

The following paperback and magazine dealers sometimes offer L'Amour collectibles. Many of them publish catalogs aimed at the collector's market. It is recommended in writing away for catalogs to send one dollar to help cover the cost of catalog and mailing.

*Pandora's Books Ltd,* PO Box 54, Neche, ND 58265 (monthly paperback catalog)

*Books Are Everything,* R.C. & Elwanda Holland, 302 Martin Drive, Richmond, KY 40475 (paperbacks)

*Attic Books,* 707 S. Loudoun St., Winchester, VA 22601 (paperbacks)

*Black Ace Books,* 1658 Griffith Park Blvd., Los Angeles, CA 90026 (paperbacks)

*Gorgon Books,* 102 Joanne Drive, Holbrook, NY 11741 (paperbacks)

*Jack Deveny,* 6805 Cheyenne Trail, Edina, MN 55439-1158 (publishes a pulp catalog twice a year)

*David T. Alexander,* PO Box 273086, Tampa, FL 33618 (pulp magazines)

*The Pulp Collector,* 4704 Col. Ewell Court, Upper Marlboro, MD 20772 (pulp magazines)

*Black Lodge Books,* PO Box 423, Oak Forest, IL 60452 (rare books and pulp magazines; ask for their special Louis L'Amour catalog)

# Appendix 2:
# Suggestions for Further Reading

THERE have been hundreds of newspaper and magazine articles written about Louis L'Amour. Surprisingly, however, very little has been done in the way of critical commentary or criticism of his work. The following list is a small sampling of a cross-section of material (not included in this book) of interest to the L'Amour fan:

**1.** "Among Word-Spinners of the Old West, Louis L'Amour is the Top Gun" by Brad Darrach, *People*, June 9, 1975.

**2.** "He's No Rhinestone Cowboy" by Ned Smith, *American Airways*, April 1976.

**3.** "Interview with Louis L'Amour" by Jeff Sweet, *Gallery Magazine*, June 1978.

**4.** "Driving Through the Old West, L'Amour's Novels are Roadmaps" by Susan Price-Root, *US*, July 25, 1978.

**5.** "The Fastest Typewriter West of the Pecos, Pardner" by Pete Hamill, *New York Daily News*, January 31, 1979.

**6.** "L'Amour Rides the Range" by Ben Yagoda, *Esquire*, March 13, 1979.

**7.** "Louis L'Amour: Range Writer" by Hank Nuwer, *Country Gentleman*, Spring 1979.

**8.** "A Conversation with Louis L'Amour" by Michael T. Marsden, *Journal of American Culture*, Winter 1980.

**9.** "Louis L'Amour: Storyteller of the Wild West" by John G. Hubbell, *Reader's Digest*, July 1980.

**10.** "The Real-Life Romance of Louis L'Amour" by Norma Lee Browning, *Success Unlimited*, October 1980.

**11.** "The West of the Story" by Louis L'Amour, *Writer's Digest*, December 1980.

**12.** "Introduction to *Crossfire Trail*" by Keith Jarrod in the hardcover *Crossfire Trail*, Gregg Press, 1980.

**13.** "Introduction to *Kilkenny*" by Wesley Laing in the hardcover *Kilkenny,* Gregg Press, 1980.

**14.** "Introduction to *Utah Blaine*" by Wayne C. Lee, in the hardcover *Utah Blaine,* Gregg Press, 1980.

**15.** "Introduction to *Showdown at Yellow Butte*" by Scott McMillan, in the hardcover *Showdown at Yellow Butte,* Gregg Press, 1980.

**16.** "The West—The Greatest Story Ever Told" by Louis L'Amour, *The Roundup,* September/October 1981.

**17.** "An Interview with Louis L'Amour" by Francis Ring, *American West,* July/August 1982.

**18.** "The Men Who Made the Trail" by Louis L'Amour, *American West,* July/August 1982.

**19.** "Louis L'Amour" by Michael T. Marsden, in the hardcover *Twentieth Century Western Writers,* Gale Research, 1982.

**20.** *The American Frontier: Yesterday and Today; A Teacher's Guide for the Novels and Short Stories by Louis L'Amour* by Lou Willett Stanek, Bantam Books, 1982.

**21.** "Louis L'Amour" by Jon Tuska, in the hardcover *Encyclopedia of Frontier and Western Fiction,* McGraw-Hill, 1983.

**22.** *Louis L'Amour: America's Storyteller,* Bantam Books, 1983.

**23.** *Louis L'Amour* by Robert L. Gale, Twayne Publishers, 1985.

**24.** "L'Amour of the West" by Bodie Thoene, *American West,* November/ December 1986.

**25.** "World's Fastest Literary Gun: Louis L'Amour" by Donald Dale Jackson, *Smithsonian,* May 1987.

**26.** "A Guide for Collecting L'Amour Paperbacks" by Dean L. Mawdsley, *Paperback Parade,* August 1987.

**27.** "We All Called Him Louie" by Loren D. Estleman, *Mystery Scene,* #16 (1989).

**28.** *Louis L'Amour, His Life and Trails* by Robert Phillips, Paperjacks, 1989.

**29.** *The Works of Louis L'Amour: An Annotated Bibliography and Guide* by Halbert Hall, Borgo Press, 1991.

# Copyright Extension

**305**

## *Part Three*

## *Part Four*